The author's stated goal in writing this book was to "disrupt conventional thinking" related to the idea of "mercy," and to replace it with a concept that was itself "radically disruptive." This is exactly what the author achieved in this beautifully written book that breaks down this greatly misunderstood notion to its essence through his analysis of biblical passages and his and his wife's own personal experiences and observations. For readers that want to go far beyond the superficial, this is the book for you. As a human trafficking practitioner, I will use the lessons learned in this book in the way I relate to both the survivors and criminals alike.

—**Matt Friedman**, human trafficking expert and author of *Be the Hero: Be the Change*

Contrary to Shakespeare's famous dictum, in too many hearts, the quality of mercy is severely constrained. That's why Matthew Clarke's new book is so important. He advocates and inspires readers first to imagine and then to embody a quality of mercy that doesn't just fit in quietly around the edges, but rather goes to the heart and disrupts everything from there. A book for this critical moment—highly recommended.

—**Brian D. McLaren**, author of *Faith After Doubt*

Matthew Clarke invites the reader into a sustained reflection on the most radical, subversive claim in biblical faith. He shows how pervasive mercy is in scripture, how urgent it is in our society, and how up-stream to our world context it is. He intends to lead the reader to serious active engagement in ways that may be a practice of rescue for a society propelled by hardened hearts. This is a welcome read and a compelling imperative.

—**Walter Brueggemann**, professor emeritus of Old Testament at Columbia Theological Seminary

Disrupting Mercy is a fine book on an urgent and critical theme. We live in an age driven by transactional accounts of human behaviour, fixated on blame and revenge and seriously lacking the will or capacity to act from a compassionate heart. Mathew Clarke offers an alternative way to live. In a provocative, reflective, insightful and practical book the author captures the richness of the biblical and gospel tradition of mercy. Clarke locates mercy within an ecology of love and an economy of gift. Mercy appears as a prophetic act and gift of extreme kindness impelled by compassion. This most accessible, readable and practical book is grounded in the best contemporary theological scholarship. I found it uplifting, informative and challenging. A great book for individuals and small groups.

—**Rt. Rev'd Dr. Stephen Pickard**
Australian Centre for Christianity and Culture

In *Disrupting Mercy*, Matthew Clarke is like an experienced trekker: a wise and thoughtful guide who invites us on a carefully chartered journey through the perilous landscape of mercy. Perilous, because to enter each chapter means to risk being challenged, turned upside-down, and our understandings of mercy disrupted. And the landscape he leads us into exposes us to different perspectives on mercy, giving vistas of mercy at work, and pointing out what gets in the way of mercy 'landing' as we would hope. This landscape is clearly well-known to Clarke, as he turns our eyes toward real examples of possibility and hope that lead us toward seeing mercy as a true bringer of shalom. This really is a full-orbed exploration, disturbing and enlightening at almost every turn, and yet at every point, we know we are in wise hands that offer ways forward into mercy and true shalom.

—**Dr Sally Longley**
Spiritual Director and author of *Conversations with Silence*

DISRUPTING MERCY

THE GIFT OF EXTREME KINDNESS MOTIVATED BY COMPASSION

MATTHEW C. CLARKE
WITH ANNABELLA ROSSINI-CLARKE

Turning Teardrops into Joy
Newcastle, Australia

Copyright © 2022 by Matthew C. Clarke.

All rights reserved. No part of this publication may be reproduced, distributed or transmitted in any form or by any means, including photocopying, recording, or other electronic or mechanical methods, without the prior written permission of the publisher, except in the case of brief quotations embodied in critical reviews and certain other noncommercial uses permitted by copyright law. For permission requests, contact the publisher.

Published by Turning Teardrops into Joy
www.turningteardropsintojoy.com/books

Most scripture quotations are from the New Revised Standard Version Bible, copyright © 1989 National Council of the Churches of Christ in the United States of America. Used by permission. All rights reserved worldwide.

Where noted, some scripture quotations are from The Holy Bible, New International Version® NIV®
Copyright © 1973 1978 1984 2011 by Biblica, Inc.™
Used by permission. All rights reserved worldwide.

Disrupting Mercy / Matthew C. Clarke—1st ed. (IS)
Paperback ISBN 978-0-6487248-2-7
Ebook ISBN 978-0-6487248-3-4

Contents

Preface vii
1. Up a Tree with Zacchaeus 1
2. The Essence of Mercy 13
3. Mercy in the Old Testament 37
4. Mercy in the New Testament 67
5. Mercy and Justice 97
6. Mercy and Brokenness 119
7. Sin and Forgiveness 135
8. Bondage and Liberation 163
9. Exile and Return 181
10. Putting Mercy to the Test 201
11. Obstructions to Mercy 217
12. Zacchaeus, Mercy and Evangelism 243
Appendix: Alternative Conceptions 253
Notes 291
Bibliography 311

Preface

A SOCIETY WITHOUT MERCY is harsh and unforgiving. But the dominant landscape of the modern Western world has become a merciless vista in which we have not only allowed, but promoted, unkindness and oppositional thinking to invade every aspect of our lives. I am not just referring to military heavy-handedness, violent crimes, the rape of our environment, and massive prison populations, but also to the underlying social dynamics that make such extremes seem normal. I mean our propensity to find someone else to blame so that we can sue them. Oppositional politics that require constant one-upmanship and character assassination. An online culture of trolling (deliberately provoking people into an argument) and doxxing (embarrassing or harassing people by leaking their private information to the public) that often hides behind anonymity. Verbal abuse under the banner of free speech, and the counterpoint of so-called "cancel culture" that shuts down alternative viewpoints rather than engage in meaningful conversation.

These pernicious mechanisms are often deliberately contrived to generate insecurity and fear. They are both symptoms and drivers of an unhealthy society that demonstrates a deep need for kindness. The bar depicted in mass media and in social media has dropped so low that any expression of kindness can seem out of the ordinary and mercy is seen as naive, old-fashioned, impractical, and weak.

In defiance of dominant forces that dehumanize us all and an anemic view of mercy, we have created opportunities for people to receive this book for free. This is a deliberate step away from the pervasive economy of exchange and toward the more nourishing ecology of love. Why? Because God desires mercy rather than sacrifice, and mercy is free. Properly understood, mercy disrupts our preconceptions about giving and taking, about what constitutes worth and whether or not we should ever get what we deserve, and about the relationship between God's good news and human flourishing.

My dual goal is to disrupt conventional thinking about mercy, and to replace it with a concept that is itself radically disruptive. Mercy is not magnanimously throwing a few dollars to the poor from a position of superiority. Nor is it a naive failure of justice that lets an offender "off the hook." Such insipid notions are common but need to be disrupted. They are not the image of mercy portrayed in the Bible. As we shall see, the mercy of God, and the network of reciprocal mercy that God invites us into, is extravagant, outrageous, and even scandalous.

Everyday kindness is the relational glue enabling us to be a society rather than a mob. We need more of that everyday kindness. But we also need something more. Above the base level of everyday good deeds, we need surprising and generous forms of forgiveness and compassion that are offered with no strings attached. We need the disruption of mercy, given freely and beyond what anyone could expect.

Mercy is multi-layered. It responds to people's immediate needs for physical healing, but also addresses the core forms of human brokenness: it enables forgiveness of sin, liberation from bondage, and finding a way home from actual or metaphorical exile. Mercy also offers each of us disruptive opportunities for personal transformation and redemption, just as it did for Zacchaeus when Jesus called him down from the sycamore tree in Jericho. Ultimately, mercy is God's strategy for removing enmity, not only between people but also within each person, between people and God, and between people and the created world so that, with true and full *shalom*, all things in heaven and on earth may be reconciled in Christ. Mercy is the passion of God that powers the Good News.

As Australian-born musician Nick Cave points out, we need the safety net of mercy to allow us to take risks. Cave showed extraordinary insight as an observer of human capacity and fragility when he wrote:

> *Mercy is a value that should be at the heart of any functioning and tolerant society. Mercy ultimately acknowledges that we are all imperfect and in doing so allows us the oxygen to breathe—to feel protected within a society, through our mutual fallibility. Without mercy a society loses its soul, and devours itself.*
>
> *Mercy allows us the ability to engage openly in free-ranging conversation—an expansion of collective discovery toward*

> a common good. If mercy is our guide we have a safety net of mutual consideration, and we can, to quote Oscar Wilde, "play gracefully with ideas."
>
> Yet mercy is not a given. It is a value we must nurture and aspire to. Tolerance allows the spirit of enquiry the confidence to roam freely, to make mistakes, to self-correct, to be bold, to dare to doubt and in the process to chance upon new and more advanced ideas. Without mercy society grows inflexible, fearful, vindictive and humourless.[1]

The Christian church has often promoted the importance of mercy, as have Judaism and Islam. Pope John Paul II made a heartfelt appeal for mercy, which he said, "Humanity and the modern world need so much ... even though they often do not realize it."[2] In doing so, he noted three duties of the church regarding mercy: to proclaim God's mercy, to show mercy in its own actions, and to call on God for mercy. More recently, one of the first acts of Pope Francis was to declare an Extraordinary Jubilee of Mercy to highlight "the love of God who consoles, pardons, and instils hope."[3]

I attended an Anglican service of Holy Communion one Sunday and counted fifteen times that mercy was mentioned in the standard liturgy. Each week, Australian Anglicans repeatedly hear that God is merciful, but what does that mean? In two cases, the word was used declaratively, as in the sentence, "You are the same Lord whose nature is always to have mercy." All other cases were in the context of calling on God to show us mercy, such as "Lord, have mercy. Christ, have mercy. Lord, have mercy."

Preface

And yet, although mercy is mentioned many times, in my experience our Christian tradition has rarely cultivated within its members a deep, life-changing engagement with the concept.

By the time you reach the end of this book, I hope you will have seen that acts of mercy, and the predisposition or posture that undergirds those acts, are the foundation stones of a society in which all can flourish. I hope those of you who identify as followers of Jesus will see something else as well: that the expression of mercy is not an optional extra but an essential element of God's redemptive plan for the world.

If I succeed, then the title of this book will become doubly true, having not only disrupted the common views of mercy as "nice," naive, and optional, but having also replaced those simplistic and dismissive attitudes with the idea that mercy itself is deeply disruptive—not weakly domesticated but bold, challenging, and transformative.

Three important influences have intersected in the process of crafting that message: the Anabaptist tradition, research into the ongoing global problem of modern slavery, and my collaborator Annabella.

ANABAPTIST PERSPECTIVE

This biblical analysis of mercy is heavily influenced by Anabaptist understandings of theology and ecclesiology. The Anabaptist tradition arose in the midst of the Reformation during the sixteenth century. Small groups of Christians across Europe thought that Luther and Zwingli had not gone far enough in their rethinking of biblical faith, especially around understandings of priesthood, baptism, and the alignment of church and state. Some of these groups, in which adults baptized each other, became known derisively as "Anabaptists," literally the re-baptizers.

Anabaptist theology evolved to emphasize the importance of local worshipping communities as the site of spiritual discernment, the importance of discipleship based on the life and teachings of Jesus, and a commitment to non-violence. In response to these practices, Anabaptist groups were violently suppressed by both Catholics and the Reformers. Anabaptists were arrested, burnt, and sometimes subjected to "the third baptism," that is, drowning.

The Anabaptist movement continues today in a variety of groups such as the Mennonites, Amish, Bruderhof, Hutterites, and the Church of the Brethren. These varied expressions of church are neither Catholic nor Protestant. What unifies them is not a set of agreed beliefs (orthodoxy) but a commitment to faithful living that reflects right behavior (orthopraxy) and the right heart (orthocardia).

As you read this book, distinctively Anabaptist ideas will seep through in the way I engage with the Bible, in my understanding of the interaction between the church and the surrounding world, in the way I draw on the life and teaching of Jesus as normative for the ethics of his followers, and in my non-coercive approach to ecological, social, and spiritual reconciliation.

Preface

MODERN SLAVERY

Several years ago, my wife and I founded the Freedom Keys Research Project to investigate the apparent ineffectiveness of anti-slavery strategies in the past two decades. According to the best estimates we have, there may be fifty million people living with the types of abuse, exploitation, and coercion that fall within the category of modern slavery, also called human trafficking. That is a huge number of people, and the evidence suggests that, despite massive amounts of effort to reduce the problem, the number is increasing.[4] Our project generates innovative strategies for addressing modern slavery during the next two decades and tests the effectiveness of those strategies. We have been developing the idea that the key to ending modern slavery is not rescuing victims, nor putting the traffickers in jail—important as these tasks may be—but understanding the external socio-economic drivers and internal motivations of traffickers so that meaningful alternatives can be created that enable them to change their own behaviors.

In 2019, we visited friends in Fiji who do rehabilitation work with prisoners. In our conversations with them, the concept of mercy repeatedly came up. In both contexts—the global blight of modern slavery and personal rehabilitation in Fijian prisons—we saw the importance of changing perpetrators' perceptions of themselves, of finding forgiveness, and of being given opportunities to live differently. This set me on a journey to find out more about historical and biblical notions of mercy, and to think through how mercy might apply to the difficult social problems of today.

As a consequence, modern slavery is an important thread woven through this book. Modern slavery exemplifies sin, bondage, and exile, and demonstrates the extreme lack of mercy in the way some people treat others. It becomes a plumb line against which to test any claim about mercy. If mercy is as transformative as I think it is, how would it operate within contexts of horrendous evil such as the abuses, exploitation, and coercion of modern slavery?

ANNABELLA AND OTHER SUPPORTERS

My wife, Annabella, is the silent voice behind this book. Together, we run a sustainable social enterprise selling coffee in urban Australia, to raise funds for various international development projects. This business, and the supportive community around it, has been the context for me to read, ponder, and write about mercy.

Although the writing of the words has been my task, the ideas have arisen from our life and work together. Everything in this book springs from conversations between the two of us. She is my Muse and my Grace, my Thalia. Like the two Greek goddesses named Thalia, which means flourishing, Annabella brings joy, abundance, lavish banquets, comedy, and inspiration. She disrupts me with questions I would never have thought of, and mental pathways quite orthogonal to my own. Our lines of thinking often approach an idea from quite different angles. Which is the right angle? When we esteem both lines and follow them with curiosity, the point of insight is often uncovered at the intersection. So, this book is the outcome of a deeply collaborative process.

I am also grateful to numerous people who read early drafts, and to friends who provided accommodation and nourishment, physical and spiritual, during writing retreats. As will be clear from the many citations in the book, I am also infinitely indebted to a myriad other people whose experiences and writings have influenced my own.

AN INVITATION

Mercy is an action rather than a feeling or a belief. To inspire action, I have tried to make this book interactive to the extent the form allows. I invite you into personal reflection and action rather than just engaging cognitively. Each chapter commences with a suggestion—a quote, a song, or some artwork—for you to meditate on before reading the chapter. Each chapter ends with a page on which you may record your responses to what you have read. I have included specific questions on those pages in the hope that we all move past polite affirmations, so that, through deeper personal reflection, we allow mercy to change us. If you dislike my questions, just skip them, but please take time to reflect on how the ideas about mercy can be put into practice.

The publisher's website also points readers to a community space where you can share your own stories of mercy. My hope is that, through such sharing, we will nourish and encourage each other on our journeys within God's web of mercy.

[1]

UP A TREE WITH ZACCHAEUS

> *An initial thought to ponder:* Please open a web browser and search for images of mercy, kindness, compassion, or forgiveness. Pick two or three that resonate with you. Include one that is not from your usual way of thinking: perhaps an image from a religious tradition other than your own, an image from Japanese anime, or from a computer game. Bookmark or print those chosen images and keep coming back to them as you read this book. How do those images of mercy make you feel?

FROM HIS VANTAGE POINT in a sycamore tree, Zacchaeus hoped to see Jesus without drawing attention to himself. The encounter with Jesus did not turn out as Zacchaeus expected, but provides us with a perfect example of mercy. The incident exemplifies a way of thinking about mercy as a proactive blessing with the power to transform the recipient's life rather than simply a reactive deliverance from suffering or guilt. It may seem a simple story. It is one we often present neatly to children. But I'd like to explore this encounter a bit further to uncover its richness. As you will see, most of the themes of this book find their roots under this sycamore tree.

The interaction between Jesus and Zacchaeus appears in Luke's account of the life of Jesus, as part of an extended discussion on the nature of salvation. The theme picks up momentum when "a certain ruler" approaches Jesus and asks, "Good Teacher, what must I do to inherit eternal life?" (Luke 18:18).[5] After some banter about what it even means to be "good," Jesus disappoints the man by saying it is almost impossible for a rich person to enter God's kingdom. (Today, the word "kingdom" carries the negative connotations of patriarchy and feudal domination, but those were not the images intended by Jesus. If the word is too tarnished for you, I suggest replacing it with the more modern term "society.")

People who watch this interchange are surprised enough to ask, "Then who *can* be saved?" (18:26, my italics). Luke weaves an answer to this question by narrating three consecutive interactions between Jesus and his close disciples (18:28-34), an unnamed blind man (18:35-43), and Zacchaeus (19:1-10). In these encounters, we find out not only who can be saved and the varied forms that salvation can take, but also about the close relationship between salvation, eternal life, and participation in the kingdom of God.

> Then Peter said, "Look, we have left our homes and followed you." And he said to them, "Truly I tell you, there

is no one who has left house or wife or brothers or parents or children, for the sake of the kingdom of God, who will not get back very much more in this age, and in the age to come eternal life."

Then he took the twelve aside and said to them, "See, we are going up to Jerusalem, and everything that is written about the Son of Man by the prophets will be accomplished. For he will be handed over to the Gentiles; and he will be mocked and insulted and spat upon. After they have flogged him, they will kill him, and on the third day he will rise again." But they understood nothing about all these things; in fact, what he said was hidden from them, and they did not grasp what was said. (Luke 18:28-34)

To the people already committed to following him, Jesus acknowledges that they have already given up what the rich man was unwilling to relinquish. They have left everything, including homes and family, "for the sake of the kingdom of God," and are already on the path to inheriting the eternal life that the rich ruler may never find. But then Jesus confuses them by noting that the path they will travel together also leads to being mocked, insulted, spat on, flogged, and killed—not the kind of salvation they expected!

Who can be saved if not the rich and powerful? Those who give up all and suffer along with Jesus. For them, salvation means being blessed within their lifetime with more than they have given up, and the future blessing of eternal life.

Jesus and his disciples then continue their walk toward Jerusalem via Jericho.

> *As he approached Jericho, a blind man was sitting by the roadside begging. When he heard a crowd going by, he asked what was happening. They told him, "Jesus of Nazareth is passing by." Then he shouted, "Jesus, Son of David, have mercy on me!" Those who were in front sternly ordered him to be quiet; but he shouted even more loudly, "Son of David, have mercy on me!" Jesus stood still and ordered the man to be brought to him; and when he came near, he asked him, "What do you want me to do for you?" He said, "Lord, let me see again." Jesus said to him, "Receive your sight; your faith has saved you." Immediately he regained his sight and followed him, glorifying God; and all the people, when they saw it, praised God. (Luke 18:35-43)*

On the outskirts of Jericho, they are accosted by a blind beggar who calls out repeatedly, "Jesus, Son of David, have mercy on me" (18:35-43). He is told to shut up by the crowd, but Jesus responds to his marginalization by asking, "What do you want me to do for you?" In asking this question, Jesus acknowledges the man's request for mercy and pauses to listen and to understand what mercy would mean to such a person. The blind beggar confirms what we expected: he wants to see. In response, Jesus says to him, "Receive your sight; your faith has saved you" and immediately the man can see.

The Greek word *sesōken* is often translated as "healed" in this verse, but its root *sózó* has the primary meaning of "saved" and is the same word as used in the crowd's earlier question "Then who can be saved?" The word is applied later to Zacchaeus, although the nature of his salvation is very different from the physical healing of the blind man.

Up a Tree with Zacchaeus

Who can be saved if not the rich and powerful? Those who are physically broken and socially outcast. For them, salvation may mean, first and foremost, physical healing.

Having received the mercy he asked for, the man follows Jesus, praising God. Nothing in Luke's account implies that mercy was shown because the man deserved it, or did not deserve it, nor because of any prior repentance or future debt. Jesus' own explanation is that the man's *faith* saved him: a faith demonstrated by calling out to Jesus in the belief that Jesus could, and would, show mercy.

From the outskirts of Jericho, Jesus and his followers, including the once blind man, now move through the city, where they meet another man in need of mercy.

> *He entered Jericho and was passing through it. A man was there named Zacchaeus; he was a chief tax collector and was rich. He was trying to see who Jesus was, but on account of the crowd he could not, because he was short in stature. So he ran ahead and climbed a sycamore tree to see him, because he was going to pass that way. When Jesus came to the place, he looked up and said to him, "Zacchaeus, hurry and come down; for I must stay at your house today." So he hurried down and was happy to welcome him. All who saw it began to grumble and said, "He has gone to be the guest of one who is a sinner." Zacchaeus stood there and said to the Lord, "Look, half of my possessions, Lord, I will give to the poor; and if I have defrauded anyone of anything, I will pay back four times as much." Then Jesus said to him, "Today salvation has come to this house, because he too is a son of Abraham. For the Son of Man came to seek out and to save the lost." (Luke 19:1-10)*

Disrupting Mercy

Zacchaeus has a different social standing from the rich ruler who started this whole conversation about salvation. In Matthew's account, the rich ruler is referred to as a "young man" (Matthew 19:22) and is probably a naive youth with inherited money from a well-respected family. On the other hand, Zacchaeus has probably been shunned by the Jewish townsfolk because, as a tax collector, he is a collaborator with the occupying Roman forces. He is a man of considerable power, not just a tax collector but the local *chief* tax collector—probably the head of a tax collecting company who won a contract to collect taxes on behalf of the Romans—with wealth that came from exploiting his fellow Jews.

Zacchaeus is a short man, looked down upon both literally and figuratively. He wields a lot of power and is consequently disliked, despised, and feared. Though privileged and wealthy, Zacchaeus lives just as much on the edge of the crowd as does the blind beggar. Zacchaeus too is broken and in need of salvation. Although curious, he does not have the faith to call out for mercy.

Nevertheless, Jesus sees him ... deeply sees him ... sees beyond the wealth and beyond the status of social pariah. In a display of proactive mercy Jesus calls out above the babble of the crowd and invites himself to Zacchaeus' home. It is a simple request, but one that reverberates through the hearts of both the crowd and Zacchaeus.

The crowd is aghast and cannot make any sense of this travelling preacher sullying himself by contact with a known sinner. This tax collector, they are sure, does not deserve any favors. Furthermore, in the normal practice of

Up a Tree with Zacchaeus

Middle Eastern culture, the *community* would have selected the most suitable host to honor a visitor, but Jesus had chosen to avoid that hospitality and instead insulted them by preferring the hospitality of their oppressor! Where previously they were hostile toward Zacchaeus, now they are angry at Jesus.[6] Such is often the effect of mercy on jealous observers.

Zacchaeus, on the other hand, is transformed. The details of what caused that transformation are not related by Luke. Perhaps Jesus and Zacchaeus held a longer conversation that evinced the change. But the brevity of Luke's account suggests that the core reason was simply Jesus' act of inviting himself to Zacchaeus' house. This unexpected act highlights several important aspects of mercy. It went against the social current. It was dignifying. It was a gift. It upended the idea of debt.

First, Jesus' compassion for Zacchaeus motivated him to reject the dismissive attitude of the crowd toward Zacchaeus. According to Kenneth E. Bailey,[7] the text and the legal restrictions on the placement of large trees imply that Jesus had passed through Jericho at this point and was on his way out of town toward Jerusalem. Earlier on, Luke says that Jesus was just passing through Jericho (19:1) but, having seen Zacchaeus, changes his mind about continuing to Jerusalem. Despite his own plans, and despite (or perhaps because of!) the antagonism of the townsfolk to Zacchaeus, Jesus repeats his habit of embracing the outsider.

Second, Zacchaeus would have seen the reaction of the crowd. Like them, he would have noted the violation of hospitality customs and recognized that the invitation to eat with him was a slight against the honor of the community. He would understand that Jesus was risking ritual uncleanness by entering the house of a "sinner" the day before Passover. He heard the crowd muttering against Jesus, but whereas the crowd was affronted by Jesus, Zacchaeus "was happy to welcome him" (19:6).

Zacchaeus immediately understood that Jesus' simple act affirmed his dignity and value. Jesus' acceptance of Zacchaeus denied his status as an outcast and acknowledged him as "a son of Abraham" (19:10), meaning, in this context, that he too was a member of the Jewish community. We should not deduce that Jesus invested him with some new value but rather than he recognized and affirmed the value Zacchaeus already had, even if that value had been forgotten. The true Zacchaeus had indeed been "lost" and needed to be "saved" but all along he remained a beloved child made in the image of God.

Zacchaeus was not the only person on the margins who Jesus treated that way: Jesus dealt the same way with the woman at the well (John 4:1-42), the thief on the cross (Luke 23: 39-43), the woman who wiped his feet with her hair (Luke 7:36-50), people with leprosy (e.g., Matthew 8:2-4), people supposedly possessed by demons (e.g., Matthew 8:28-34), and countless others. Showing mercy in this way was clearly his normal practice.

Third, this tendency or natural posture of Jesus was not a result of anything Zacchaeus deserved or did not deserve, nor was it conditional on any prior repentance or subsequent response from Zacchaeus. It was a free gift.

Fourth, Jesus showed mercy to Zacchaeus in a very strange way: by putting himself in debt to Zacchaeus. On the surface, he did not give Zacchaeus anything but instead asked Zacchaeus to give him something. He invited himself to Zacchaeus' house where he presumably ate a meal and perhaps even slept overnight.[8] In the normal course of social interaction this would mean he now owed Zacchaeus something. The fact that he took the same approach with the woman at the well—whom he asked for a drink of water (John 4:7)—suggests that this is a deliberate strategy. I will say more about this in a later section on mercy as gift.

In this context, the process of asking for help contributed to Jesus' affirmation of Zacchaeus by declaring him worthy of being a host.[9] Jesus denied the judgment of the crowd that Zacchaeus was a taker and gave him an opportunity to prove them wrong. Jesus placed himself in a position of need and asked Zacchaeus to serve him, saying in effect "I don't care that others spurn you, I would be honored to walk by your side and be a guest at your table."

The effect of this act of mercy was a radical shift in thinking for Zacchaeus that led to a radical shift in his financial and relational intentions. He spontaneously decided to give half of what he owned to the poor and to repay fourfold anyone he has cheated. This response was in no way required by Jesus. The reparations were not a condition of Jesus' mercy but a result of it.

Disrupting Mercy

Luke does not spell out the thought process that led to this radical change but I imagine Zacchaeus' self-talk going something like this:

> *Jesus risked his own reputation for me. For me, whose own reputation is a crock of camel dung! Why have I been so proud of making myself rich? Proud of how everyone fears me. What have I become? They all hate me. And they're right: I've got more money than I know what to do with but I am worthless. An outcast like that blind beggar I walk past every day. (Blind no more it seems! I wonder what happened to him?) Where was I? Oh yeah ... outcast and ashamed of myself. But Jesus doesn't see me that way. He's not blind to what I do but seems to think I'm worth spending time with. I wish I was. Maybe I am. But if I want to lead a household worthy of giving hospitality to someone like Jesus, I'll have to be a better me than I've been. Maybe that needs to start with being more generous.*

Whether or not this imagined reflection is accurate, there was a change at the root of Zacchaeus' identity. Jesus' mercy sparked a re-evaluation by Zacchaeus that resulted in true repentance: not a heavy sense of moral guilt or even remorse, but a change of mind accompanied by a change in behavior. He started to think of himself differently and as a result realized that he had to act differently. Such a transformation deserves the label "salvation." Jesus comments "Today salvation has come to this house." Today, Jesus has come to this house. Today, mercy has come to this house. Today, the real Zacchaeus, a son of Abraham, who had been lost, has returned to this house.

Jesus has been asked, in effect, "Who can be saved if not the rich and powerful?" He assures his disciples, who have already given up their past lives to follow him, that they will receive more than they have given up, and they already share a place in the kingdom of God. He responds to a blind beggar's cry for mercy with healing. Jesus responds to Zacchaeus in an act of mercy that transforms his whole outlook. Salvation looks different to each person as God's mercy is applied to their specific needs.

Who can be saved? Those who follow Jesus, the oppressed and the oppressor, and, despite the difficulty of pushing a camel through a needle's eye, even the rich, for "What is impossible for mortals is possible for God" (Luke 18:27).

The salvation of the blind beggar and Zacchaeus highlights the centrality of mercy in Jesus' strategy. He came "to seek and save what was lost" (19:10) through such acts of proactive, non-transactional mercy.

The story of Jesus' encounter with Zacchaeus is one of many that show the transformative potential of mercy. Mercy is not simply letting someone off the hook so that they "get away with" their failings. It is a generous gift that can lead to a radical reorientation in the life of the recipient. If we were to live mercifully, it would also require a radical reorientation of our attitudes as givers.

WHAT EXPERIENCES OF MERCY HAS THIS CHAPTER BROUGHT TO MIND: OCCASIONS WHEN YOU HAVE RECEIVED, WITNESSED, OR SHOWN MERCY?

[2]

THE ESSENCE OF MERCY

An initial thought to ponder: Please listen to the song "Mercy Now" by Mary Gauthier. There is a video of a live performance on YouTube and I am sure the song will be available elsewhere too. Does it seem to you as though too many of our modern social interactions lack the mercy we all so deeply need?

JESUS' INTERACTION WITH Zacchaeus highlights many features of mercy, and in the context of Luke's larger narrative, shows mercy to be a key ingredient in Jesus' recipe for human flourishing. We will see many more examples of mercy throughout this book that share three essential features with the story of Zacchaeus. Those three features are summed up in this definition:

Mercy is a gift of extreme kindness motivated by compassion.

Disrupting Mercy

My definition differs significantly from how the word is often used. More commonly, people use "mercy" to describe the leniency shown by someone in a position of power. They imagine a sword fight in which one combatant has been knocked to the ground. The victor's sword point is dramatically poised above the fallen one's neck. Will the loser be dispatched, or will the victor show mercy? Or they imagine a court room. The charges have been laid, the evidence weighed, and the verdict pronounced: "guilty as charged." In a final plea, the guilty party throws themselves on the mercy of the court. Will the just punishment be pronounced, or will the judge show clemency?

These archetypes of mercy on the battle field and in the court room have been passed on to us from ancient literature like the return of Ulysses in Homer's *Odyssey*, to modern storytelling like the 2000 movie *Gladiator*. They are shown in real-life cases such as Adolf Eichmann's trial after World War II, and the trial for drug transportation of the so-called Bali Nine in Indonesia.

What links those two images together is the idea of letting someone off the hook. In both cases, one party has failed: they have been insufficiently skilled in the fight or found to be morally blameworthy. They have lost, and their fate depends on another. That other is always depicted as physically higher—standing over the fallen combatant or elevated behind the judge's bench—to emphasize that they hold all the power.

In some religious contexts mercy is a synonym for almsgiving, that is, for charitable acts towards the poor and needy. That too suggests a power imbalance between the magnanimous giver and the pitiable receiver.

The appendix to this book delves into various conceptions of mercy in more detail, but my primary aim is to explore a conception that I think more accurately reflects its portrayal in the Bible, and that generates deeper insight into the transformative potential of mercy today.

A better starting point for understanding mercy than the battle field or court room is to consider its position within the ecology of love. In a natural ecology, plants, animals, soil, air, rain, and sunshine operate in synergy with each other. The health of the whole depends on the interactions between all the components. In the same way, mercy, pity, compassion, kindness, forgiveness, grace, clemency, justice, humility, empathy, generosity, caring, friendship, faithfulness, and love all jointly contribute to the practice of healthy interpersonal relationships and social cohesion, as well as to our understanding of God. We can think of this whole network of concepts as the ecology of love that sustains all life.

We must not, however, mistake mercy for the whole of that ecology. Mercy is always a manifestation of love, but although love provides the context for mercy, not every expression of love is an act of mercy. The romantic notion of "falling in love," for instance, bears little or no relation to mercy. We don't fall in love with someone because they are needy and we are able to offer them leniency from some position of superiority ... or at least I hope nobody does that! Putting aside that romantic meaning of "love," many other expressions of love are also outside the category of mercy. For instance, when we say we love God, we are not claiming to show mercy to God. Children may bring their mother breakfast in bed because of their love, but that is not mercy.

When we think of God as merciful, the idea springs from God's fundamental nature of love. Mercy is not the whole of God's love, though it is an important, perhaps even the most important, expression of it. Mercy includes God's compassion for our suffering, God's posture of grace that blossoms into kindness, and God's non-coercive generosity toward us.

Which brings us back to Zacchaeus, and to my non-standard definition of mercy. In the actions of Jesus toward Zacchaeus, we see God's compassion blossoming into a surprising act of non-coercive generosity to someone who does not appear to deserve it. Let's look more closely then at the three essential features of mercy: that it is motivated by compassion, that it is an unconditional gift, and that it is an extreme or surprising form of kindness.

MERCY IS MOTIVATED BY COMPASSION

My definition positions compassion as the motivation, the impulse, or the fuel, behind acts of mercy. Mercy is a gift of extreme kindness *motivated by compassion*.

Compassion is a heart-felt, or gut-level, yearning for another's well-being which starts with being able to truly notice them: not to look past them but to see them as a real person. Through this attentive seeing, you become more able to perceive the brokenness of the person's situation. You witness their suffering—their injury, guilt, shame, grief, or misfortune—or simply their need for food, companionship, shelter, etc. Having seen, compassion moves you from being a dispassionate observer to someone who *feels for* that person, and who wishes something better for them. I like the linguistic movement from "dispassion" to "compassion." Whereas "dispassion" means detached and undisturbed, the etymology of "compassion" relates to *suffering with*. To truly see another person is no longer to be detached from or unaffected by their suffering. You are stirred inwardly, with a yearning for the one in need.

This is easier in some cases than others. We find it easier to feel compassion for those close to us: family members and friends rather than strangers. When we perceive that a person's suffering is undeserved, we are more likely to feel compassion for them than when it seems they brought on the suffering by their own choices.

An act of mercy occurs when those precursors of compassion in our mind and heart are converted into action. Compassion does not always lead to mercy. Sometimes we can feel compassion for someone but be unwilling or unable to do anything about it. Our unwillingness may be simply hypocrisy, as James wrote, "If a brother or sister is naked and lacks daily food, and one of you says to them, 'Go in peace; keep warm and eat your fill', and yet you do not supply their bodily needs, what is the good of that?"—it is dead faith (James 2:15-16). There are, however, situations where we are not unwilling but rather unable to act on our compassion. This has become increasingly common in a globalized world where we see on TV and the internet a hundred different examples of human need every day. We see the need, feel compassion, and yet we cannot act to meet even 1 percent of that need.

Some may ask, "But can't I *act* with compassion? Can't I *feel* merciful?" That semantic difference depends on your personal language usage. Some people do indeed use "compassion" to refer to actions rather than an inner yearning. Some people do use "mercy" emotively, in forms like, "I am feeling merciful today." But to use the words as clearly as possible, I invite people to accept the distinction I am making, at least while reading this book. That allows me to separate the feeling from the action without laboring the point repeatedly.

True mercy is never founded on any motivation other than compassion. Suppose two people see a group of refugees dying from thirst. One responds, out of compassion, by providing tankers of water at their own expense. The other, seeing a commercial opportunity, provides similar tankers of water but finds a way to profit financially in the process. It's the same act but, because of differing motivations, the former is an act of mercy while the latter is not.[10]

Of course, the motivations for any decision or behavior are complex mixtures, often unconscious, and often self-serving. It is impractical to judge whether any human action arises purely from compassion. We can hardly evaluate our own motivations accurately let alone those of others. But at least in theory, if not in practice, the inner mechanism that drives mercy is compassion, however much the purity of that motivation might be muddied by other factors. God may be the only one whose mercy is motivated purely by compassion rather than self-interest.

Although compassion and pity are often used as synonyms, I avoid using the word pity because it has such a strong connotation of looking down on someone contemptuously. By emphasizing moral superiority, pity maintains the distance between people whereas compassion and mercy draw us together. As Friedrich Nietzsche pointed out,[11] pity demeans the receiver by implying that they are not able to deal with their own suffering. To show pity takes away the possibility of the sufferer learning and growing through their suffering.

The phrase "motivated by compassion" establishes the social context for mercy. To speak of compassion implies someone experiencing a need and someone noticing that need. Compassion implies an internal, often empathic, sorrow that becomes the motivation to act for the good of the other.

MERCY IS A GIFT

One of the challenges for actions motivated by compassion is how to avoid them being patronizing reinforcements of a power imbalance. How can one act in mercy without implying that we are the magnanimous rescuer of some poor wretch? I will return to that question several times in this book and will underline the importance of humility. Mercy operates from a stance of solidarity, that is, an understanding of our shared humanity, and a recognition that we all need each other. We all need mercy and are all able to show mercy.

Disrupting Mercy

An important reason why the giving and receiving of mercy is problematic in our culture is that we are so deeply influenced by a transactional view of interpersonal relationships. By "transactional," I mean the mindset in which there must always be an exchange. For everything we give we expect to receive something in return. We go to the shops expecting to take home some food in exchange for giving the shop owner some money. We go to work, giving our time and expertise in the expectation that we will be rewarded with a weekly salary. Both parties expect to receive something of equal or greater value to them than what they give, and when that does not occur feel either cheated by or indebted to the other.

We apply the same transactional thinking to non-financial contexts as well. When someone invites us to their home for dinner, we feel obliged to reciprocate or "return the favor" by inviting them to our home for dinner. When someone drops our kids off at school, we try to "balance the books" by looking after their dog when they go away for a weekend.

Transactional thinking is conditional: I'll scratch your back if you'll scratch mine. I'll forgive you but only after you say sorry. I'll wash the dishes today but I expect you to do it tomorrow. You'd better be good, or Santa won't bring you any presents.

In a world dominated by such thinking, the most radical contribution of mercy is that it is non-transactional and non-conditional. Mercy is a gift that does not *result* from debt. Mercy is never a repayment of something previously done for us, nor a responsibility that falls on us because we owe something to the other person. Mercy can never be demanded. It can only be given freely. Conversely, mercy does not *incur* any debt either. Mercy is a gift that does not need to be repaid, and in many cases cannot be repaid. Mercy can never be coercive, as though my goodness to you could force you to do something in return. To the extent that such an exchange occurs, it ceases to be mercy.

We all engage in transactional and non-transactional behavior. But living a life of mercy means giving greater space to the non-transactional, so that over time it increasingly crowds out the transactional.

Defining mercy as a gift is a challenging idea in the face of philosophical debates about the impossibility of any pure gift. Let's look briefly at why the idea of a gift is contentious.

French anthropologist Marcel Mauss (1872-1950) published a book in 1925 titled *The Gift: The Form and Reason for Exchange in Archaic Societies*. In that book he described gift exchange practices across several cultures and noted that gift-giving predated other forms of economic activities. Mauss documented three crucial features of gift-giving in those cultures: the socialized obligation to give, the obligation to receive, and the obligation to reciprocate.

French postmodernist Jacques Derrida (1930-2004) subsequently affirmed Mauss's study but claimed that *The Gift* "speaks of everything but the gift."[12] By this he meant that if there are obligations to exchange gifts then they cease to be gifts at all. "For there to be a gift, there must be no reciprocity, return, exchange, countergift, or debt."

Consequently, the practices Mauss had documented were not in fact examples of gifts. In Derrida's view true gifts are impossible: there is no such thing as a free gift because all supposed gifts imply obligations.

We are all aware of false gifts: gifts that are actually payments or rewards; gifts that come with strings attached. We are not fooled by retailers who distribute "free gift vouchers." But does the abundance of such false gifts mean that no true gift can be given?

In claiming that gifts are impossible, Derrida is not saying that is the end of the story. On the contrary, as John Caputo and Michael Scanlon note in a commentary on Derrida, "everything *interesting* for Derrida is impossible. ... Being impossible is what ignites our passion, gets us off dead center, and drives our desire to make it happen."[13] Having met Derrida in 1998, I can personally testify to that observation. At the time I was writing a Master's thesis on the topic of forgiveness while lecturing at the University of Natal in South Africa. Although the thesis was never completed, the experience clarified my own thinking about the relational, social, psychological, legal, religious, and philosophical aspects of forgiveness, and in a sense laid the foundation stones for this current book. Derrida delivered a lecture at my university, titled "Forgiving the Unforgivable." I introduced myself to him after the lecture and he was kind enough to listen to the ideas I was working on. In his view, we misuse the label "forgiveness" for relational mishaps that are too trivial to really need forgiving. In fact, the idea of forgiveness only becomes relevant when something is truly unforgivable, but at that point forgiveness can no longer be applied. For Derrida, the notions of both gift and forgiveness suffer from internal inconsistencies that make them rationally impossible.

Regardless of how impossible gift, forgiveness, or mercy may seem *to reason*, and regardless of how much we misunderstand them or spoil their purity, they are nevertheless part of our human experience. In my own understanding, gifts tend asymptotically[14] toward an ideal. Every actual gift falls short of the ideal, but for any difference you might point out between an example of a gift and the ideal, there will be another example closer to the ideal. For all practical purposes, actually occurring events come as close to the ideal of a gift as you could ever want. That observation makes any argument about the impossibility of a true gift irrelevant.

Certainly, our human acts of mercy may all be tainted with other less than noble motives. Even when our attempts to bless others are unalloyed with self-interest, we may receive something in return. That may have nothing to do with our ability to give freely, but with the recipient's inability to receive. As we will see later, the ideal of pure mercy is demonstrated by God in Christ. Followers of Jesus are called to imitate that mercy, and the fact that we do so only imperfectly does not detract from the ideal.

A wonderful example of a simple gift that comes close to the ideal is recounted by Paul Salopek. Salopek set out from Ethiopia in 2013, intending to walk twenty-one thousand miles to the southern tip of Chile. While in Uzbekistan, he recorded this incident:

> *The Fergana sky is waxy, overcast and cold. The sun hangs dully in it, a pale cocoon. On the frozen road ahead strides Tolik Bekniyazov, our lanky donkey driver. A taciturn nomad. At some old trailside camp he must have noticed me squinting, with book-ruined eyes, toiling to spear a licked thread—the cheapest nylon, not silk—through the eye of a needle, perhaps mending my coat. Soon we will part ways at a new border. And I will discover many days later, shaking my head in wonder, that he has threaded and knotted every needle in my sewing kit.*[15]

The donkey driver was a travelling companion for only a brief time. His simple act of kindness was performed in secret with no expectation of reward. Surely he knew that Salopek would not discover the threaded needles until after they had parted. There was virtually no chance that they would ever meet again, and whatever joy he experienced was found in the act of kindness itself, not in anything that Salopek might give in return. It was a simple gift, with no pre-conditions, no debt to repay, and without expectation that he would even be thanked. There were threads in the needles, but there were no strings attached to the gift!

Such examples are not rare, although it may seem that way within the "economy of exchange" that dominates patriarchal thinking. As Derrida admits, and Jean-Luc Marion emphasizes, it is only within that economy of exchange that gifts are impossible.[16] While they muddle

The Essence of Mercy

around striving to find the right way to account for the gift as an impossible concept, I am more convinced by the approach of Genevieve Vaughan, who points out that outside the economy of exchange there is a parallel "economy of gift" familiar to every mother. The mothering role has *always* relied on a non-calculating response to a child's needs.[17] A mother holding a baby at her breast gives milk freely without any expectation of payment or reward. (Fathers and others can also care for children in this way, but the pattern is shown archetypically by mothers.) Those parental interactions precede any historical social expression of transactional exchange, and our personal experience of receiving a gift precedes any sense of payment or debt psychologically. If that parental attitude had been sufficiently valued, Vaughan suggests we might now think of ourselves as fundamentally *Homo donans*—the humans who give—rather than *Homo sapiens*, and what a world of difference that would make![18]

From a theological perspective, God's mothering of us is perhaps the most fruitful image of the genesis of mercy. I will say more about that connection in the later section on the Hebrew word *racham*, but I want to dwell here for a while to emphasize the importance of Vaughan's account of gift-giving.

We have become so enmeshed in the transactional way of interacting, as required by an exchange economy, that we forget our fundamental dependence on gifts. In an economy, the primary social act is the exchange of goods or services. This may be a direct exchange—I give you a chicken and you give me a kilogram of potatoes—or an

25

exchange mediated by money—I give you a chicken, you give me five dollars, and I know I can exchange that money for a kilogram of potatoes in a subsequent transaction. Every object and service is valued according to what it can be exchanged for. Embedded in a world driven by exchange, we easily start to think that the many expressions of love must also involve exchange: that expressions of love incur a debt to be repaid, that kindness is conditional, that mercy must be deserved, that forgiveness must be earned.

But think of all the gifts we receive. Putting aside birthday presents and the like, consider the gifts of light, air, water, warmth, birdsong, potatoes, scents, and flavors that the earth gives us, all for free. We take such things for granted, as givens, as simply being there in the background of our lives. They are present to us with or without our attention. They are presents to us without any requirement that we give in return. They are gifts from creation that reflect the givingness of the Creator.

Consider the gift of language: of words, meanings, and sentence structures that enable an infinite variety of communication. We do not earn or pay for language, but as children we receive it as a free gift from our families. Consider the gifts of wonder, insight, and joy given to us by art, music, and poetry. Of course books, music, and art can be sold to us, but I'm not talking about how *access* to those things can be controlled through exchange: I'm talking about how the story itself, the painting itself, or the photo, the song, the movie, the poem, all give us something, whether that be an emotion, a memory, or a new idea. Like many aspects of life, such experiences come to us freely, unilaterally, without any possibility of us paying back. Consider the gifts of unpaid labor: of volunteers who deliver Meals on Wheels, of homemakers who cook, clean, and create welcoming spaces, of counsel and comfort from friends.

In an exchange economy, all such gifts are dis-counted. They are not *undervalued*, but literally *not counted* in economic measures. But the exchange economy could not operate without that substrate of gift-giving. The apparent necessity of exchange is an illusion that acts as a curtain behind which is hidden the myriad gifts that enable human flourishing.

The exchange economy, and the transactional thinking that is inextricably linked to it, is driven by what each party deserves, that is, on what is earned by the perceived value of things being exchanged. Whatever I give, I deserve to receive something back of at least equal value. If I pay $50 for a massage then I deserve to receive $50 worth of massaging services. If I work for a day then I have earned a fair day's wages. In contrast, a gift economy operates on the basis of needs rather than deserts.

The exchange economy is parasitic on the underlying gift economy. The former could not operate without the latter, but the narrative power of the exchange economy makes the host it devours appear of no value. Giving freely without any demand for payment or imposition of debt seems like an irrational weakness, an exception to the rule. The truth, however, is that the gift economy is the natural, sustaining reality of life.

Assumptions from exchange economics have come to dominate much of our thinking, including much of our so-called Christian theology. In part, this book is an attempt to undermine that influence by promoting a gift-based theology of mercy. Our decision to offer this book freely to anyone who requests it is an attempt to make the possibility of a gift economy more visible. Our hope is that at least some readers will catch the vision and "pay it forward" through their own giving to others.

Mercy is a powerful antidote to transactional thinking. Mercy is a demonstration of God's givingness, the foundation stone of a gift economy, and a vital tool for undermining our enchantment with the exchange economy. Mercy may be the scissors that cut the curtain of illusion from top to bottom, so that we can once again see the hidden treasure of gift-giving. Because it is unexpected in the context of an exchange economy, the gift of mercy has the disruptive potential to reveal the centrality of giving in human experience, and to save us from the tyranny of transactional thinking.

To avoid a misunderstanding about gifts and transactions, I need to clarify my use of the word reciprocity. In some of the literature about gifts, reciprocity is understood in terms of a bidirectional exchange: I give to you and you reciprocate by giving to me, and we both understand the mutual obligation implied by the transaction. In drawing on the concept of gift economy, however, I will normally use the phrase "network of reciprocity," which means something quite different. Participants in a gift economy form a tapestry of relationships in which giving and receiving are uncoupled. In a network of reciprocity, giving is undertaken freely and without any requirement for repayment. The community shares its abundance "in an endless choreography of generosity and care,"[19] ensuring that all can flourish together. Experiencing this nourishing circularity leaves an entirely different flavor from transactional exchange.

God is the architect of that network of reciprocity, and God invites us into that web of love, grace, and mercy. Notice that 1 John 4:11 says, "Since God loved us so much, we also ought to love one another." This instruction to pass on the love we receive is the biblical foundation for a pay-it-forward strategy. The verse does not say, "Since God loved us, we ought to love God back." God's love is a gift to be passed on rather than a debt to be repaid. Similarly, Peter wrote that "Like good stewards of the manifold grace of God, serve one another with whatever gift each of you has received" (1 Peter 4:10). In other words, we receive God's grace as stewards rather than owners or debtors, and are expected to share the gift with others.

God is also a participant in the network of reciprocity. God donates to us and also receives from us within that circular reciprocity. That may sound controversial, because God surely needs nothing from us. God is not "served by human hands, as though he needed anything" (Acts 17:25). But the fact that God does not *need* anything from us does not mean God does not *receive* anything from us. God receives our praise, even though if we did not give our praise the very earth would call out its praise instead (Luke 19:40, Psalm 66:4). God receives our prayers

(Revelation 5:8, 8:4) and David suggests that God even collects our tears (Psalm 56:8). Nicodemus provided a tomb for Jesus, a Samaritan woman gave Jesus water, a woman washed Jesus' feet with her hair. Surely as a mother, Mary showed mercy to her son. According to Jesus, when we do good or bad to those in need, God counts it as though we did it to God. In all these ways, the Bible shows God receiving from people.

MERCY IS EXTREME KINDNESS

The world desperately needs more kindness. Kindness is a fundamental need for any stable human society, and a virtue we are sorely missing. Many voices today are calling for a recovery of kindness, empathy, gratitude, and tolerance.[20]

Although those voices are important, in this book I start with an assumption of kindness as the base level. Civilization has not survived and cannot survive without people helping each other, smiling, apologizing, mentoring, and by being honest, gentle, and caring toward each other. Many of those acts may be motivated by compassion and offered as gifts. Even so, they may be acts of kindness without being acts of mercy.

Followers of Jesus are called to something more. That is why I define mercy as *extreme kindness*. Mercy goes beyond what is morally required, what can be reasonably expected, or what is essential to social stability.

I suggested a situation earlier where a group of refugees were dying for lack of water, and someone responded compassionately by providing tankers of water, without

The Essence of Mercy

cost to the refugees. To add another nuance to that scene, compare the case where the person providing the water paid for it out of their own savings, to the case where the person applied for a government grant that covered the costs. In both cases the motive is the same, but we are more likely to think of the latter case as simply kindness. The person has arranged to help but at no great personal cost. The self-sacrifice in the former case, however, goes beyond what anyone could ethically require. By acting "above and beyond" what could be expected, the person has acted with true mercy.

I use the word "extreme" with caution because mercy can still be shown by people who apparently have nothing to give. The extremity of kindness can be situated along many dimensions. It may be sacrificial, entailing personal risk, offered toward an enemy or toward someone whom everyone else dismisses. It may be extravagant in its persistence or generosity. But extreme does not mean expensive, as though only the rich, got-it-all-together, healthy, successful people can afford to show mercy. We dishonor and disempower too many people if we ever imply that the poor or broken cannot show mercy. Mercy is not charity in the sense of giving as much money as you can. As Jesus once observed, two small copper coins can be a greater gift than wads of hundred dollar bills (Mark 12:41-44; Luke 21:1-4). The size of the gift does not define mercy, but the size of the heart and the nature of the giving.

Mercy is like this. Once there was woman walking from Jerusalem to Jericho, when she fell into the hands of some robbers who beat her until she was almost dead. They were laughing at her when suddenly a priest came into view. The robbers freaked out and ran away, but one tripped and was trampled by the priest's horse as he too tried to get away from the scene as quickly as possible. The woman passed out, but when she came to, the injured robber still lay there, twenty meters away, screaming in agony. After she slowly and painfully crawled over to him, she could see the massive amount of blood he had already lost, pooled around him. Unable to do anything else, she lifted his head onto her leg and stroked his brow until he died.

The woman's kindness was simple and inexpensive, yet in the context surprising and extreme. Mercy is located not in the cost of the gift but in the heartfelt way she affirmed the dying man's worth.[21] Maybe "surprising" is just as good an adjective as "extreme."

WHY THIS DEFINITION?

The term "mercy" has been interpreted in many ways and often covers a much broader concept than what my definition based on compassion, gift, and extreme kindness allows. From one perspective, any definition of mercy will be inadequate, because it is more of a visceral than an intellectual concept. Nevertheless, at the risk of over-intellectualizing, I want to avoid equating mercy with everything that is loving, good, or godly. If mercy is taken to encompass too much then it ends up meaning nothing.

The idea that mercy is *motivated by compassion* situates mercy within the context of need, and clarifies the relational motivation that responds to that need. Defining mercy as *a gift* moves the concept out of the economy of exchange and into the ecology of love; out of the realm of bilateral transactions and into a network of reciprocity. Defining mercy as *extreme kindness* repositions it from being merely nice to being unexpected and extravagant.

People who think that mercy is *nice* have most likely not understood mercy at all. Mercy is neither passive nor weak, but rather proactive, bold, and risky. Mercy is disruptive and outrageous to the point of being scandalous. Mercy takes human needs seriously, as it does evil and human brokenness. Mercy does not let people off the hook or sweep evil under the rug. But neither does mercy turn its back on human needs or run away from evil.

Mercy does not confront evil with evil, as though the most powerful will win. It does not punish violence by imposing another form of violence. On the contrary, aren't we all familiar with cases of mercy that deny or even reverse an established power structure? What of the mercy shown by an oppressed group to their oppressors: patiently waiting in hope for the oppressor to find their own humanity? What of a child caring for an alcoholic parent: bearing their abuse while daring to believe that something good may yet be loved back into wholeness?

Mercy plays a vital role within a network of reciprocity. The network itself is a fabric woven with threads of kindness, generosity, and mutual care. Regardless of how strong such a fabric may be, there will still be broken threads that can lead to gaping holes. People trip up physically or relationally, they become sick and unable to give, they become fearful and unable to receive, they will be hurt and will hurt others. The job of mercy is to repair the fabric so that those in need do not become disconnected from the nurturing community. A tapestry protected by mercy can be seen not so much in the beauty of the front face, but in the tangle of knots on the underside that have repaired the many broken threads. We need more people committed to tying knots.

You might disagree with this way of defining mercy. But there is *something* that is central to God's character, central to the gospel, central to God's intention to reconcile all things in heaven and earth, central to the possibility of human community, and consequently central to the project of human flourishing. That *something* is a gift. It is a form of extreme kindness. It is motivated not by duty or any external obligation, but by compassion. I cannot think of a more appropriate word for that *something* than mercy. I invite you while reading this book to be open to that *something*, so that the transformative potential of mercy seeps through for you too.

Which aspect of mercy—compassion, gift, or extreme kindness—most resonates with you? Which aspect most challenges you?

[3]

MERCY IN THE OLD TESTAMENT

An initial thought to ponder: In The Merchant of Venice, Shakespeare's character Portia says:
> The quality of mercy is not strain'd
> It droppeth as the gentle rain from heaven
> Upon the place beneath; it is twice blest,
> It blesseth him that gives, and him that takes.

Have you been blessed as the recipient of mercy? Have you felt the blessedness of showing mercy to someone else?

A LONG TIME AGO, in a culture far, far away, a young ploughman was chosen to replace Israel's leading prophet. The chosen one was Elisha and he was born during a violent period of Jewish history after the commonwealth of Kings Saul, David, and Solomon had collapsed. Internal political machinations had led to the breakup of the kingdom, with Jehoram ruling in the north, Jehoshaphat in the south, and Mesha in the south-east, while the external forces of Aram threatened from the north-east. Elisha lived through that time and eventually died peacefully as an old man. But what happened between 1 Kings 19 and 2 Kings 13 was a remarkable life of mercy.

Elisha took up the mantle of Elijah—he literally picked up Elijah's cloak and thus created the metaphor we still use today to signify a change of leadership. Elijah had been an outspoken critic of his own king and queen, a man with political and religious power who did not shy away from violence to protect religious purity. When Elisha saw Elijah mysteriously taken up to heaven in a fiery chariot, he received a "double portion" of the spirit of his mentor. He had watched Elijah at work and learned from his words about both politics and faith. But how well would Elijah's mantle sit on the shoulders of this ploughman apprentice?

Virtually all the stories recorded about Elisha show him helping people in need, with kindness and peace. He made poisoned food safe. He miraculously fed one hundred men with a few loaves of bread. He raised a friend's dead son to life. When an army with horses and chariots attacked from Aram, Elisha prayed for them to be blinded—not as a punishment but so that he could safely lure them away. The blind army followed him to Samaria and when their eyes were opened again, behold, they were captured! Although others urged him to kill the prisoners, Elisha instead hosted a feast for them and sent them home. The result? No more raids from Aram!

Elisha's attitude to enemies is shown even more in his interaction with Naaman, a commander of the enemy Aramean army, who had some dreadful skin disease. Naaman's wife had a personal slave, a young Israeli girl, who said in effect, "Your husband should go to the prophet in Samaria; I'm sure he could heal him." Naaman's wife told Naaman, and Naaman told the king of Aram. The king, surely realizing what a political storm it would cause, wrote a letter to the king of Israel politely asking his enemy to cure Naaman. The king of Israel metaphorically pulled his hair out pondering how to avoid the trap: he had no way to heal Naaman, but just as clearly, if he did not then the offense to the king of Aram would escalate to further violence.

On hearing about the problem, Elisha said very coolly to the king, "What's your problem? Just send Naaman to me." The king complied and, to cut a long story short, Elisha arranged for Naaman to be healed by washing in the Jordan River.

Although Naaman had come with chariots full of silver and gold, Elisha refused to accept any payment. In fact, Elisha became angry when his personal assistant took payment behind his back. However, although Elisha's act was a gift, this did not mean it was without intent or effect. Elisha said to Naaman, "Go in peace," and I am sure that a broad smile graced his face, because Naaman was not only physically healed but also transformed. Through the water of the Jordan River Naaman was born again and went home a servant of the true God.

Disrupting Mercy

All these incidents show Elisha responding compassionately to people's immediate physical needs with a double portion of kindness. He repeatedly opens new opportunities for people, giving them a second chance to flourish. Even after his own death, the final mention of Elisha underscores the same pattern of mercy: when a dead man was hastily thrown into Elisha's tomb, the man miraculously bounced back to life!

On the other hand, Elisha was not always so merciful. Soon after taking over from Elijah, Elisha was travelling to Bethel when a gang of boys accosted him with an obscure taunt: "Go away, baldy" or some such insult. Incensed, Elisha cursed them and, perhaps to everyone's surprise, "two she-bears came out of the woods and mauled forty-two of the boys."

What are we to make of such unwarranted violence? Jewish commentary in the Talmud suggests that Elisha was later punished for this overreaction. Other people argue that the insult was more significant than I have described and that the boys deserved what they got.[22] The biblical text, however, does not say that. In fact, it makes no commentary on the incident whatsoever, which leaves an opening for many interpretations. In the narrative flow, one clear result of the incident is that it cements Elisha's authority as Elijah's successor.

In my own view, the inclusion of this incident in the biography of Elisha's life reminds us that even people with moral failures may still feel empathy and on their better days offer gifts of extreme kindness. The ability to show mercy is not limited to those who are morally perfect.

Further, I think this early outburst of arrogance disrupted the trajectory of Elisha's ministry. The tragic result of being unmerciful to those boys may have been the prompt he needed to turn aside from the violence of his predecessor and toward the compassion of his God.

CHESED, RACHAM AND OTHER HEBREW WORDS

Readings of the Bible that juxtapose an angry God of the Old Testament with a merciful God of the New Testament do not do justice to the rich theology of mercy within the Old Testament. To understand that heritage, our first step will be to understand the key Hebrew words within the ecology of love.

Given the overlap between English concepts such as mercy, compassion, pity, sympathy, love, and kindness, we will not be surprised to find that in other languages, multiple words for these concepts display the same ambiguity. As is normally the case with language translation, the words for these concepts in Hebrew do not relate to English words in a one-to-one correspondence. As a result, the suite of Hebrew words used in the Old Testament to describe these concepts are translated inconsistently in English versions of the Bible.

The two most significant and relevant words are *chesed* (or *hesed*) and *racham*. *Chesed* and its variants occur over 280 times in the Old Testament, usually translated as loving-kindness or steadfast love, though some English versions of the Bible frequently use mercy, and the NRSV even opts for "clemency" in Micah 7:18. Although love is an essential component of *chesed*, *chesed* is not the normal

Hebrew word for love, which is *aheb* (verb) or *ahabah* (noun). *Chesed* is that type of love most clearly shown in the abundance of God's enduring kindness and faithfulness. *Racham*, in various forms as verb, noun, and adjective, occurs over one hundred times. It too can mean love, but primarily that form of love shown in compassion or mercy.

In the vast majority of Old Testament uses, *chesed* and *racham* relate to God's posture toward us, but they emphasize different aspects of that posture. The two complement rather than oppose each other, and are often found together, as in the well-known verse "The steadfast love *[chesed]* of the LORD never ceases, his mercies *[racham]* never come to an end" (Lamentations 3:22), and repeatedly in Psalm 103.

Chesed is mostly associated with God's covenant with humanity—especially Israel—and is expressed through God's faithfulness to that covenant. *Chesed* has legal, contractual connotations, but this does not imply that God's loving-kindness results from a pre-existing covenant, as though the covenant obliges God to be faithful, loving, and kind. Rather, it is the reverse: the covenant with Israel flowed from God's pre-existing *chesed*. This is clear from an oft-repeated pattern in the Bible where God's loving-kindness continues to rescue Israel (and others) even when they violate their side of the covenant.

Racham, on the other hand, emphasizes the heart-felt compassion typified by a parent's love for their child. As Pope John Paul II expresses it, "Of this love one can say that it is completely gratuitous, not merited, and that in this aspect it constitutes an interior necessity: an exigency of the heart."[23] *Racham's* linguistic root means womb. A womb is the original safe place where we all once sheltered in warmth and nourishment. In Arabic, the same linguistic link is evident, with *rahim* (womb) and *rahma* (mercy) sharing the same root. Consequently, in Islamic thinking, God is the womb from which we were born. The prophet Hosea says much the same thing. When calling Israel to return to the Lord, he writes, "In you the orphan finds mercy" (Hosea 14:3): in God, even the motherless finds a womb!

A contemporary Jewish understanding of this relationship between mercy and womb adds that no merit is required of a baby in the womb. The baby neither deserves nor does not deserve to be taken care of. The mother provides food, safety, warmth, and love because of her joy in the *potential* of the unborn child, not because of anything that the child has done. The child is given care in the hope that the child will grow up to be worthy of it. When we call for mercy, we are in effect saying, "Please God, don't look at me for what I have done, please judge me based on my potential for the future; treat me like the unborn, like a baby in the womb."[24]

However, while I agree with the thought that mercy does not depend on the merit of the recipient, this particular Jewish understanding does not capture the essence of parental love, and hence misses something important about mercy. A mother cares for the child in her womb because it is *her child*, flesh of her flesh. Her love does not depend on the future potential of the child. Future merit is still merit, turning the mother's love into a delayed transaction. The child does not earn the mother's care through future worthiness. Although a parent hopes their child will flourish, the love for the child is in no way dependent on that hope coming to fruition. If a mother magically knew that the child in her womb would grow into a mass murderer, she would still love and nurture it. Womb-like love, if it is "because" of anything, is because of the nature of being a mother, just as God's love and mercy toward us is because of who God is rather than because of anything we have done, will do, or even might do.

Those covenantal and parental aspects of mercy are augmented by several other Hebrew words:

- *Salach* occurs 51 times, meaning forgiveness.
- *Chus* occurs 23 times and is translated as pity, to look on with compassion, and sometimes as the concept of sparing someone.
- *Chamal* and its variant *chemlah* occur 43 times and although their primary meaning is to spare, they are also translated as pity, mercy, and compassion. In nine verses, *chus* and *chamal* are used together in the negative to emphasize that no leniency should or will be shown.
- *Chanan* occurs in various forms about two hundred times, mostly in the sense of pleading or beseeching, though sometimes as a gracious response to such pleading. Occasionally this is interpreted specifically as an appeal for mercy (e.g., in Job 9:15). The

Mercy in the Old Testament

idea of grace or favor is repeated in variants such as *techinnah*, which is also sometimes translated as mercy (e.g., Joshua 11:20).

- *Nasa* occurs many times in the sense of taking something away, and sometimes has the moral sense of pardon or forgiveness, through which our guilt or punishment is taken away (e.g., 1 Samuel 15:25; Exodus 34:7; Micah 7:18).
- *Kapporeth* is often translated as mercy-seat but the association with mercy is indirect. The word literally means a covering and always refers to the gold slab on top of the ark of the covenant. The *kapporeth* plays a key role in the Day of Atonement ritual described in Leviticus 16, and in the New Testament Paul refers to Jesus as the mercy-seat (Romans 3:25).[25]

Last, a central concern in the Old Testament that overflows into the New is the maintenance of *shalom*. This Hebrew word, often translated "peace," encompasses all aspects of things being right: physical well-being, social harmony, moral goodness. *Shalom* is the state in which individuals can flourish because relationships are whole and good, including relationships with each other, with God, and with the created world. *Shalom* is never translated as mercy, but it provides the teleological context in which mercy becomes important. I make that point clearer in Chapter 5, "Mercy and Justice."

Keeping in mind the distinctions and the overlaps between all these words, I now turn to how they are used in the Old Testament depiction of mercy. Rather than exegeting the role of mercy through the whole Old Testament, I will focus on two exemplary passages, first the book of Hosea, and then the well-known verse, Micah 6:8.

THE MERCY OF GOD IN HOSEA

The disturbing set of prophecies by Hosea forms one of the Old Testament's most extravagant portrayals of mercy. Hosea lived in the northern kingdom of Israel about two hundred years after it split from the southern kingdom of Judah. He was keen to show how far the northern kingdom had moved away from God, and the dire consequences of the nation's unfaithfulness for them as well as for the world around them.

> *There is no faithfulness or loyalty [chesed],*
>   *and no knowledge of God in the land.*
> *Swearing, lying, and murder,*
>   *and stealing and adultery break out;*
>   *bloodshed follows bloodshed.*
> *Therefore the land mourns,*
>   *and all who live in it languish;*
> *together with the wild animals*
>   *and the birds of the air,*
>   *even the fish of the sea are perishing. (Hosea 4:1-3)*

The idea comes to Hosea that God's people are acting like an unfaithful wife, and worse: like a wife who acts as a prostitute.[26] In a provocative and problematically patriarchal move, Hosea sees the nation's unfaithfulness reflected in the unfaithfulness of his own wife Gomer. This powerful,

Mercy in the Old Testament

emotional, and deeply personal anguish pushes the metaphor toward hyperbole. Hosea believes God told him to marry Gomer even though she was a prostitute who would inevitably be unfaithful. He names his daughter Lo-ruhamah, which means literally "no mercy," and one of his sons Lo-Ammi, "not my people." Hosea curses his adulterous nation, calling on God to "give them a miscarrying womb and dry breasts" (9:14).

Hosea's attitude is deeply offensive. Imagine being either his wife or his children, thrown under the bus by your husband/father in the name of God! Imagine being pushed onto the social stage as an object lesson in faithlessness, unforgiveness, and disinheritance.

Fortunately, that is not the end of the story. As often happens, the biblical text subverts its own bias so that we are left thinking that the "righteous" anger of Hosea is given center-stage so that it can be contrasted with a radical revelation of God's mercy. The text claims that God will punish Israel for her unfaithfulness (2:13) but also that God will woo her (2:14). The future hope is that Israel will relate to God as a wife to a husband rather than as a slave to a master (2:16), and that the nation will once again know itself to be God's people on whom God has mercy (2:23).

The truth is that all along, while unfaithful Israel pursued other lovers, God continued to give her food and silver, and even the gold she threw away to her lovers (2:7-8). Such unfaithfulness inevitably results in hunger and barrenness (4:10) but God loves even those who turn aside to other gods (3:1). Israel, and by implication all of us, will remain in desolation until they acknowledge their guilt and turn to seek God (5:15).

In the meantime, it can seem as though we live under God's wrath. Hosea writes in the voice of God, "Woe to them, for they have strayed from me! Destruction to them, for they have rebelled against me!" (7:13). God will punish their sins, even to the point of returning them to slavery in Egypt (8:13). "I will love them no more" (9:15).

But then comes a surprisingly anthropomorphic turn: the husband and father—God—cannot maintain such anger. The turn starts with the word "yet" in 11:3. Despite Israel and Ephraim's unfaithfulness, God recalls the father-like joy of teaching a child to walk, and of lifting a child to cuddle. How could a father subject their child to anger and desolation?

> *How can I give you up, Ephraim?*
> *How can I hand you over, O Israel? ...*
> *My heart recoils within me;*
> *my compassion grows warm and tender.*
> *I will not execute my fierce anger;*
> *I will not again destroy Ephraim;*
> *for I am God and no mortal,*
> *the Holy One in your midst,*
> *and I will not come in wrath. (Hosea 11:8-9)*

To clarify the naming confusion, recall that Abraham's grandson Jacob was later renamed Israel and subsequently the label "Israel" was applied to all of Jacob's descendants. Ephraim was one of Jacob's grandsons and so the label

"Ephraim" refers to one significant tribe within the Israelite people.

"My heart recoils" can be translated literally as "My heart is overturned." When God contemplates giving up on Ephraim/Israel it is as though God's heart is upside down. To reject Israel would create a divine cognitive dissonance that Hosea recognizes could not prevail. Why not? Because "I am God and no mortal." God's holy essence is not expressed in wrath, but in mercy.

This is the central revelation of Hosea and one of the convictions that animate the Old Testament's whole trajectory. God is not fundamentally wrathful. God's nature, God's heart, is warmed by compassion rather than by the fire of wrath.

Walter Kasper expresses this conviction well (apart from the gendered language):

> *This deeply moving passage shows that God already in the Old Testament is not an angry and righteous God, but rather a merciful God. Nor is he an apathetic God, who sits on his throne, oblivious to all the sin and distress of the world. He is a God who has a heart, which flares up in anger, but which then overturns itself out of mercy. With this "subversion," God shows himself, on the one hand, to be moved in a seemingly human way and, on the other, he reveals himself as being completely other than mortals. He reveals himself as the Holy One, the Wholly Other. The constitution of his essence, which fundamentally distinguishes him from human beings and elevates him above everything mortal, is his mercy. It is his sublimity and sovereignty; it is his holy essence.*[27]

There is certainly an element of anthropomorphism in the claim (by Hosea and Kasper) that God has a heart that can change, but we should not imagine this as a naive projection of human emotional volatility. The intended direction of this metaphor is the reverse: God's proclivity for mercy rather than wrath acts as the model for the highest ideal of our human hearts.

Those who seek God, find mercy. Those who seek to honor God will find their heart turned in the same way as God's: away from wrath and toward mercy.

HOSEA, COVENANT, AND CONDITIONALITY

The prophecy of Hosea starts with an understanding embedded in covenantal thinking. The covenant between God and Israel, operating like a marriage, has been violated. Hosea thinks of Israel's plight in terms of adultery and prostitution. The problem is relational: like an unfaithful wife, Israel has broken a covenant (8:1).

"Covenant" is explicitly mentioned five times in Hosea: the promise of a new covenant (2:18); that Israel has violated the covenant (6:7, 8:1); that Israel too easily makes empty promises to (10:4), and treaties with, other nations (12:1). In a covenant, the parties pledge themselves to each other: this is not a business contract in which certain actions and payments are agreed, but a mutual giving of oneself to the other. This idea of covenant underpins Hosea's whole approach. Israel has traded a husband-and-wife relationship with God for a slave-and-master relationship with Baal, but God persists in the hope that the earlier

Mercy in the Old Testament

covenant can be renewed (2:14-16). God woos Israel toward peace and safety with the promise:

> *I will take you for my wife for ever; I will take you for my wife in righteousness and in justice, in steadfast love, and in mercy. I will take you for my wife in faithfulness; and you shall know the LORD. (Hosea 2:19-20)*

Walter Brueggemann noted that these verses encapsulate the five key characteristics of a covenant: righteousness, justice, steadfast love *(chesed)*, mercy *(racham)*, and faithfulness.[28] I would also add the characteristic of "for ever" that is part of what distinguishes a covenant from a contract. Despite the patriarchal language (the implication of female inferiority and the right of a male to "take" her), this hoped-for covenant reflects God's self-giving in the context of mutuality. Within that mutuality, Israel will come to know God truly and intimately.

The story gets more theologically interesting when Hosea reflects on why God withholds wrath and gives Israel another chance. God sees Israel's unfaithfulness—their rejection of God (7:13) and the moral corruption (9:9) that arises from that rejection—as well as their suffering (4:2-3, 7:9) and responds in mercy. That mercy encompasses both the forgiveness of their guilt and the easing of their suffering. But what prompts God's mercy?

Thinking about covenant sheds light on what can seem to be an ambiguity of conditionality in the Bible. What I mean by the "ambiguity of conditionality" is that at times the Bible speaks in conditional terms about how God relates to us while at other times it voices unconditional promises. There seems to be some equivocation in the Bible about whether God's love, forgiveness, and mercy are conditional or not. In some cases, they appear transactional, based on reciprocal obligations, and with conditional blessings and curses. In other cases, God appears to act unilaterally with no pre- or post-conditions, and seems to make commitments to act without regard for anything we might do.

As a simple example, God's word to David (through the prophet Nathan) in 2 Samuel 7 ends with the unconditional promise that "Your house and your kingdom shall be made sure for ever." In Psalm 132, however, that assurance is qualified: "If your sons keep my covenant and my decrees that I shall teach them, their sons also, for evermore, shall sit on your throne" (v. 12). So, will David's kingdom stand for ever or does its future depend on David's sons' faithfulness to the covenant?

The ambiguity may be resolved in various ways. Perhaps under the verses that seem unconditional lie unstated conditions, so that all of God's promises are dependent on our acceptance of them and our faithfulness to God. Perhaps Paul's claim that "you reap whatever you sow" (Galatians 6:7) shows that what can look like a conditional promise is often a statement of natural consequences.

The ultimate reality is that God can show mercy toward whomever God chooses to show mercy (Exodus 33:19). But another dynamic at play is that the conditionality of some biblical statements depends on whether they are situated within the context of covenant or not. A covenant imposes obligations on the parties, e.g., "I will walk among you, and will be your God, and you shall be my people ... But if you will not obey me ..." (Leviticus 26:12, 14). Conditional statements, requirements, and consequences are natural within such a legal context.

Outside of covenant obligations, however, the relationship between God and humanity is less conditional. Even when people violate their covenant obligations, God can remain faithful, because that is the nature of God (Romans 3:3; 2 Timothy 2:13). God's covenants with humanity are themselves motivated by *chesed*. As I noted before, covenants are not the cause of God's loving-kindness toward us but one of its results. Beyond covenant, God's posture toward us is one of freely given and unconditional grace. Mercy may prompt a covenant and be expressed through covenant, but mercy predates covenant and is independent from it. God can be, and is, merciful outside the obligations of covenant.

That might lead some to question why God bothers with covenants. If unconditional mercy always trumps the conditional requirements of a covenant, what is the point of a covenant? Why does God institute a covenant with us if God knows it is going to fail but will step in with unconditional mercy and love anyway? The reason becomes clearer once we understand that the covenants between God and humanity were established for our sake rather than for God's. As parents, we know how important boundaries are for our children. By defining boundaries, parents provide a scaffolding for developmental growth and safety. God uses covenants in the same way for us all.

Boundary setting is itself an act of mercy: a kindness toward the needs inherent in immaturity. When a child pushes the boundaries or violate a covenant, a good parent may allow the consequences or punishments of the covenant to affect them. That too is a form of mercy to the extent that the child might learn from the discomfort. But a good parent would never allow the covenant boundary to be the final word, especially when that puts the life or health of their child at risk.

Might it be that the notion of covenant obligations captures the conditional aspects of God's interaction with humans, while mercy captures the unconditional aspects? That is certainly the case in Hosea, where God's response to Israel's need springs from two sources: God's heartfelt compassion for them and God's covenantal pledge to be faithful to them.

When kindness is enacted solely because of an obligation, it ceases to be mercy. Mercy is a free gift, not a contractual transaction. Mercy is prompted by compassion, not duty. Yet there is no contradiction between the obligation and the free act. An act of kindness may be simultaneously an obligation and a free gift. God may show kindness to Israel both because God has pledged to do so *and* because God chooses to out of compassion for their suffering. Either motive may be sufficient on its own. One act of kindness, by God or by us, may result from a prior promise. Another act of kindness may result from compassion toward a specific instance of suffering. A third act of kindness may lie within the intersection of both:

compassion for a specific instance of suffering by a person to whom we have pledged ourselves.

The third case is exactly what the prophet Micah concludes about God. God "delights in showing clemency," he will "have compassion upon us" and "cast our sins into the depth of the sea," and in doing so God shows faithfulness to what was "sworn to our ancestors" (Micah 7:18-20).

Nothing should seem strange about those dual motivations. They are the same as occur within a human marriage: I act kindly toward my wife when she is suffering both because I have made a pledge to her and because I have compassion on her. There is no need to see any conflict between God's commitment to a covenant and God acting mercifully, nor between the conditional and non-conditional elements of God's promises to us. God does not need to express just one or the other and there is no contradiction in God expressing both. That situation is clearer in relation to children. Parents do not make a conscious covenant with their children in the same way as a husband and wife do to each other.

Hosea starts with covenantal thinking—that Israel has been an unfaithful wife—but in the watershed moment of Hosea 11 God's reason to withhold wrath is phrased in terms of God's relationship with Israel as a parent rather than as a husband. In the logic of Hosea, the rift between God and Israel arises from a violation of covenant but the reason God withholds wrath and shows mercy is explicitly not God's obligation to Israel as wife, but God's compassion to Israel as child.

The same thought was voiced by the prophet Jeremiah toward the tribe of Ephraim:

> *"Is Ephraim my dear son?*
> *Is he the child I delight in?*
> *As often as I speak against him,*
> *I still remember him.*
> *Therefore I am deeply moved for him;*
> *I will surely have mercy on him,"*
> *says the LORD. (Jeremiah 31:20)*

God shows mercy toward Ephraim because God's heart is moved with parental compassion.

That understanding helps to disentangle the confusion about whether God's love, forgiveness, and mercy toward us is conditional or not. The biblical evidence is that God's actions are both: sometimes conditional and sometimes not. God acts toward us in loving-kindness within the context of covenant, and in that context, mutual obligations prescribe a conditional framework for the relationship. But God also acts toward us with unconditional mercy, outside any bounds of covenant obligation.

LOVING MERCY

The mercy that flows from the very nature of God, and was demonstrated in the way Jesus treated everyone he met, is supposed to be a foundational trait of God's people as well. This is most famously expressed in a verse from the prophet Micah, written perhaps in the late eighth century BCE:

> *He has shown you, O mortal, what is good. And what does the* LORD *require of you? To act justly and to love mercy and to walk humbly with your God. (Micah 6:8, NIV)* [29]

To act justly. To love mercy. To walk humbly with God.

What does it mean to love mercy? At one level everyone loves mercy ... when they are its recipient! We all appreciate being treated kindly: for others to act toward us with compassion for our struggles, empathy for our eccentricities, and forgiveness for our failures. As long as those attitudes toward us do not smell of pity, we love being the beneficiaries of mercy.

Rather than encouraging us to enjoy receiving mercy, however, Micah is of course referring to the converse: that we should love mercy being expressed to others. One aspect of that love applies to how we react when we see someone else receiving mercy.

During the COVID-19 pandemic in 2020, the Australian government offered financial assistance to any small business that could show at least a 30 percent drop in income from the same period in the previous year. There are good economic reasons to keep as many small businesses solvent as possible, but such schemes can also be viewed as acts of mercy from society as a whole to those struggling at the lower end of the capitalist eco-structure. It was Australia as a whole who decided, through their leaders, to offer that assistance, and to foot the bill through taxes and public debt.

My wife's takeaway coffee business is our sole source of income and we worked hard during COVID lockdown to provide a service to the local community. We worked longer hours and, at considerable personal cost, starting a delivery service to support people who could not leave their homes. As a result, our income dropped only 22 percent during that first wave of lockdown—less than the 30 percent threshold—and so we received no government assistance at all.

Other businesses saw their income drop far more than ours, sometimes through no fault of their own, sometimes through a lack of initiative, and sometimes through deliberately holding their business back. Through the public mercy of financial assistance, they received substantial amounts of money while we did not.

The point of the story is to ask myself how I feel when someone else receives a cash handout or a tax break in times of financial hardship but I do not? Do I rejoice in their good fortune or complain that it is not fair?

How do you react when a family member gets a better Christmas present than you do? When someone sick becomes well but you or those you love do not? When a political prisoner is granted clemency? When a death sentence for a horrendous murderer is commuted? Do you criticize the giver for being overly generous to someone who did not deserve it? Do you begrudge the gift because someone else received it but you did not?

Micah suggests that God would have us rejoice. Fostering that attitude involves some complex psychology, for it requires us to be satisfied with what we have rather than envious of what others receive, and it requires us to rethink what it means to deserve something.

Ultimately, Micah 6:8 calls us to something beyond rejoicing when others are shown mercy. We are not called to just love mercy from afar as a spectator. What God requires of us is to love the process of practicing mercy ourselves.

The word "love" has many meanings. The way we love our partner is different from how we love our pet dog and how we love a good coffee and how we love being on holidays. The Hebrew word used by Micah, *ahabah*, is just as versatile as our English word love. This verse is the only time *ahabah* appears in Micah, and in this context, it means something like to treasure or cherish, to revere or honor, and to engage with excitement. The same thought is emphasized in the next chapter of Micah, where we read that God "*delights* in showing clemency *[chesed]*" (7:18).

That is, we are not being told to act mercifully out of duty, or fear, or for what it might gain for us, but to act mercifully because we love doing so, because it delights us. Mercy ought not be a rare exception but a way of living. If we loved mercy, we would always be looking for opportunities to express that love by actively showing mercy to others.

JUSTICE, MERCY, AND HUMILITY GO TOGETHER

Micah 6:8 commends not only mercy but also justice and humility. These three intertwine in the lives of those who seek to lead a good life. That may seem odd, because common conceptions of justice, mercy, and humility place them in conflict with each other. I need to tease out a few nuances to see how they function together.

Mercy is often imagined in opposition to justice. In the stereotypical cases, justice demands some punishment, recompense, or restitution, but mercy steps in and lets the person off the hook. Writers from various traditions claim that justice and mercy are in conflict.

As an example, disagreement about the relationship between God's justice and mercy was a key issue in the Reformation split between Roman Catholics and Protestants.[30] Since 1999, however, Lutherans and Catholics affirm that "God's justice is his mercy."[31] In line with that declaration, Pope John Paul II saw in God's mercy evidence that love holds primacy over justice. "This seemed so obvious to the psalmists and prophets that the very term justice ended up by meaning the salvation accomplished by the Lord and His mercy. Mercy differs from justice but is not in opposition to it."[32]

In Chapter 5, I will say much more about justice and mercy, and how the relational intention of both concepts reasserts their essential harmony. For now, I just plant the seed of this thought: biblical justice is not about getting what one deserves, and biblical mercy is not about being let off from some deserved punishment.

Mercy in the Old Testament

In the Old Testament, justice and mercy cooperate rather than compete. In the context of a relational breakdown between Israel and God, Psalm 85:10 asserts that mercy *(chesed)* and truth meet, justice and peace kiss. Covenant violation and the resulting conflict do not prevent the cooperation between mercy, truth, justice, and peace, but necessitate it. If there is to be reconciliation, the voices of all four must be heard. When we see the four as contradictory, we are forced to choose between them. But if they meet and kiss, the synergy can create deeper understanding and unexpected possibilities.[33]

Humility also plays an important role in clarifying how we are to apply justice and mercy. Sometimes people try to impose justice and mercy within a power structure. Justice is often mediated by an authority figure who declares guilt or innocence and imposes consequences. In mercy too, the normal picture is of a magnanimous giver and an undeserving recipient. In both cases there is a power imbalance that implies, or at least permits, moral superiority.

Humility is the antidote to such superiority. To "walk humbly with your God" is to have a right view of oneself as dependent, to recognize that we too need mercy, and to position ourselves as peers with all humanity. From that position, alongside rather than above others, we can act with justice and mercy in our relationships without being judgmental or patronizing.

Pope John Paul II called particular attention to the importance of mutuality in mercy. Patronizing attempts at kindness that flow in one direction from the powerful to the needy fall short of the ideal of mercy. The humility in our posture comes from a recognition that every time we show mercy, we also receive mercy.

> *An act of merciful love is only really such when we are deeply convinced at the moment that we perform it that we are at the same time receiving mercy from the people who are accepting it from us. If this bilateral and reciprocal quality is absent, our actions are not yet true acts of mercy, nor has there yet been fully completed in us that conversion to which Christ has shown us the way by His words and example, even to the cross, nor are we yet sharing fully in the magnificent source of merciful love that has been revealed to us by Him.*[34]

The words "bilateral and reciprocal" in this quote do not imply a transactional debt. The Pope was not proposing that mercy requires something to be paid back. His point was that an appreciation of our own fragility leads to an approach to caring for each other that is mutual rather than one that maintains separateness and superiority. In the process of blessing others we bless ourselves as well.

NOT AN OPTION

Mercy is often considered to be supererogatory: a morally good action that is not obligatory.[35] To be merciful is to go above-and-beyond what one morally must do. In contrast to this good-but-optional view, Micah 6:8 is phrased as what the Lord *requires*. In what sense should we understand love, mercy, and humility as requirements?

In my youth I used to play tennis, though not very well! One of the rules of tennis is that the server must stand behind the base line until they have hit the ball. If you step over the line the umpire will call a "foot fault." Two such faults in a row and you lose the point. Serving from behind the line is in that sense a requirement.

Can you play tennis without standing behind the line? Certainly. Many people play tennis for fun without imposing all the rules. As a boy I was so hopeless at serving that my father would often let me serve "illegally" just to enjoy the game together. Even in a professional context you *could* play a whole match without adhering to that rule: it would just mean that you lost every point when you were serving. That would not be a particularly good game!

Micah says that God has shown us what is *good*. Goodness is demonstrated by God's character revealed in creation and in God's covenant history with Israel. The Hebrew word translated "good" here is rendered elsewhere as beautiful, better, and prosperity. Rebekah was beautiful in this sense (Genesis 26:7), as was the young David (1 Samuel 16:12). Further, the Hebrew word translated as "requires" is more usually rendered as "seeks" or "cares for." So, the sense here is not that God has shown us what we must do to be morally good, but that God has shown us what to seek if we mean to live well.

To play a good game of tennis you need to serve from behind the line. To follow God toward the good life you need to act justly, love mercy, and walk humbly. Those three are what God cares about, what God seeks, and hence they become a requirement for any who share God's heart.

To bring in a New Testament image, showing mercy may well be supererogatory in the sense that it is "going the extra mile." There are times when following the example of Jesus means that we go beyond the formal requirements of any law. The law might require you to carry a Roman soldier's pack for a mile when asked to, but the follower of Jesus will carry it two miles (Matthew 5:41).

Jesus came to free us from the coercive constraints of law (see, for example, Paul's discussion of our freedom from the law in Galatians 3:23-25), and yet those who decide to follow the way of Jesus will *of necessity* love mercy because otherwise they would not be following the example of Jesus. For us, the behavior and attitudes of Jesus become normative. Our own ethics and character are to become conformed to his example.

Although a legalistic way of thinking was familiar to Jesus, his own ethical approach was relational rather than defined by the strict application of law. Acts of kindness that are commonly understood as optional are precisely the things that define mercy in the biblical sense. Mercy is always above-and-beyond anything that can be legislated. If Jesus' instructions to "go with him two miles" became a rule, then mercy would have us go three miles. In most ethical approaches, such actions are optional, but for followers of Jesus, they become an essential part of discipleship. The life of Jesus, including his consistent expressions of mercy, is normative for those who want to follow his lead.

Mercy in the Old Testament

IN THE LIGHT OF MICAH 6:8 ...
WHAT DOES "LOVING MERCY" LOOK LIKE IN YOUR LIFE?
WHAT DO YOU HOPE IT WILL LOOK LIKE IN FIVE YEARS?

[4]

MERCY IN THE NEW TESTAMENT

An initial thought to ponder: Please read the Peace Prayer, often attributed to Francis of Assisi, or listen to one of the many musical renditions. I especially like the version by John Michael Talbot. What does this prayer say to you about the posture of mercy? What does it say about the idea of being-for-others discussed in this chapter?

IN SOME WAYS, THE NEW TESTAMENT re-presents the same notions of mercy as the Old, but there is novelty as well. This chapter highlights those new aspects, particularly the way the incarnation of God in Christ shows God's solidarity with us, the way Jesus' ministry extends mercy beyond tribalism to the entire world, and the way Jesus' death and resurrection places mercy at the center of God's mission to reconcile all things.

Disrupting Mercy

To begin with, let us note that in the context of God's covenant with the Jewish people, instructions like those in Micah 6:8 refer to more than just their treatment of fellow Jews. God's mandate to the nation of Israel was always to care for the foreigner in their midst (Exodus 22:21, 23:9; Leviticus 19:10, 19:33-34, 23:22; Deuteronomy 10:18-19, 14:29, 24:19-22, 26:12-13, 27:19; Jeremiah 7:5-7, 22:3; Ezekiel 47:21-23; Zechariah 7:10), and to bless all nations (Genesis 12:3, 18:18, 22:18, 26:4, 28:14).

Jesus confirms the same universal scope. For instance, in a conversation about the instructions in Leviticus 19:18 to "love your neighbor as yourself," Jesus was once asked "And who is my neighbor?" (Luke 10:29). Rather than reply directly, Jesus told a story: the now famous parable of the Good Samaritan (Luke 10:30-35).

In that story, someone walking from Jerusalem to Jericho is attacked by robbers and left half-dead by the side of the road. Two fellow-Jews see the beaten one but both decide not to get involved. Then a Samaritan—a marginalized Jewish ethnic group—saw the person and, moved by a gut-level compassion, stopped to help.

At the end of the story, Jesus turns the original question back to the inquirer, "Which of these three, do you think, was a neighbor to the one who fell into the hands of the robbers?" The man answers, "The one who showed him mercy" and Jesus concludes, "Go and do likewise."

The movement of ideas here is fascinating. The conversation starts with a question about eternal life, but quickly moves to the Law and then on to love. But the conversation ends with an instruction to show *mercy*. By connecting mercy to love and to eternal life, Jesus is not saying that we are each individually responsible for rescuing everyone in the world. But if we love our neighbor as ourselves, we will show mercy to whomever we encounter, not just those like us, nor just to those we like. We will act mercifully toward all, regardless of beliefs, culture, race, sexuality, social status, or any other factor we might hold in common with them or not. Importantly for those of us who read this parable as followers of Jesus, the hero of the story does not even comply with any notion of correct religious doctrine. Samaritans were not seen by Jesus' listeners as belonging to the true religion. By depicting a Samaritan as the hero, Jesus is highlighting that you do not have to be a Christian or Jew to show mercy. Mercy is not dependent on right theology.

Many have noticed that Jesus flipped the inquirer's question from "Who is my neighbor?" to "Who will you be a neighbor to?" In doing so, Jesus emphasized the continuity of his message with God's promise to Abraham that through him all nations would be blessed (Genesis 12:2-3, 22:15-18). The mercy of God is to be offered not just to your own people but to everyone, so that through us all will be blessed. Part of Jesus' game plan is to dislodge our habit of erecting tribal boundaries based on race, culture, politics, ideology, religion, or any wall we are tempted to erect around "us" to keep us separate from "them."

ELEOS, OIKTIRÓ AND OTHER GREEK WORDS

In most cases, when we see "mercy" in the New Testament it is a translation of the Greek noun *eleos*, or the associated verb *eleeó*. The variant *eleémosuné* is often translated as alms in the sense of giving to the poor (e.g., Matthew 6:1-3). That word cluster occurs 74 times and signifies an active expression of compassion: "sympathy manifested in act."[36]

Although it is a Greek word, *eleos* also plays an important role in the Old Testament. In the second and third centuries BCE, the Hebrew Scriptures were translated into a Greek version known as the Septuagint. In the Septuagint, the Hebrew *chesed* was nearly always translated as *eleos*. As usual with language translation, this is not a perfect match, but nevertheless very revealing: it shows that the Jewish scholars prior to Jesus' birth felt that the essence of the Hebrew word for God's loving-kindness was best captured by the Greek word for mercy.

A slightly stronger word translated as compassion or mercy is the Greek verb *oiktiró*. This word, along with its noun and adjectival forms, occurs ten times, for instance in Romans 12:1 "I appeal to you therefore, brothers and sisters, by the mercies of God ..."

Thirdly, the Greek noun *splagchnon*, which literally means the bowels, is sometimes translated as mercy. This word has a visceral feel to it, as though the experience of compassion burns within one's inner organs.

New Testament writers sometimes add emphasis by combining those three terms. For instance, "By the tender mercy [*splanchna eleous*] of our God, the dawn from on high will break upon us" (Luke 1:78). Paul also uses the evocative phrase *splanchna oiktirmou* in Colossians 3:12, which may be best translated as "heartfelt compassion."

Mercy in the New Testament

Those primary words for mercy are closely related to several other Greek words in the ecology of love:

- *Hileós*, whose primary meaning is propitious (favorable, forgiving), occurs eight times and is occasionally translated as mercy, e.g., "For I will be merciful toward their iniquities, and I will remember their sins no more" (Hebrews 8:12, quoting Jeremiah 31:34).
- *Agape*, meaning God-like love, occurs over three hundred times and often expresses God's gracious, merciful kindness to us.
- *Charis*, which occurs almost two hundred times, is normally translated as grace, but also has connotations of gift and kindness.
- *Aphiémi* occurs over 160 times. Its literal meaning is to release or dismiss, but in over a third of cases it clearly refers to forgiveness.

If you go by word counts, the NRSV translation uses mercy/mercies/merciful 65 times in the New Testament, compared to 98 in the Old Testament. Just counting "mercy" in English, however, can be quite misleading. As we have seen, a variety of words in Hebrew, Greek, and English orbit around the idea of mercy. If we count the whole constellation of mercy, grace, forgiveness, compassion, pity, and loving-kindness then the statistics are more like 570 instances in the New and 770 in the Old.

Trinity

The doctrine of the Trinity is a distinctively Christian foundation for understanding the nature and source of mercy. The communal identity of God as three-in-one can be read back into the Old Testament but only became fully articulated as the young church sought to understand the nature of God in the light of Jesus. In the New Testament, numerous verses show overlapping characteristics between God as Creator and metaphorical father, the human Jesus, and the promised Spirit who would comfort and guide. Several verses bring all three aspects of God together (e.g., Matthew 3:15-16, 28:19).

None of those biblical sources claims that the Father, Son and Spirit are all coequally God. Yet as the community of Jesus' followers sought to make sense of their experiences, they concluded that although there is only one God, God exists in three distinct persons. Their Jewish theological heritage emphasized that God is a person in the sense that God has a personality, an individual identity as a subject rather than just an object, a "who" rather than a "what," an "I" who is able to relate to other persons. Standing firmly within that monotheistic worldview, their experience of the life, death, and resurrection of Jesus led them to believe that Jesus was not only a human but also truly God. Layered on top of that, their interactions with the ongoing presence of God after Jesus' Ascension led them to believe that the Holy Spirit was also a person and truly God.

A variety of Jewish, Islamic, and Christian theologians claim that mercy is an essential attribute of God. By "essential," they mean God is merciful independent of anything outside God. Whether that can be true depends on your conception of both mercy and God. A Christian Trinitarian conception approaches the issue slightly differently than other monotheistic positions.

To the Lutheran Oswald Bayer, "The triune God's entire being is merciful."[37] But, says Wilhelm Löhe, that only works if mercy is not a response to misery, for "Insofar as it is a relation of love and mercy to misery, it [mercy] cannot be older than misery itself."[38] Likewise, Tim Keller believes that the first act of mercy was when God provided clothes for Adam and Eve, following the Fall.[39] If mercy is defined as a response to misery, then mercy can only come into existence after misery, and hence can only be a contingent rather than a necessary attribute of God.

In Catholic discussion, this same contradiction was noted by Daniel Moloney in response to Walter Kasper's claim that mercy is *the* fundamental attribute of God. Says Moloney:

> *This sounds profound, but does not withstand examination. Mercy is a virtue that requires someone who needs mercy, someone with some sort of sin or other imperfection. The Father is not merciful to the Holy Spirit. He loves the Holy Spirit, but there's nothing imperfect about the Holy Spirit so that he needs the Father's mercy. For mercy to be essential to God, as Kasper holds, it would mean that God could not exist without expressing mercy. But since God does not show mercy to himself, it would not be possible for*

Disrupting Mercy

him to exist without there also being sinners in need of his mercy—and that notion is absurd.[40]

Moloney is fine with *love* being an essential attribute, because the persons of the Trinity can express love to each other. God's love predates creation, but mercy, which can only be expressed in the compassionate response to a need, only became evident after creation.

There is no theological problem, in a Trinitarian framework, with mercy flowing from the eternal love of God. That is not so easy to argue from a Jewish or Islamic framework, because within non-Trinitarian monotheism even claiming love as an essential attribute of God is problematic. For love to be an essential attribute, it must have always been an attribute independent of any other being. But before the creation of someone other than God, there was nothing for God to love except God, and narcissistic love cannot easily be described as a virtue worthy of God. In a Trinitarian framework, however, the source of love is not narcissistic but other-centered. Love is not a means of addressing imperfection, but of caring in relationship with others, and of maintaining community. The mutual relationships within the Trinity were sustained by love prior to the creation of this world, and prior to any mercy shown toward the needs in this world.

This is similar to the approach of John Barclay, who sees grace rather than mercy as an essential attribute of God. To Barclay, grace—a stance of loving favor toward all things—is expressed within the Trinity, but the manifestation of grace in the form of mercy depends on the existence of someone in need external to God.[41]

My own definition of mercy—a gift of extreme kindness motivated by compassion—places me on the side of Löhe, Keller, Barclay and Moloney rather than Kasper, Luther and Bayer. Mercy can only be expressed once one has seen someone in need and felt compassion for them.[42] The Christian concept of Trinity sees relationship in the heart of divinity, and in that relational dance sees pure love. Creation too is an expression of God's love, even grace and kindness, but not an example of God's mercy.

Contrary to Moloney and Keller, however, I do not think mercy depends on the Fall. Sin is not a prerequisite, for mercy takes many forms apart from the forgiveness of sin. Mercy can be a compassionate response to any need: certainly to the suffering of sin, but also to physical, emotional, and social needs. God showed mercy to Adam in providing food to eat, air to breathe, and a companion in Eve, prior to any moral need arising from sin.

As Creator and metaphorical father, God shows mercy in giving us all that is physically needed for life. As Jesus, God shows mercy through living among us, pronouncing forgiveness to us, and removing the fear of death. As Holy Spirit, God shows mercy by guiding us toward truth, raising our awareness of our own brokenness, comforting us in times of need, and empowering us to overcome evil with good.

The Bible depicts the whole world as infused with God and with God's grace. As a consequence of that common grace, even people who do not align their beliefs and practices to God can experience and show mercy. But if you grant that the whole world was designed and created by the Judeo-Christian God, then whatever the proximal cause of mercy might be in each person's life, the ultimate cause is, by necessity, God.

INCARNATION

Against a backdrop of God communicating with humanity through dreams, angels, and prophets, the primary innovation proclaimed in the New Testament is the coming of God onto the world stage in person. In the Incarnation, the eternal and infinite God, who created all things, became embodied and finite to share our human existence. Jesus, "the reflection of God's glory and the exact imprint of God's very being," became truly human. The great high priest, greater than Abraham and even Moses (who was the only person since Adam and Eve who had seen God's face and lived), pitched his tent among us (Hebrews 1-4; John 1:14).

Such claims should still stagger our minds and hearts. The idea that God became human is virtually incomprehensible: a stunning revelation that turns our conception of God upside down.

The Incarnation was itself an event of mercy, the wildest act of mercy conceivable. Jesus was the gift of God, from God to us: a gift of extreme kindness inspired by God's compassion for us. This gift of God's own self was an act of solidarity with us: a sign that God did not consider the human form repugnant or a failed experiment to be thrown into the garbage. No, God came among us to affirm

Mercy in the New Testament

our value and to show us what abundant life can look like (John 10:10). First-century Israelites were waiting for God to show them mercy, and just prior to the birth of Jesus, Mary (Luke 1:46-55) and Zechariah (Luke 1:67-79) both declare that the promised mercy has come. In an early Christian hymn, the depth of God's compassion and humility is shown through God giving up the privileges of divinity to take on the very nature of a servant (Philippians 2:6-7).

Pope John Paul II correctly observed that "Christ confers on the whole of the Old Testament tradition about God's mercy a definitive meaning. Not only does He speak of it and explain it by the use of comparisons and parables, but above all He Himself makes it incarnate and personifies it. He Himself, in a certain sense, is mercy."[43] As we saw in the previous chapter, God's mercy is evident in the Old Testament, but in the New we see demonstrated in Christ the fullness of that mercy.

From the earliest of Jesus' recorded speeches, mercy played a central role. In a synagogue at Nazareth, he read the words of the prophet Isaiah and applied them to himself: "The Spirit of the Lord ... has sent me to proclaim release to the captives and recovery of sight to the blind, to let the oppressed go free, to proclaim the year of the Lord's favor" (Luke 4:18-19). In this declaration of mercy, Jesus deliberately omitted the concluding phrase in the passage from Isaiah: "the day of vengeance of our God." In doing so, Jesus implied that he came to fulfill Old Testament prophecy through mercy rather than through vengeance. Similarly, in the Sermon on the Mount, he asserted that one characteristic of a blessed life is the ability to give and receive mercy (Matthew 5:7), an idea that may be the keynote of everything he proclaimed.[44]

That theme is carried forward in Matthew's Gospel by Jesus' repeated references to Hosea 6:6—"Go and learn what this means, 'I desire mercy not sacrifice.'" In Matthew 9:11, Jesus was castigated for hanging around tax collectors and sinners, but in his defense Jesus said his mission was to show mercy to the sick and sinners rather than to expel them as the Pharisees do. Later, in Matthew 12:2, Jesus was reprimanded for allowing his followers to harvest corn to eat on the Sabbath, but in his defense Jesus pointed out precedents in the Old Testament and said his desire was to nourish his followers rather than force them to continue to be hungry. In both cases, the Pharisees wanted to apply a law strictly for the sake of ritual purity, but Jesus claimed that responding to people's need with mercy is more important.

This is another example of Jesus quoting the Old Testament in a way that reinterprets its original meaning. To a reader of Hosea, the verse meant "I, God, desire my people to show mercy rather than making sacrifices to me." But Jesus uses the verse to mean "I, God, prefer to show mercy rather than demand sacrifice." In other words, the God incarnated in Christ wants to save people rather than sacrifice them.[45] Stephen Pickard sees this movement highlighting "the deeper scandal of God's mercy" because "it entirely overturns received notions of what God desires."[46]

The gospels repeatedly describe Jesus as being moved with compassion for the people he meets: a man with leprosy (Mark 1:41), a widow whose son had died (Luke 7:13), a hungry crowd (Matthew 15:32), and so on. Paul used the Hebrew linguistic device of parallelism to emphasize that the God of Jesus was the God of all comfort, and that the Father of Jesus was the Father of compassion *[oiktirmōn]* (2 Corinthians 1:3 NIV).

Note, however, the distinction I have already made between the *feeling* of compassion and the *action* of mercy. Simply looking on compassionately is not mercy. Mercy requires a certain type of action in response to that compassion. Pope John Paul II described this well when he wrote:

> *The true and proper meaning of mercy does not consist only in looking, however penetratingly and compassionately, at moral, physical or material evil: mercy is manifested in its true and proper aspect when it restores to value, promotes and draws good from all the forms of evil existing in the world and in man. Understood in this way, mercy constitutes the fundamental content of the messianic message of Christ and the constitutive power of His mission.*[47]

Mercy is not just the fundamental content of Jesus' message, but the underlying power animating all that he did. Jesus not only *preached* mercy, and *felt* compassion, but also *demonstrated* mercy consistently. His willingness to die for our sakes is clearly the most remarkable act of mercy, and I will say more about that shortly. But let us not undervalue the many acts of mercy he showed during his life toward a wide variety of needs, spiritual, social, and physical.

For example, recall the man with paralysis whose friends lowered him through a roof (Mark 2:1-12). Jesus both healed his legs and forgave him. There was no precondition, nor did Jesus request that the man should respond in any way. The healing was not even based on the man's faith, but on that of his friends!

Recall the two blind men who cried out, "Have mercy on us, Son of David!" (Matthew 9:27-31). They were not asking for forgiveness, but physical healing, and Jesus responded to that specific need by enabling them to see. His only condition was that they should tell nobody ... a condition they ignored!

Likewise, Jesus calmed storms, healed many physical ailments, provided wine at a wedding, fed crowds of followers, and raised the dead. All these were signs of his authority and filled with layers of symbolic meaning, but they were also displays of mercy: gifts of extreme kindness motivated by compassion in response to the immediate needs of people around him.

In all these ways, Jesus showed a way of being that differs radically from normal human self-centeredness. Jesus is not unique in this, for other people have also lived (and died) for others. Many great saints and humanitarians set aside opportunities for self-advancement because of a philosophical commitment to some higher purpose. In contrast, most of us live for ourselves, for our own survival, our own benefit, with perhaps some extension of that benefit to the people closest to us. The motivation for the

Incarnation was that God loved the entire world (including, but not limited to, its human inhabitants) and so for Jesus that higher purpose was to seek and save the lost (Luke 19:10).

Whereas the very essence of most people's existence is being-for-self, the Incarnation shows the most radical example of being-for-others. In this other-centeredness, the Incarnation demonstrates God's recipe for human flourishing.

The doctrine of Incarnation goes beyond the theological mystery of God becoming human, and beyond the mercy shown in the life and teachings of Jesus. The Incarnation is also a call to us, individually and communally, to express mercy. Thus, Jesus said to his disciples, "Be merciful, just as your Father is merciful" (Luke 6:36). Notice that in this verse Jesus did not call us to merely *act* mercifully but to *be* (or even *become*) merciful. In other words, we are to take on, or grow into, the merciful character of God. We are to live with a posture of mercy, or, as we have already seen in the words of Micah, we are to love mercy. As the body of Christ, we too live incarnationally, embodying the Spirit of God in our own communities. In that way, we too become the site of God's mercy in the world.

MERCY AND CONDITIONALITY ACCORDING TO PAUL

In the earlier discussion of Hosea, I considered a certain type of ambiguity around whether God's relationship with us is conditional or not. We saw that two motivations coexist comfortably within God: a conditional component situated within covenant, and a parent-like component outside the bounds of any covenant obligation. Mercy sits within the second component. In the context of the New Testament, there is now something further to note about mercy as an unconditional gift.

The depiction of divinity in the Bible is of a giving God who loves creation and who pours out grace upon grace to bless everyone. Many of God's gifts we easily take for granted: air to breathe, food to eat, warmth, water, birdsong, companionship, starry nights, moonlight over a clam sea, and a thousand other marvels that nourish our bodies and souls. According to James, God gives generously to all who ask, without finding fault (James 1:5) and Paul repeatedly notes that God's giving is without favoritism (Romans 2:11; Ephesians 6:9).

Beyond the givens that form the background and context for life itself, the gifts of grace and mercy are a key theme in the writings of Paul. "What do you have that you did not receive?" he asked the believers in Corinth, "And if you received it, why do you boast as if it were not a gift?" (1 Corinthians 4:7).

British academic John Barclay provides the most sustained analysis of this theme in his highly influential 2015 book, *Paul and the Gift*, and its later companion, *Paul and the Power of Grace*. In both books, he treats "gift" and "grace" as virtually synonymous, and periodically throws in "mercy" as a third synonym. After I wrote to him to ask for a clearer statement on the relationship between grace and mercy, his return email included this helpful statement: "I see grace as the more all-embracing term, a stance of loving favour toward all things that is expressed

Mercy in the New Testament

in a variety of forms. Mercy is a form of grace, as compassion on the suffering or the sinful."[48]

Keeping that distinction in mind, we can read what he wrote about grace and think about how it applies to mercy. First, he notes that grace (and hence mercy) is used in the New Testament to encompass three things that we might otherwise think were different. Grace can be something that is charming, attractive, or an object of favor. Grace can be a gift, favor or benefit, or an attitude of benevolence. Grace can also be the returning of gratitude or thanks.

Barclay then considers what the perfection of a gift, or grace, might look like. Every Christian theological tradition acknowledges the importance of grace, but there has been considerable disagreement about the shape of that grace. Part of that disagreement springs from differing understandings of gift, which, as I have already discussed, has been a topic of much recent philosophical debate. Consequently, my own take on the nature of gift will influence how I respond to Barclay's understanding of Paul's understanding of grace. (Perfectly straightforward really!)

To make sense of the differing opinions, Barclay proposes six possible attributes of the perfect gift/grace:[49]

- Superabundance: gifts that are huge, lavish, unceasing, extravagant, etc.
- Singularity: that the giver's character is *purely* giving, consistently good and beneficial.
- Priority: when the gift comes prior to anything the recipient does, rather than a response to a request.
- Incongruity: when giving is not based on the recipient's worthiness.

- Efficacy: gifts that change the recipient with a good and lasting effect.
- Noncircularity: gifts that require no reciprocity, return or exchange.

Barclay does not propose that all six of those attributes apply to the biblical picture of grace, only that they are *possible* ways to discuss the perfection of grace. Many of the varied historical positions on grace can be described in terms of which combination of these six features a person believes apply to God. Augustine, for instance, emphasized the incongruity of grace (that nothing we could do would make us merit God's grace), its priority (that grace comes to us before we move toward God), and its efficacy (that God's grace is irresistible). Martin Luther, on the other hand, emphasized the incongruity of grace alongside its noncircularity (that grace is given for our own sake with no expectation that we could do anything to benefit God in return).

Next, Barclay undertakes a close reading of Galatians and Romans to document Paul's view on grace. In both letters, he finds grace to be at the center of Paul's theology, and the gift of Christ to be at the center of that grace. "For Paul, the Christ-gift is most fundamentally not the giving of a thing but the giving of a person: 'The Son of God loved me and gave himself for me'." [50]

In both Galatians and Romans Paul shows the incongruity of God's grace. It is not only given without regard to one's social status, gender, or ethnic background (Galatians 3:28), but actively given while we were still sinners (Romans 5:8). This is so fundamental that Barclay asserts that "The gospel stands or falls with the incongruity of grace."[51]

Barclay also understands Paul to be saying that the gift of Christ is necessarily circular, that is, it must be followed by a different set of orientations, allegiances, and obligations.

> *The grace of God is unconditioned (without prior considerations of worth) but not unconditional, if we mean by that the noncircular perfection of grace that expects nothing in return. Grace, for Paul, is not a gift from a disengaged benefactor who would rather be left alone; it is not a donation 'with no strings attached.' To the contrary: personal and social practice aligned to the good news is integral to what Paul means by 'faith' or 'trust.'* [52]

At first glance, Barclay's claim that grace is unconditioned but conditional refutes my own stance that mercy is a free gift that incurs no debt. We agree that God's gift, whether viewed as grace or mercy, is offered to all people without pre-conditions. But where Barclay sees post-conditions, I do not. The difference, however, may not be as significant as it first appears.

Part of what looks like a difference of understandings reflects the differing scope of Barclay's "grace" and my "mercy." *Paul and the Power of Grace* explicitly addresses Paul's instructions to readers who are already believers in the Christ-gift, and focuses on that specific epitome of grace which is the salvific life, death, and resurrection of Jesus. To that audience, Paul's presentation of what it means to have received God's gift most certainly includes expectations of how they should now live in the light of that gift. "Jesus makes clear that strong expectations are laid on those who are welcomed into the kingdom: the forgiven are expected to forgive (Matthew 6:12), the fig tree is expected to bear fruit (Luke 13:6–9), the disciples are called to serve (Mark 10:41–45), the wealthy are expected to give (Luke 19:1–10), and the loved are commanded to love (John 13:34–35)."[53]

Grace and mercy, however, are far broader than that context. Having received the Christ-gift, you will inevitably live differently, but such inevitability does not apply to grace or mercy in general, because they are often given without being fully received.

Offering mercy certainly entails a hope for its future effect. Mercy is shown to someone in the hope that the act will alleviate their immediate suffering, in the hope that the recipient will appreciate the compassionate intention behind the gift, even in the hope that the person will be transformed into becoming more merciful themself. But such hopes are not requirements. The lack of appropriate response to mercy should not prevent it being given, nor does a lack of response mean that the gift of mercy ceases to be mercy. The free gift of mercy is not retrospectively annulled by the presence or absence of any post-condition.

To be as clear as possible, my belief in mercy as a gift implies that it cannot depend on any pre- or post-conditions. Mercy is nevertheless an intentional act. Mercy is offered with a purpose, with hopes and even with expectations about its effect, but intentions, purposes, hopes, and expectations do not constitute conditions. The gift is given regardless of whether the hopes or expectations are met.[54]

A further reason why Barclay's analysis has led him in a different direction from mine is our interpretive lens. In *Paul and the Power of Grace* Barclay reads the work of Jesus through the lens of Paul, whereas my Anabaptist stance reads all Scripture, including Paul's letters, through the lens of Jesus. If we accept Paul's words that Jesus is the visible image of the invisible God (Colossians 1:15), and Jesus' own words that "Whoever has seen me has seen the Father" (John 14:9), then the grace and mercy of God will be illuminated by what we see in the life and teaching of Jesus.

As an example, recall the ten lepers who called out to Jesus to show them mercy (Luke 17:11-19). Luke makes no suggestion that Jesus evaluated their worthiness before healing them all. When only one returned to give thanks, there is no indication that Jesus rescinded his healing of the others. Their praise might have been hoped for but did not constitute a post-condition.

The same can be said for virtually all Jesus' miracles. He met people's needs with the hope that they would be transformed by the experience, but his mercy was never conditional upon such transformation. To the contrary, the gospels explicitly record cases when Jesus knew people would not respond positively to his kindness, and yet he continued to show them grace. The prime example is Judas: Jesus washed his feet and shared an intimate meal with him knowing he would betray him (John 13, notably vv. 11 and 26).

Disrupting Mercy

Through his actions and words (e.g., Luke 6:35) Jesus encouraged us to do good without expecting anything in return. Since Jesus is God incarnate, we must deduce that *God* gives without requiring anything in return.

When Barclay digs into the shape of what he sees as Paul's post-conditions, he notes that they primarily relate to how believers should live within a new community in which grace is central. When Paul instructs the Galatians and Romans about their response to the grace of God, he says they should nurture the fruit of the Spirit (Galatians 5:22), refuse to require circumcision (Galatians 2:3, 5:12-15), care for each other (Galatians 6:2; Romans 12:10), offer their bodies as living sacrifices (Romans 12:1), bless those who persecute them (Romans 12:14), etc. These are not ways that believers repay God for the grace they have received, but ways that they participate in that grace. Instead of "paying it back," we are enjoined to "pay it forward" so that God's grace is shared and passed around. "Paul expects the grace of God in Christ to cascade through the life of communities"[55] and that cascade of grace is exactly what I have referred to as a network of reciprocity. In this sense I can completely agree with Barclay's use of the term "circularity" as one dimension of the perfect gift. To participate in God's grace is to be part of a joyful community of giving in which cascading generosity brings both joy and sustenance to all. This is a hoped-for result of grace and mercy, but not a post-condition. It is not a debt incurred or a requirement to pay God back, but the acceptance of an invitation to flourish within a community of grace.

REDEMPTION AND RECONCILIATION

Two more interlocking themes in the New Testament show the centrality of mercy to God's mission. God's work in the world is teleological: its intent, or purpose, is the redemption of humanity and the reconciliation of all things in heaven and on earth. Both of those outcomes—redemption and reconciliation—are enabled by God's mercy, brought to us through Christ.

Paul wrote in a letter to his apprentice Titus, "When the goodness and loving-kindness of God our Savior appeared, he saved us, not because of any works of righteousness that we had done, but according to his mercy" (Titus 3:5). We are saved through the goodness and loving-kindness of God, that is, through God's mercy. Such a claim immediately raises the question of what we are saved *from*, and to that question the New Testament gives many answers.[56] In the context of the letter to Titus we are saved from our foolish enslavement to various passions, our disobedience to God, and the resulting envy and hatred that mar our relationships with each other (see v. 3).

In a similar verse that links several aspects of mercy, Paul wrote, "In [Jesus] we have redemption through his blood, the forgiveness of our trespasses, according to the riches of his grace that he lavished on us" (Ephesians 1:7-8). Paul himself is one of the Bible's paramount examples of God's lavish grace. After approving of the murder of the first Christian martyr, Stephen (Acts 7:54 - 8:1), Paul became a leading persecutor of the fledgling community of Jesus' followers (Acts 9:1-2). Paul calls himself the foremost of sinners, and noted that he received mercy from God not because of being good, nor in spite of being bad, but explicitly *because* he was so bad (1 Timothy 1:12-17).

As discussed in a later chapter, forgiveness is God's response to our moral waywardness and one of the primary expressions of mercy. Paul understood that this forgiveness is a gracious gift, not doled out begrudgingly but expansively "lavished on us." The conduit for this mercy is Jesus' "blood," that is his death, and the result is our redemption.

In Christian thinking, redemptive salvation comes through Jesus, and Jesus alone (Acts 4:12). The "riches of God's grace" are shown in Jesus' self-sacrifice on the cross, through which we see the very essence of mercy, its ultimate expression. Let's consider for a minute how that self-sacrifice works.

First, part of our understanding of the Incarnation is that Jesus' humanity enables him to empathize with us, and yet take the role of high priest to atone for our sins. "He had to become like his brothers and sisters in every respect, so that he might be a merciful and faithful high priest in the service of God, to make a sacrifice of atonement for the sins of the people" (Hebrews 2:17).

Second, notice that the New Testament repeatedly asserts that Jesus "*gave* himself for us" (Luke 22:19-20; Galatians 1:4, 2:20; Ephesians 5:2; 1 Timothy 2:6; Titus 2:14). That is, although people deserted, betrayed, accused, arrested, convicted, and crucified Jesus, there is a deeper sense in which Jesus consciously chose to be killed.

Mercy in the New Testament

In his life and his death, Jesus acted *for us*. He gave himself over to a torturous death on our behalf.

Third, notice an important distinction between two uses of the word "sacrifice." In many contexts, including the sacrificial system of the Old Testament, to sacrifice means to forcefully take something and violently destroy it. But there are other contexts in which sacrifice is neither coercive nor violent. Parents, for instance, may give up their time, their sleep, even their career, for the sake of their children. According to Jesus, the greatest expression of love would be to give up your life for your friends. These are true sacrifices, but willingly chosen rather than coerced. To think that Jesus' death was a sacrifice of the first kind, a violent murder demanded by God, is a mistake. Rather, Jesus' death was a sacrifice of the second kind. He willingly gave up his life for his friends, and even for those who position themselves as enemies. In doing so, he solidified the Old Testament intimations that God has no interest in sacrifices of the first kind (e.g., Psalm 51:16, Isaiah 1:11, Hosea 6:6), and abolished the need for any future sacrifices of that kind (Hebrews 10:1-18).

Fourth, the self-sacrifice of Jesus was one act in a deliberate plan. Jesus allowed himself to be killed, in some ways precipitated his own death, in order to bring salvation to all (Titus 2:11), to bring us back to God (1 Peter 3:18), to redeem us (Ephesians 1:7), to set us free from the fear of death (Hebrews 2:15), to release us from the tragedies of our lives, and instead become enthusiastic about doing good (Titus 2:14).

Last, compare the self-sacrifice of Jesus to my definition of mercy: a gift of extreme kindness motivated by compassion. Jesus' voluntary self-sacrifice was a gift: the greatest gift of love (John 15:13). It was an extreme kindness, made especially surprising by the fact that we were unworthy of it (Romans 5:6-8). It was motivated by God's never-ending love and compassion for us and for all creation (John 3:16; Romans 8:19-23).

In all of those ways, the self-sacrifice chosen by Jesus testifies to his fundamental being-for-others. His whole life and death were other-directed, *for us.*

The New Testament passages discussed above show that one of the central purposes of God's mercy through the life, death and resurrection of Jesus is the redemption of individual people, indeed of *all* people (e.g., Titus 2:11; 1 Timothy 2:4-6; 1 John 2:2). Individual salvation is not, however, the whole of the Good News. Regardless of how important the theme of redemption is, that is only part of a bigger picture.

In Zechariah's song of praise to the infant John the Baptist (Luke 1:67-79), he not only claims that God's mercy has finally arrived (vv. 72, 78), but also explicitly links that mercy to redemption (v. 68), rescue (v. 74), salvation (v. 77), the forgiveness of sins (v. 77), and peace (v. 79). The following verses from Paul's hand make the same connections, but also extend our understanding by claiming that the ultimate goal of God's mercy is the restoration of everything throughout all creation.

> *[The Father] has **rescued** us from the power of darkness and transferred us into the kingdom of his beloved Son, in whom we have **redemption**, the **forgiveness** of sins. He is the image of the invisible God, the firstborn of all creation; for in him all things in heaven and on earth were created, things visible and invisible, whether thrones or dominions or rulers or powers—all things have been created through him and for him. He himself is before all things, and in him all things hold together. He is the head of the body, the church; he is the beginning, the firstborn from the dead, so that he might come to have first place in everything. For in him all the fullness of God was pleased to dwell, and through him God was pleased to **reconcile** to himself all things, whether on earth or in heaven, by making **peace** through the blood of his cross. (Colossians 1:13-20)*

Note how this passage starts with an assertion that the purpose of the Father is to redeem individuals, but after describing the essence of the Incarnation it then reveals God's deeper plan to reconcile all things in heaven and on earth. Clearly, this goal is achieved *through Jesus*. The fullness of God dwelt in Jesus, and it is God-in-Jesus who both redeems and reconciles.

The term "reconcile" has several interrelated connotations. One is about the restoration of an original intention: making things as they were supposed to be. Another connotation is shown in the way two friends who have drifted apart because of some conflict are brought back together: we say they have reconciled their differences. A third connotation is financial: a bank reconciliation process starts with two sets of records, two versions of the truth, and attempts to bring them into alignment. So it is with the work of God through Jesus: the whole creation is restored to God's intention, enmity is resolved, and everything brought into alignment with Jesus, "reconciled to himself."

Each of these connotations add something to our understanding of God's plan to reconcile all things through Jesus. Through the mercy of God, everything in heaven and on earth will be drawn into harmony so that all creation, including each of us, finally plays the same glorious tune. This grand plan sits behind every act of mercy. The mercy depicted in the New Testament not only deals compassionately with people's immediate physical needs, but also addresses our deeper existential need to be saved from all manner of brokenness and alienation. Even more, mercy in the New Testament draws all creation into God's ultimate goal in which heaven and earth are reunified and every creature can flourish.

This is the salvation we are to announce, by words and actions, to the ends of the earth (Acts 13:47). It is why Paul calls us "ministers of reconciliation" (2 Corinthians 5:18-21). We are part of this grand scheme to proclaim the mercy of God so that all may be redeemed, and so that everything in heaven and on earth may be reconciled to God's original intention in Christ.

WHAT CONDITIONS DO YOU PLACE ON MERCY?
IN PRACTICAL WAYS, HOW MIGHT DEVELOPING A HABIT OF
MERCY MAKE YOU AN "INSTRUMENT OF PEACE"?

[5]

MERCY AND JUSTICE

An initial thought to ponder: Please search the web for photos of the statue "Justice Tempered by Mercy" at Samford University's Cumberland Law School. As usual, Justice is blindfolded so that she must weigh the evidence and pass judgment without seeing either the accused or the accuser. What do you think Mercy might whisper to Justice?

CHLOE STOOD IN COURT to hear the judgment, which would almost certainly include jail time.[57] She was 22, on a good behavior bond from previous convictions, and now charged with assaulting her partner, possessing illegal drugs, and trying to bribe a police officer.

Chloe's early life had been far from smooth. Her parents' marriage broke up when she was three, and over the next ten years she lived sometimes with her mother, who was alcoholic, and sometimes with her father, who was physically abusive. Both parents encouraged her to fight back when she was threatened, and between eight and twelve she was part of a competitive fighting club. At thirteen she moved in with her boyfriend, then another, and another. She took one of those boyfriends to court for beating her, but the police lost the photographic evidence and the case was dismissed. She left one school because of being bullied and was expelled from two others. At nineteen she was pregnant and reliant on government welfare payments.

At twenty, as a single mother who had not completed high school, Chloe had little social support and no job prospects. Although she loved her young son and wanted his life to be better than hers, she lived with self-protective anger in survival mode. She often exploded with uncontrollable rage.

Two events gave her the opportunity to turn her life in another direction. The first was enrolling in a high school that ran a program specifically for young parents. The school campus included a child-care facility where Chloe could drop off her son while she attended classes. Today she is still studying part-time at that school and will soon complete her final year.

When she started at that school, she was quite aggressive, though grateful for the opportunity it gave her. The school program is founded on the idea that all students are loved and valued. The child-care facility, an on-campus psychologist, alternative classroom formats, and assessment processes all contribute to an environment that supports the difficult journey of people like Chloe. She says the school was the first place that accepted her and believed in her. By aptitude and training, the staff are attuned to the challenges of the students and provide explicit emotional coaching. Always looking for the best in the students, the staff do not rescue them but draw out the potential from within them, teaching them to look after themselves without hurting others, and without cutting themselves off from help. In Chloe's case, their kindness and the skills of self-awareness they have nurtured are helping her learn to control her explosive tendencies.

At times that progress has been interrupted by damaging outbursts, like the time Chloe punched a worker in the gym next to the school. The gym owner demanded she be expelled, but the school's senior staff worked hard to find a better solution. The incident scared Chloe and prompted her to rethink her trajectory. She knew that if she were expelled, it would be the end of her hope to complete high school, and a bad prospect for the rest of her life, with serious consequences for her son. At school she had tasted something good and now might lose it. She had been told she was worth it, and maybe started to believe it herself. She was allowed to study from home for several months with remote supervision, and then returned to the campus with the requirement that she goes nowhere near the gym.

Chloe is not one to give up easily! She started to see a drug counsellor and a recent series of fifteen random drug tests have all come back negative. She pays with her own money to see a psychologist, focusing on anger management. At the end of 2021, Chloe received the

Principal's Award for her attitude and application to her studies.

However, none of that altered the charges against her and the looming court hearing, which could negate all the progress she had made. The charges were serious and, given that Chloe was already living under a good behavior bond, jail time was the most likely outcome.

Clearly, she was guilty, and the requirements of law dictate that she be punished. But would that be truly just? Would it resolve anything? Would imposing further hardship on Chloe somehow balance the crime and the damage done by her? Or is there a deeper justice that sees the damage done *to* Chloe and seeks to bring back some fairness and dignity to her life?

The judge had driven to court that day thinking about the devastating statistics of crime and social disfunction in the area. Without meeting Chloe, she was already thinking about youth like her, and about how important education was in breaking past cycles of abuse. Having read of Chloe's commitment to the school program, to counselling, and to giving up drug use, she surprised everyone with her verdict. Her closing comments were, "You should be very proud of yourself. I will be dropping all your charges. Good luck with [your studies]."

Institutions such as schools and courts are not generally known for showing mercy. Institutions have too many rules that dictate what is required and prescribe what their staff are allowed to do. In Chloe's case though, the best aspects of institutional diligence have been shown. People within those institutions—the staff at Chloe's school and the judge in the court—embody the heartbeat of *shalom*. They see Chloe through eyes of compassion and choose to push the boundaries of institutional rules to give her another chance. Those types of actions are always risky because the new opportunity might be squandered.

For Chloe, however, the dual mercies of the school and the judge gave hope. Hope that the ill-treatment she received as a child can be overcome. Hope that she can finish high school, find a job, and move away from dependence on welfare payments. Hope that she can properly care for her son and give him a more nourishing upbringing than her own.

After reading my summary of these events, Chloe asked me to add:

> *Without the compassion, understanding and forgiveness I have been shown I wouldn't have the life I do now. I wouldn't have learnt to be the resilient person I am today if it wasn't for others giving me that opportunity. I have learnt forgiveness from being forgiven and I will always be grateful for the opportunities I can now have, thanks to my school and others in my life.*

That's the outcome of mercy. When compassionate people go out of their way to give someone a new opportunity, and the person receiving that kindness recognizes the gift, remarkable transformation can occur.

ARE MERCY AND JUSTICE IN CONFLICT?

In this chapter I return to one of the repeated debates about the nature of mercy, namely, its relationship to justice. More than one perspective on mercy positions it in direct opposition to justice, but to me they operate collaboratively.

At least one contemporary Jewish rabbi, Dr. David Gottlieb, takes the view that mercy is *fundamentally* in conflict with justice.[58] To him, mercy is by definition the suspension of justice. In a court, a plea for mercy only arises *after* one is found guilty. Mercy presupposes that a person is guilty but asks that the full extent of justice not be applied. Gottlieb attempts to align this to the Hebrew Scriptures by making both justice and mercy subservient to God's love *(chesed)*. Love, he claims, is the whole purpose of all creation, and in different contexts God uses either justice or mercy to serve the goal of love. Justice establishes laws and punishments to provide a structure for human life that enables us to live together harmoniously and to experience love. There are times, however, when justice is inadequate for that purpose and the higher goal of love requires justice to be over-ruled by mercy.

In my view, Rabbi Gottlieb has mis-framed the issue. Yes, justice and mercy both serve the goal of love. But justice and mercy cooperate rather than compete. To frame them as being in conflict shows a misconception of both concepts.

First, note that mercy applies not only in the context of the court room. Contrary to Rabbi Gottlieb, mercy does not always imply guilt. Mercy is certainly expressed at times as the withholding or reduction of punishment. But mercy can also be the alleviation of someone's pain, financial assistance, being present in times of grief, or

Mercy and Justice

other responses to someone's need. In such cases, there is no conflict with justice, regardless of how justice is conceptualized.

Second, even in the court room setting, where guilt has been established, conceptualizing justice as the imposition of punishment is a very shallow view that trivializes the depth of biblical examples. Many people today certainly see justice primarily in terms of punishing lawbreakers: a criminal violates some law, harming some victim in the process, and the role of justice is to punish the criminal and, perhaps, compensate the victim. From this perspective, justice involves balancing the books: those who do bad things get punished, those who do good get rewarded, and perpetrators are required to repay their victims for whatever damage was done.

When justice is viewed as getting what you deserve, and you are found guilty of some criminal or moral failure, then justice would seem to require that you pay somehow. You may need to repay the cost of whatever damage you did. Perhaps justice requires your deed to be exposed to the public to bring your name into disrepute. Or perhaps justice requires you to suffer in order to balance the scales through some eye-for-an-eye exchange.

From that perspective, showing mercy is a denial of justice. If someone is guilty, then justice requires one thing, but mercy permits the opposite. Mercy lets the offender off the hook by not imposing the just penalty. Mercy holds back the hand of justice.

However, that is not the only way to frame the concept of justice. Although it is the dominant approach in our modern Western culture, there are several philosophical, criminological, and theological alternatives. Justice is not equivalent to the law; in fact some laws are patently unjust.

A central concern in the Bible is the maintenance of *shalom*: the state in which humanity can flourish because relationships are whole and good, including relationships with each other, with God, and with the created world. The Bible depicts justice as God's means of addressing the lack of *shalom*. God's justice aids the weak, the poor, and the oppressed, and breaks the power of the oppressor. God's justice reverses people's fortunes so that inequality is transformed: the feeble are strengthened, the hungry find food, the barren have children, the weapons of the mighty are broken, the proud are brought low. "God's justice makes things right by transforming the status quo of need and oppression into a situation where things are as they should be. ... God's action for justice is not based on the merits of individuals, but on their need."[59]

Such a view of justice may still make use of laws, law enforcement, court room judgments, and punishment, but this biblical view is so much larger and more redemptive than the retributive view. *Shalom*-oriented justice works hand-in-hand with mercy. The intention of both is to maintain *shalom*, and to restore *shalom* after it has been lost by accident or by deliberate harm. Neither mercy nor justice are final goals but coworkers in the construction of *shalom*. Rather than pulling in opposite directions, mercy and justice are both expressions of love that act in the service of *shalom*.

Chris Marshall, a leading theological advocate for restorative justice, makes this point very clearly:

> *We often think of mercy and justice as opposites. To show mercy when wrongdoing has occurred means suspending or disregarding the penalty which justice requires. Mercy thus represents a kind of injustice. But this is only the case if we think of justice in strictly arithmetical or legalistic terms. If instead we understand justice in terms of restoring healthy relationships, then mercy is often the best way to get there. Mercy helps to bring about, rather than to interfere with, justice. Compassionate acceptance of human fallibility is essential to the functioning of healthy relationships. Where failure occurs, justice must be seasoned with mercy, or it is not true justice.*[60]

DOING WITHOUT DESERT

Through a long history in both philosophy and law, justice has been based on an ideal of everyone receiving what they deserve.[61] Although there have been compelling arguments against this "desertist" view of justice, it remains a popular conception. This view is incompatible with what I have been saying about mercy, and to genuinely love mercy one has to give up believing that the concept of desert bears any relevance to how we treat others.

A brief comment is needed about the word "desert" because it is a rare use of that word and easily confused with several other words. It is pronounced the same as the "dessert" you might have at the end of a meal and is the noun form of "deserving," as in the sentence "The criminals got their just deserts." I do not mean arid areas with sparse vegetation! Nor do I mean to run away from something ("deserting a friend in times of trouble").

The idea that there is a moral necessity for people to get what they deserve is deeply embedded in Western thinking, and often read back into the Bible. That is, if you already believe justice to be a matter of good people being rewarded and bad people being punished, then you can justify that belief by citing verses from the Bible. Proverbs 14:14, for instance, says "The perverse get what their ways deserve, and the good, what their deeds deserve" and Galatians 6:7 says "you reap whatever you sow."

One *could* argue that humanity is totally depraved, sinful to its core, at enmity with God, and as such deserves God's just retribution. One *could* argue that Jesus, the one person who did not deserve punishment, took the weight of God's wrath so that God would not have to punish the ones who did deserve it.

But do not imagine that this telling of the "good news" is the only "Christian" understanding or the one true way of reading the biblical narrative. Many dedicated followers of Jesus have interpreted the gospel differently from that. I will not repeat their arguments here,[62] but I will point out some biblical counterexamples to the misconception of deserved retribution.

Part of the misconception is a confusion between consequences and moral desert. For instance, how you read Romans 6:23—"the wages of sin is death"—depends on your preconceptions. For one who believes in moral desert, it seems to be saying "because you sin, you deserve to die." If you put aside moral desertism, however, that punitive

Mercy and Justice

interpretation falls away and the verse can be read as "the inevitable consequence of sin is death." Many verses commonly used to support the desertist view depend on that same presuppositional mistake.

On the other hand, many biblical passages note how often people do *not* get what they deserve. Good people do not get good things (Job 2:3; Ecclesiastes 8:14, 9:11; Psalm 73:13-14; and even Jesus in Luke 23:41) and bad people do not get bad things (1 Samuel 26:16; 2 Samuel 19:28; 1 Kings 2:26; Psalm 73:12, 103:10). Many of those passages express a hope, or even a firm belief, that God will eventually bring about the writer's conception of what each person deserves: Psalm 37 is a prime example.

And yet Jesus repeatedly questions the whole concept of getting what you deserve. He presented, in word and deed, a God who causes the sun to shine on all people regardless of whether they are evil or good (Matthew 5:45). John reported an incident in which Jesus encounters a man born blind, and the disciples, operating on the basis of a getting-what-they-deserve paradigm, ask Jesus whether it was the man's own sin that caused his blindness or his parents'. Jesus replied that it was neither, and refuted any sense of desert by healing the man on the spot (John 9). On another occasion, Jesus confronted the same paradigm by pointing to two events of the day: the murder of some Galileans by Pontius Pilate and the collapse of a tower that killed eighteen people. Did such catastrophes happen to particular people because they morally deserved it? Jesus says a clear "No!" (Luke 13:1-5). In Jesus' parable of the Good Samaritan, there is no indication at all that the person who

Disrupting Mercy

was beaten and robbed either deserved such treatment or not. What was important was that they should be shown mercy, regardless of any desert one way or the other.

I used to believe that the proper response, the just response, to wrongdoing is to punish the wrongdoer. That assumption was so deeply ingrained that the younger me was unable to question it. It is woven into our legal system, into a pervasive understanding of God, into our approach to parenting, international relations, the "war on terror," asylum seekers, and human traffickers. But it is foreign to the attitude shown by Jesus, and foreign to the image Jesus presents of God.

The turning point for me—though the power of the idea had been crumbling for many years—was a comment by Darrin Belousek[63] about these words of Jesus:

> *But I say to you, Love your enemies and pray for those who persecute you, so that you may be children of your Father in heaven; for he makes his sun rise on the evil and on the good, and sends rain on the righteous and on the unrighteous. (Matthew 5:44-45)*

How does Jesus respond when betrayed by friends, unjustly treated in a legal system, and treated violently to the point of death? Does he show any signs of revenge? Any sign that the people harming him should fear punishment? Of course not! He says, "Father forgive them" (Luke 23:34).

Jesus told his followers that the appropriate response to evil is love rather than retribution. But what Belousek showed me for the first time was the reason Jesus gives.

Mercy and Justice

Why should followers of Jesus not seek revenge? "That you may be children of your Father in heaven." That is, since God does not seek revenge, neither should God's children! God sends sun and rain equally on all people, not just those who deserve it. When we see someone metaphorically striking God on the cheek, we should never expect or hope that God will smite them, nor that God will swing to hit the "sinner" and clobber Jesus instead. Those who strike God on the cheek can expect God to turn the other cheek. To be God's children we should be merciful, just as God is merciful (Luke 6:36).

This view is at odds with the belief of many Christians who feel able to show mercy now only because of an assurance that God's retributive justice will correct it later on the final day of judgment. "In the meantime," writes James R. Harrison, "because God will carry out a definitive eschatological accounting, believers are able to act mercifully toward their enemies and persecutors amid inexplicable evil."[64] This makes mercy temporary and second best, as though we are called to be merciful because God's wrath will come later. That is a far cry from Jesus call to be merciful because God is merciful.

Perhaps many find giving up the idea of retribution difficult because in that case people who commit horrible acts will just "get away with it." To eschew retribution can seem too soft and too tolerant of evils that really should be opposed. That misses the point. I agree that one alternative to retribution is to just accept any behavior and not judge anything to be evil. But that is certainly not the alternative Jesus promotes. His life stands in clear opposition to evil, and his death displays the power of love over evil. We can take the horror of real evil seriously and seek with all our heart, mind, and strength to prevent, expose, and oppose evil, and to heal its consequences, without needing revenge or retributive punishment.

To avoid being misunderstood, I need to differentiate a couple of concepts that can be confused with desert. One is human rights. I do not think it is necessary to say "she deserves a fair trial" or "he does not deserve to be enslaved" since those are basic human rights, equally applicable to all people. All people have a right to a fair trial and a right not to be enslaved. People have rights by virtue of being people and such rights can be neither earned nor forfeited. So, when I recommend that we stop using the word "deserve" I am not implying that human rights go away. People have rights quite independently of whether we wish to say they deserve either rewards or punishments. To deserve is a moral judgment based on something we do, whereas a right is inherent in our humanity regardless of what we do.

Second, there are some cases where we use the term "deserve" without attaching any moral judgment. I remember watching a running competition in which a water bottle, thrown by a spectator, hit one of the athletes just a short distance from the finish line. Now suppose the athlete had been coming first and, purely because of missing a stride when the bottle hit them, finished in second place. We might say quite truly that they deserved to win, but that is not a moral judgment.

It would not be so true, however, to say that some kind but poor person deserved to win the lottery. Or that a school student deserved to get a better grade because they had tried so hard. Or that someone deserved to be raped because they dressed provocatively. Or that someone deserved HIV/AIDS because they were a promiscuous homosexual.

No one deserves AIDS. No one deserves to win the lottery. No one deserves heaven. No one deserves hell.

As long as we are stuck in the mire of what people deserve, we cannot fully appreciate the grace or the mercy of God. The biblical God seeks to restore *all* things (Acts 3:21), wishes that *all* would be saved (1 Timothy 2:4), sends sunshine and rain on both the righteous and the unrighteous (Matthew 5:45), and has no favorites (Acts 10:34, Romans 2:11). This is a God whose posture of grace extends to all, regardless of any reward or punishment they may seem to deserve. This is a God who releases the oppressed (Luke 4:18), who creates a home for us (John 14:1-4, Hebrews 11:16), and who forgives even those who would prefer that God was dead (Luke 23:34).

Grace is not blind to evil, nor does it condone the harm we do to ourselves, each other, and our world, but is continually expressed in acts of mercy that undermine evil by enabling a better alternative. "From [Jesus'] fullness we have all received, grace upon grace" (John 1:16). It is this grace that says, "there is neither Jew nor Gentile, neither slave nor free, nor is there male and female" (Galatians 3:28). There is no "us and them." There is no deserving nor undeserving. God's mercy is extended to all irrespective of any such category. It is all gift.

Disrupting Mercy

May our posture be the same as God's, blind to any cultural or religious notion of what people deserve or do not deserve. The posture of grace from which mercy springs does not say, "I'll be nice to you even though you don't deserve it." God's acts of justice and mercy are based on compassion for people in need, not on whether the recipient deserves or does not deserve it. Grace and mercy deny any sense of what someone deserves, and surprises people with blessings anyway.

To love mercy in the way Micah 6:8 suggests forces us to eschew any attribution of desert. If mercy is the main course, you cannot have desert!

JUST MERCY, STONECATCHERS AND MALADIGARRA

In 2014, Byran Stevenson published the book *Just Mercy: a Story of Justice and Redemption*, which was later turned into a highly acclaimed movie. The book documents Stevenson's work with the Equal Justice Initiative to provide legal assistance to prisoners condemned to death in the USA.

The book's main narrative tracks Stevenson's advocacy on behalf of Walter McMillan, who had been convicted of murder in 1988 and was waiting to be executed. The case against McMillan was flimsy at best and, largely because of Stevenson's advocacy, was finally overturned in 1993.

Alongside McMillan's case, the book assigns chapters to numerous other death row cases against a backdrop of a country that has the highest rate of incarceration per capita of any nation in the world.[65] As of April 2021, the USA has 2,504 prisoners facing the possibility of execution, and since the reinstatement of capital punishment in 1976, the penal system has executed 1,532 people.[66]

In the case of McMillan and most of the others Stevenson reports, the actions of police, public prosecutors, and court officials were prejudicial rather than fair or thorough. The case against McMillan relied on the obviously fabricated and coerced evidence of two people that placed McMillan at the location of the murder. Contrary evidence from at least a dozen witnesses who saw McMillan at a church event at the time of the murder was ignored.

What struck me most while reading *Just Mercy* was not the need for mercy in these cases, but the need for justice. McMillan and others described in the book were, in varying degrees, denied justice. They were convicted and condemned to death without a fair hearing of the evidence. The so-called justice system did nothing to promote *shalom* or to return things to how they should be. Justice was obscured by selective investigation, coercion of witnesses, hiding evidence, stacking juries, and systemic racism. It was not that the legal system imposed justice without mercy, but rather that the legal system was pathologically unable to act justly.

A similar observation could be made about an act of rape when a person cries out for their attacker to have mercy. Mercy is not really what they need but fairness and simple human dignity. If the assailant heard such a plea and decided to desist, there would be nothing morally laudable about that: it would be just re-establishing equity. A cry for mercy in such cases is a cry for the abuser to be

Disrupting Mercy

human. The cry for mercy begs the abuser to rethink who they are and who the victim is. It is a call to treat the victim as a person who is equally human and as valuable as the attacker.

Although *Just Mercy* demonstrates repeated failures to act justly by the law enforcement system, the book is full of mercy from other sources. Mercy sits in the background of the whole book in the life of the author and others who expend their time, emotional energy, reputation, and career to counter the indignity and injustice imposed on the prisoners they care for.

That source of mercy is made wonderfully clear in a later chapter of the book, which draws on the story of Jesus' engagement with the woman caught in adultery (John 8:1-11). While wandering the halls of a courthouse, Stevenson encounters an older woman he did not know, who hugged him and asked to speak with him. Fifteen years previously her grandson had been murdered, and she had sat in this very courthouse when the killers were sentenced. As she recalled that day, she said to Stevenson:

> *"I sat in the courtroom after they were sentenced and just cried and cried. A lady came over to me and gave me a hug and let me lean on her. She asked me if the boys who got sentenced were my children, and I told her no. I told her the boy they killed was my child." She hesitated. "I think she sat with me for almost two hours. For well over an hour, we didn't neither one of us say a word. It felt good to finally have someone to lean on at that trial, and I've never forgotten that woman. I don't know who she was, but she made a difference."* [67]

Mercy and Justice

Since then, she often came to the courthouse to comfort others in the way that unknown woman had comforted her so many years before.

> "It has been wonderful, Bryan. When I first came, I'd look for people who had lost someone to murder or some violent crime. Then it got to the point where some of the ones grieving the most were the ones whose children or parents were on trial, so I just started letting anybody lean on me who needed it. All these young children being sent to prison forever, all this grief and violence. Those judges throwing people away like they're not even human, people shooting each other, hurting each other like they don't care. I don't know, it's a lot of pain. I decided that I was supposed to be here to catch some of the stones people cast at each other." [68]

That woman's attitude springs from deep theology and wisdom. If we follow the way of mercy, then we too will be stonecatchers, even though "it hurts to catch all them stones people throw."

A remarkably similar idea is embedded in an Australian Indigenous practice:

> *A criminal sentenced to death has to stand before the tribal men to be speared. But the defendant obtains a Maladigarra, a champion or trained deflector of spears.*
>
> *All that the Maladigarra uses is a woomera [a wooden tool normally used for throwing spears]. He tells his client: "You watch me and my movements, and do everything I do. Don't watch the spears". He places himself in front of his client,*

> *woomera in hand. He deflects all the spears and breaks them. When all the spears are broken, his client is free.*[69]

To be a stonecatcher, or a spearcatcher, is to enact both justice and mercy. Such acts recognize the humanity and inherent worth of both victim and perpetrator. While still acknowledging the wrong done by one against the other, they create new opportunities for life, health, dignity, and flourishing for both. Such acts are often surprising and controversial. As Stevenson notes, "It's when mercy is least expected that it's most potent—strong enough to break the cycle of victimization and victimhood, retribution and suffering."[70]

May we all pursue opportunities to be stonecatchers and Maladigarra. With that restorative intention, acting out of compassion for people's needs rather than based on some artificial notion of what they deserve, we see justice and mercy moving in synergy toward *shalom*.

Mercy and Justice

WHAT OPPORTUNITIES DO YOU HAVE
TO SPEAK OF MERCY INTO THE EAR OF JUSTICE?
WILL YOU BE A STONECATCHER?

[6]

MERCY AND BROKENNESS

An initial thought to ponder: Please listen to Peter Mayer's song "Japanese Bowls." There are several versions on YouTube. I have always found this an incredibly moving, even eye-watering, song. How do you feel about your own cracks?

MANY READERS WILL BE FAMILIAR with *Les Miserables*, a massive 1,400-page novel by Victor Hugo that has since been dramatized in radio plays, TV series, more than a dozen movies, and of course the incredible stage adaptation with music by Claude-Michel Schönberg. Perhaps the key to this story's ongoing popularity is the way it juxtaposes law and mercy. In this chapter I use Hugo's portrait of Jean Valjean to help us reflect on the nature of human brokenness. One of the outcomes of an astute perception of mercy is the recognition that we are all broken, so that none can authentically stand above the rest of humanity judging, or rescuing, from a position of superiority.

The central storyline of *Les Miserables* follows Jean Valjean after his release from nineteen years in prison. Originally sentenced to five years for stealing a loaf of bread to feed his sister and her starving children, the sentence was extended after he tried to escape. Escape and recapture repeat three more times and by the time he was released he was a broken and angry man. "Through suffering upon suffering he came little by little to the conviction, that life was a war; and that in that war he was the vanquished. ... At times he did not even know exactly what he felt. Jean Valjean was in the dark, suffering in the dark; hating in the dark. He lived constantly in darkness, groping blindly like a dreamer."[71]

Another key character is Javert, an incorruptible police officer who is as harsh on himself as on criminals. Javert believes Jean Valjean will always remain a morally despicable criminal. After his release from prison, when Valjean skips his parole regulations, Javert hunts him relentlessly for twenty years. I will discuss the character of Javert and his opposition to mercy later. But for now, consider the act of mercy that transforms Jean Valjean's life soon after his release from prison.

As Valjean wanders around France, his yellow passport informs everyone that he is a criminal, not to be trusted. In the town of Digne no one will give him even food or lodging, even though he has money to pay for them. With night falling, he even seeks shelter in a small hut only to discover that it is actually a kennel, and a bulldog chases

Mercy and Brokenness

him out. Late in the cold evening he knocks on yet another door and receives a surprisingly warm welcome by the local bishop, Monseigneur Charles-François-Bienvenu Myriel. The bishop gives him a meal and a bed, refusing to accept any payment.

At 2 a.m., Valjean wakes in his bed and, forever angry at his past ill-treatment, decides to steal the bishop's silver tableware and abscond. He is captured by local police later that morning and dragged back to the bishop's house. But now an amazing thing happens:

> *[The bishop] approached as quickly as his great age permitted: "Ah, there you are!" he said, looking at Jean Valjean. "I'm glad to see you. But I gave you the candlesticks, too, which are silver like the rest and would bring two hundred francs. Why didn't you take them along with your cutlery?"*
>
> *Jean Valjean opened his eyes and looked at the bishop with an expression no human tongue could describe. ...*
>
> *Then turning to the gendarmes, he said, "Messieurs, you may go." The gendarmes left.*
>
> *Jean Valjean felt like a man about to faint.*
>
> *The bishop approached him and said, in a low voice, "Do not forget, ever, that you have promised me to use this silver to become an honest man."*
>
> *Jean Valjean, who had no recollection of any such promise, stood dumbfounded. The bishop had stressed these words as he spoke them. He continued, solemnly, "Jean Valjean, my brother, you no longer belong to evil, but to good. It is*

Disrupting Mercy

> *your soul I am buying for you. I withdraw it from dark thoughts and from the spirit of perdition, and I give it to God!"* [72]

Giving Valjean a meal and bed is an act of kindness, but the bishop's response to the theft is something more than kindness. The extraordinary generosity and implied forgiveness is an act of mercy, which springs from the bishop's compassion. Rather than being blinded by what others think Valjean deserves, he calls on Valjean to become a better person.

Valjean is not immediately changed, but enters a period of confusion, resistance, tears, and reconsideration. He senses a new light shining on him: a light that both exposes the horror of who he has become, and gently illuminates a fragile hope.

The rest of the book shows how deeply Valjean is transformed by Bishop Myriel's mercy. For the remainder of his life Valjean demonstrates the same mercy to others in acts of self-sacrifice, generosity, forgiveness, and love. Note, however, that this hoped-for outcome was not a determinant of the bishop's mercy. If Valjean had remained selfish, deceitful, and angry, it would not have changed the bishop's choice.

One last point about Bishop Myriel, before moving on. In the musical version of *Les Miserables*, Bishop Myriel's character is very shallow, with this scene being his only brief appearance. In the book, however, the bishop is the main focus of the first hundred pages. It is Hugo's portrait of a man whose whole life reflects the self-giving generosity of mercy. Bishop Myriel illustrates for us a key feature of mercy: mercy is demonstrated not in single heroic acts, but through a character developed over a lifetime, out of which acts of mercy, large and small, spring naturally and frequently.

OUR OWN ENCOUNTERS WITH MERCY

Victor Hugo's portrayal of Jean Valjean shows how mercy can drastically redirect the trajectory of a person's life. Valjean is not, however, as extreme a case as it might first appear. As Peter Mayer's song "Japanese Bowls" reminds us, we are all broken. The most important question is not how to avoid being broken but what we do with our inevitable brokenness.

Like everyone else since Adam and Eve, Annabella and I have been damaged by "the slings and arrows of outrageous fortune," by things we have done, and by things done to us. We have been richly blessed as well as deeply hurt, and in the midst of all that we have experienced the gift of mercy and sought to show mercy to those around us.

I have been privileged to have friends, family, work colleagues, and a profusion of life experiences that have been positive and nourishing. I have had money, education, and career opportunities far beyond what most of the world experiences. Certainly, there have been challenges, but I am alert enough about my history to know that whatever I say about mercy is biased by unearned privilege. That is not to suggest all privilege is unearned, but that so much good just came to me. All of it is a gift, a kindness, independent of what I might or might not deserve. And such a life inevitably raises the question of why I am the recipient of such mercy when so many others are not.

At times I have extended mercy to others, and at times I have not. After an idyllic childhood on a dairy farm in the lush coastal town of Berry, my high school experience was the most destructive period of my life. I suffered through the ages of eleven to seventeen at an all-male boarding school on the south-western outskirts of Sydney, a school that seemed to me devoid of love, in stark contrast to the family environment I had known up until that point. The school culture was marked by bullying, the derision of anyone who was different, and the hierarchical bastardization or hazing that is common in many male institutions. With a youthful and idealistic sense of fairness, I actively opposed that culture, often refusing to give in to it as a junior, standing up for the underdog and, as a senior student, calling on others to break the cycle of abuse. The whole experience was traumatic for me, and many, many nights I quietly cried myself to sleep. On the other hand, I was not blameless, and my own struggles to manage adolescent sexuality were unhealthy and harmful.

During that troublesome time, great mercy was extended to me by some of the school teachers. One teacher in particular must have seen how much I was struggling. He arranged activities that helped me to release the tension and get me through the final high school exam period. Against the normal school procedures, he hosted evenings of card games for a few students. He would physically wrestle with me, normally letting me think I was winning. He took a few students off campus on abseiling and caving trips. He did not confront any of the challenges I faced or mistakes I was making, but simply gave me his time and his emotional support. At a time when my parents were not there, and the school's institutional structures offered no help, he kindly gave me the steadying hand I needed.

Other people have also helped me in hard times. I cannot imagine how I could have survived otherwise. How can anyone, or any society, survive without the safety net of mercy?

After school and university, I worked in Sydney, and lived in an intentional Christian community linked to the Uniting Church. That house had many visitors, including Malcolm[73]—a young man with severely antisocial psychological problems. He could not hold down a job, was often homeless, sometimes violent, drunk or high. We naively tried to help him, though he drove us crazy. During almost every visit he would abuse us for not giving him what he wanted, because that, he assured us, was what real Christians would do.

One day Malcolm stole some money from a jar in our kitchen that held cash for groceries—one of us saw him do it through the window. After we confronted him about the money and wrestled with him to get it back, he left saying, "You'll be sorry! I'm going to send the boys around to deal with you!" Although he was capable of violence, we were not particularly worried by his threat until there was a knock on the door a few hours later and we could see two large shapes through the frosted glass of the front door. When we opened the door, the shapes turned out to be two police officers, following up a report of someone being attacked in our house. Malcolm *had* sent the boys around ... just not "the boys" we expected! The police were easily assured that there was no problem and went away without even coming inside—leaving me wondering what would have happened if we really had been assaulting someone in the back room.

We would often get late night emergency phone calls from Malcolm. Calls that lasted hours. Though it appears heartless looking back now, we would sometimes just leave the phone with him talking and go back to bed. He could talk for an hour before realizing no one was listening. Once we had to take him to hospital to get his stomach drained of whatever cocktail he had taken. On another call he told me in a panic that his girlfriend had just slit her throat, and I drove twenty minutes to his home to help. They were both stressed and hyperactive, though the girl's injuries turned out to be minor. There was little I could do except try to calm them down.

In another situation two of us spent a night sitting with a young woman who was trying to escape a drug addiction "cold turkey." A couple of years later a young man moved in with us after being released from prison. He too struggled to escape a drug addiction, and tragically died of an overdose while living with us. Around that time, I changed my paid work from five to four days a week so that I could spend one night a week hanging out with homeless youth.

I recount those interactions to suggest that however naive we were as twenty-somethings, we deliberately positioned ourselves to be able to engage with Malcolm and others so that we could act with mercy towards them. We did not name it mercy then, and we had little idea about how to really help, but we were learning.

In my late twenties I saw the movie *Cry Freedom*, about the death of anti-apartheid activist Steve Biko and, through the organization African Enterprise, I started to learn more about the complexities of racial injustice in South Africa. I spent a month or so in South Africa at the beginning of 1990 to see some of that first-hand, and to weigh up whether I could do anything to support the processes of peace and justice there. During that trip I spent a weekend in Soweto, much to the horror of many white people I informed. "You can't go there," they would say, "You'll be killed for sure!" Instead, I found warm hospitality. A year later I sold all I had in Australia, even cashed in my superannuation, and emigrated to South Africa. I lived in an inner-city area and volunteered in African Enterprise's cross-cultural bridge-building programs. My main intention, in that context of extreme separation and fear, was not to take sides or project a foreigner's judgment, but to show by example that cross-cultural collaboration and friendships were possible.

Once again, I am recounting this to show my early and sustained willingness to act out of compassion. There is not much to boast about. None of it was driven by any sense of sacrifice, nor judgment. An inner sense of what was right, good, and kind impelled me, but I could rarely tell if my presence made any positive difference or not. My motives were, no doubt, muddied by arrogance. But the posture of acting for others, of pursuing an ideal that encompassed both justice and mercy, has been with me for a long time. And I am still learning.

My wife Annabella was raised by stricter parents than mine. According to the theology of her parents, children were born sinful and manipulative. Good parenting required those errant urges to be dislodged, using the fear of physical punishment to counter disobedience. Annabella cannot recall her parents ever singing her to sleep or reading a bedtime story. That is not the full story of course. They were loving and kind in their own ways and following parenting norms of the day. In fact, in a way that seems paradoxical now, it was their love that motivated their harshness.

Annabella recounts two childhood incidents that show her hunger for mercy and the results of her own lack of mercy. On one occasion, when she was about eleven years old, Annabella was left at home with her sister who was about three, while the rest of her family were at church for a couple of hours. During that time Annabella told her sister that their parents had died in a car crash and were not coming home. Her sister climbed into her lap and cried, while Annabella assured her she would look after her. The sister was deeply upset and soon afterwards Annabella told her it was not true and that their parents would be home soon.

One important aspect of that story is to try to understand why Annabella acted as she did. To a large extent she was yearning for comfort herself. She wanted someone to need her, someone who would sit in her lap and

Mercy and Brokenness

be comforted. She needed someone to hug and who would hug her.

Another aspect is the long-term effect on Annabella's sister who, later in life, recognized a fear of her parents dying. Although she had no conscious memory of the incident with Annabella, did it contribute to that fear? Annabella had never spoken to anyone about her deceit until that time. In her late thirties, Annabella recognized her own shadow side in that childhood event: how her own need for relational warmth and affirmation led her to exploit her sister's emotions. She described this childhood incident to her sister and apologized for it, and her sister offered forgiveness. That forgiving interchange as adults was an important relational step for both of them.

Back in Annabella's childhood, another experience highlights the confusion about love and mercy in her mother's approach to parenting. At age thirteen, Annabella was very excited about being allowed to attend a church youth group. However, two days before the event, she made some mistake that resulted in her being grounded. Her mother would not allow her to attend the youth group. Annabella thought that surely, if she were the model daughter, her mother would relent, have mercy, and allow her to go. For the next two days she did everything right and offered to do extra chores. But no, it did not matter how repentant Annabella was, a decision had been made. From her mother's point of view, any leniency would undermine her authority and encourage Annabella's waywardness. Since no backing down was possible, the punishment had to be carried out.

Disrupting Mercy

Annabella was deeply hurt as her brother's car drove off to the youth group without her, confused and angry that her best efforts could not change her mother's decision. The longer-term impact was that Annabella gave up trying to please her mother and learned how to dance around her instead. It did not instill the respect her mother intended, nor did it deter manipulation, but encouraged the reverse. The despondency that arose because there was no hope of receiving mercy led to Annabella following rules dutifully and fearfully, but lying to avoid punishment. She found other ways to meet her needs for affection and kindness rather than expecting them from her mother.

Both incidents highlight the importance of mercy in our family relationships. Mercy is like the springs of a trampoline, which allow the structure to flex and bounce back rather than break. We also need to be retrospectively merciful to our younger selves, because most of us have done things we regret that have wounded others who are dear to us.

What is clear from both Annabella's and my experiences is that without mercy, we are all stuck up the tree like Zacchaeus, alone, ashamed, and hopeless. Acknowledging our own shadows, we have learned that we, and everyone, need mercy. Without mercy we are lost. But if we allow the gold of mercy to be poured into our cracks we can embrace our brokenness and become items of great beauty.

THREE MACRO-STORIES

Brokenness is a universal part of human experience, though we are each broken in unique ways. A distinctive mark of Jesus' ministry was the way he valued people's brokenness and drew them beyond its effects into a higher purpose. He knew brokenness did not erase the image of God in us and is never the end of our story.

The Bible is full of stories: an observation that has fueled countless theological treatises on narrative style, plot, scene, symbolism, journey, and character development. But underlying all the varied plots, authorship, and styles are some recurring themes. These are important meta-narratives that provide structure to the many individual stories. Marcus Borg calls them "macro-stories" and suggests that three macro-stories are particularly important for understanding how God interacts with us.[74] These macro-stories reflect three forms of brokenness in our human condition along with God's response to them.

The first macro-story is the biblical depiction of the problem of sin: a problem whose resolution is found in forgiveness. The second is the problem of bondage, whose resolution is found in freedom. The third is the problem of exile, whose resolution is found in the journey home.

Those three macro-stories provide a helpful way to frame the role of mercy in God's mission. These three categories of brokenness are so fundamental to the human condition and such strong themes in the Bible that I allocate the next three chapters to discuss each one in turn. My intention is to show how mercy acts in contexts of sin, bondage, and exile, to bring about forgiveness, freedom, and the journey home. I am not suggesting that every story of mercy fits neatly into one of those categories. Often a person's story will involve multiple forms of brokenness, so choosing in which category to place them can be somewhat arbitrary.

At our wedding, Annabella and I placed candles and our rings on a broken plate. Although it was badly cracked, the plate had been repaired with gold—well, fake gold anyway—in the Japanese style called *kintsugi*. For us, the cracks represented the brokenness of our individual histories: our mistakes and failures, our past relationships, the disappointments that came from within, and the damage we had suffered from without. In our marriage, we did not intend to deny or whitewash those past cracks, but to explicitly honor them because they constituted, and continue to constitute, essential parts of who we are. *Kintsugi* recognizes that nothing lasts, nothing is finished, and nothing is perfect. Rather than throw away something that is broken, *kintsugi* repairs it in a way that highlights the imperfections. In the same way, we hope that our marriage will honor our individual pasts, and that we may pour gold into each other's cracks.

Mercy is like that. Mercy does not deny our need or our guilt, but neither does it discard people because they are broken. We all need *kintsugi* of the soul. Mercy is God's gold, painstakingly and expertly brushed into our cracks to make us more beautiful. Mercy gives broken people new life, infused with glory.

Mercy and Brokenness

How do you normally respond to brokenness in yourself and in others?
How would those responses change if they were infused with mercy?

[7]

SIN AND FORGIVENESS

An initial thought to ponder: Please wander through the archives of the Forgiveness Project. Their website, www.theforgivenessproject.com, contains over a hundred stories of people who have lived through abuses and tragedies, and who have experienced the magic of forgiveness. Do any resonate with you? How does that experience of forgiveness affect both the ones who were injured and the ones who caused those injuries?

AS AN AMERICA CIVIL-RIGHTS activist, the Rev. James Lawson demonstrated how non-violent resistance can confront personal and systemic sin. He was a colleague of Martin Luther King, the trainer of many who defied racial segregation laws in the USA, and in later life a pastor with the Methodist Church. Lawson spent time in prison for refusing to serve in the military forces during the Korean War, and then learned about the non-violent approach of Gandhi while working at a college in India. By 1958, aged thirty, he was teaching non-violent strategies for social change to college students in Nashville, Tennessee.

At that time, many restaurants in the USA still had segregated eating counters. To challenge that practice, groups of students started deliberately sitting at counters labeled clearly as "whites only" and demanding service. Lawson was a major facilitator of these "sit-ins" and was very keen to ensure that the protestors acted non-violently. Through lectures, workshops, and role playing, he instilled a deep sense of discipline in the movement so that even when taunted, verbally abused, physically attacked, or arrested, the participants would remain respectful and non-violent. If people did not feel able to maintain that stance, they were asked not to join the protest.

A student of James Lawson's, David Dark, recounts an incident during one such sit-in at Nashville in 1960:

> *One Saturday, Lawson was on the scene to coach students and to dissuade white passers-by from responding violently to young people whole-heartedly—and whole-bodily— committed to nonviolent witness. Lawson approached one aggressor in a motorcycle jacket at the center of a group who'd kicked Bernard Lafayette and Solomon Gort. The man directed a racial slur at Lawson before spitting in his face.*
>
> *Reverend Lawson regarded the aggressor calmly and asked if he might have a handkerchief. The man was so taken off guard that he'd handed it to Lawson before he knew what he was doing. As Lawson thanked him and wiped his face,*

he asked the man if a nearby motorcycle belonged to him. It did. And in no time, they were discussing horsepower. Within a few minutes, the man was asking how he could aid Lawson and the students in their work. The script had been flipped.

I once asked Lawson how one might develop the habit of handling people so beautifully, and he responded, as if it was just then occurring to him, "You have to keep in your mind an imagery of infinite possibility." [75]

Lawson's request for a handkerchief disarmed his opponent! Although the man approached Lawson as though the two were enemies, Lawson's eye contact and verbal interaction as equals disrupted the man's script and led to a complete turnaround in his thinking. This is the effect mercy hopes for: beyond the role mercy plays in addressing a person's immediate need, mercy hopes to be transformative. By treating his abuser with dignity and respect, Lawson prompted him to rethink whether they really were enemies. Once the enmity was disrupted, he could start to treat Lawson with dignity and respect.

Interactions like that show how a posture of mercy can foster forgiveness and reconciliation in contexts of conflict, hatred, and hostility. Maintaining an "imagery of infinite possibility" enables us to draw out from someone the best of their humanity rather than escalating the negative influence of sin. Marcus Borg sees this movement from sin to forgiveness as one of the key macro-stories in the Bible.

THE CONCEPT OF SIN

These days, "sin" is a problematic word. As a category imposed on one person by another, it is a moral judgment often designed to induce shame in order to control. Yet the theme of sin in the biblical account points to something central in universal human experience: the sense of personal inadequacy. Some brokenness comes from external circumstances and what is done to us, but the personal aspect of sin highlights the reality that part of our brokenness arises from within. To the extent that sin refers to something internal and personal, it points to our own capacity to cause damage to ourselves as well as to others.

Because sin affects other people, it inevitably includes a social dimension. As Cornelius Plantinga evocatively notes, sin vandalizes *shalom*.[76] Through sin, our relationships with other people are damaged, as are our relationships with God, with the earth, and with our own being. That brokenness bubbles upwards and creates broken systems that in turn oppress and misuse.

The bi-directionality of sin—bubbling upwards from the personal to the systemic, and flowing downwards from systems to individuals—is very clear in the arena of modern slavery. Modern slavery, or human trafficking, occurs when one person abuses or exploits another in coercive ways that severely restrict the person's freedom. The sin of modern slavery is fundamentally about broken relationships, the denial of *shalom*. In effect, the exploiter is saying that their victim is unimportant, a mere object for their own gain rather than a real person with the right to be treated with dignity. But at the same time as coercive acts dehumanize the victims, they also dehumanize the perpetrators. The people who abuse, coerce, and exploit lose their own sense of worth, their own moral integrity, their own ability to experience empathy, and their ability to either give or receive mercy.

This vandalism of God's image ripples throughout society. Families are drawn into cycles of abuse, generations are trapped in debt bondage, some victims later become traffickers themselves, law enforcement becomes corrupted, and abusive practices become institutionalized.

That is the bubble-up effect, where individual sin aggregates into systems of injustice. But the flow-down effect, where broken systems damage individuals, is equally important. Neoliberal capitalism creates the global economy in which modern slavery thrives.[77] The demand for cheap consumer goods creates supply-chain contracts that necessitate the exploitation of cheap labor. Cultural and religious beliefs normalize the exploitation of women, children, and certain social castes. The same beliefs fantasize sexuality in a way that promotes a wide variety of sexual abuse. Tribal identity politics position the pure and noble "us" above the primitive and aggressive "them." These systemic sins propagate poverty, fear, greed, and a lack of respect for others. They cultivate a body of people who are vulnerable to being exploited, and a body of people vulnerable to becoming exploiters.

Do not think of modern slavery as an extreme case that we can hold at arm's length. It is a predictable result of our individual and corporate sin. Modern slavery affects us all, for even those of us who are neither traffickers nor trafficked are beneficiaries of this system. Our prosperity in the so-called "first world" is enabled by the exploitation of other people and the earth. Furthermore, we all hold in our hearts the same tendency as human traffickers to abuse, exploit, and coerce others for our own purposes.

Modern slavery is a massive social problem, and one we have been unable to eliminate despite enormous efforts. In the context of such horrendous abuses, what does mercy look like? Certainly it means healing the harm experienced by millions of victims and survivors. But could mercy also play a role in disrupting the sin—the individual and social brokenness—that perpetuates their harm?

In the Old Testament, sin is embedded in what Borg refers to as the "temple story" or the "priestly story." The story of sin is interwoven with concepts of impurity, guilt, uncleanness, along with cleansing, covering, and sacrifice. Controlled by the priesthood, one's ritual purification depended on prescribed sacrifices at the temple. The question being addressed was how to overcome one's unworthiness before God, because it seemed that nothing impure could survive in the presence of God. How could people be cleansed of their impurity in order to become acceptable to God?

In the New Testament letter to the Hebrews, the structure of sacrifice is turned on its head. The traditional macro-story of sin requires the unworthy person to hand something of value to the priest for it to be violently destroyed. But in Hebrews, Jesus is depicted as the priest who offers *himself* as the sacrifice, and whose life turns out to be indestructible. As mentioned before, Jesus "gave himself" for us in much the same way as parents give themselves for the sake of their children. Such self-sacrifice differs starkly from the coercive, violent sacrifice it superseded. In this way, the death of Jesus subverts both the priesthood and the requirement for sacrifice.

Paul's interpretation is that "In [Jesus] we have redemption through his blood, the forgiveness of our trespasses, according to the riches of his grace that he lavished on us" (Ephesians 1:7, see also Colossians 1:14). In other words, the mercy of God—God's acts of extreme kindness to us through Christ, motivated by God's compassion toward the brokenness of our sin—results in our forgiveness. Through mercy everyone is acceptable. Because Christ is the high priest, we can stand with confidence before God knowing that we will receive mercy (Hebrews 4:16). In God's mercy, being accepted and loved is not dependent on what we deserve or do not deserve, but on who God is. The mercy of the incarnated Christ points us to a God who offers grace to all (Titus 2:11), even the ungrateful, the wicked, and enemies (Luke 6:35, Matthew 5:44-45). The mercy of the resurrection restores life to all people (1 Corinthians 15:21-22).

OVERLAPPING BUT DISTINCT

The prototypical process of forgiveness starts with someone injuring another. That may be a physical injury, some form of psychological mistreatment, a betrayal, the theft of some object, some libel that disparages the person's reputation, or a myriad of other wounds. At some point the person who caused the damage acknowledges their guilt and shows regret for what they did. Ideally, they attempt to reverse the damage to the extent that is possible. From the other side, the injured person offers to release the offender from their debt. In this process, the damage is neither condoned, forgotten, nor ignored. Rather, the guilt is acknowledged, but resentment is released and any right to retribution forgone.

The process of forgiveness is rarely as smooth as that. It becomes more complicated when it is between groups rather than individuals, and when the damage carries over from one generation to the next. In such cases, who has the relevant standing to repent or to release? Formal acts of clemency by judicial officials or heads of government present other complexities. One of the two parties may have died, in which case either the repentance or the release cannot occur. There may be no repentance and yet the injured party may sense a need to let go of the emotional trauma for their own health. Nevertheless, the process of injury, repentance and release forms the prototype from which such complexities are variations.

At the center of the process of forgiveness is the release of resentment by the injured person. When we have been hurt by another, that initial hurt is multiplied and prolonged by our own emotional response. We continue to give power to our abusers as long as we carry the anger and resentment within us. To release ourselves from that ongoing hurt, we need to forgive the other. In many people's minds that is the whole of forgiveness. For them, the purpose of forgiveness is to deal with the trauma of holding a grudge, and occurs independent of the other person. If the ability to release my own resentment relies on anything the other does, such as repenting, or promises to do, then I am still under their power, held captive by their attitude toward me.

Although there is good reason to define forgiveness as the release of resentment, God's merciful response in the macro-story about sin goes beyond that step. In the Bible, forgiveness is more than a one-sided internal psychological act by the injured person, but always relational and directed toward reconciliation. That applies to the forgiveness between two people just as much as it does to the forgiveness between us and God. Forgiveness is the path through which reconciliation is achieved.[78]

Both forgiveness and mercy seek to move us toward *shalom*, but while there is overlap between mercy and forgiveness, the two are distinct concepts. One difference is that forgiveness and mercy express different emotional directions. Whereas forgiveness might be largely the overcoming of resentment, acts of mercy aim toward the virtue of compassion.[79]

Another difference is that although you can show mercy to anyone as a compassionate response to their need, you can only forgive someone who has injured you. At least in the standard process of forgiveness, if person A injures person B, then a third person C cannot step in and say that A is forgiven. There are exceptions, such as when a representative of a group forgives a past crime committed against that group. But in general, to forgive, you must have some personal standing in the matter.[80]

Some acts of mercy are not acts of forgiveness, because mercy is a response to a wider variety of needs than just to guilt. When we see someone in need, that need may be of many kinds: a broken relationship, a broken arm, a broken heart, a broken promise, a broken bank account. When the need relates to broken relationships, the guilt of wrongdoing, abuse, exploitation, mistrust, or self-condemnation, then the form mercy naturally takes might involve forgiveness. Forgiveness itself may be the extreme kindness expressed in mercy.

However, although forgiveness is one form of mercy, many other forms of mercy are expressed toward other types of need. An example is Jesus' parable of the Good Samaritan (Luke 10:25-37). The person accosted by robbers was shown mercy (v37) by the Samaritan, not because of any guilt or sin that required forgiveness, but because he had been beaten until he was half dead and required medical assistance.

Conversely, some acts commonly labeled as forgiveness are not acts of mercy. In financial contexts, "forgiving a debt" occurs when a creditor releases someone from the obligation to repay the debt. That may occur for several reasons but normally because the effort to enforce the debt is perceived to be too great to be worthwhile. In other contexts, letting go of resentment is intended to unburden the injured party rather than for the sake of the guilty party. In either context, the act of forgiveness is not motivated by compassion for the person who is forgiven, and so is not truly merciful. Interestingly, in the case where the difficult step of releasing resentment is taken for the sake of one's own well-being, it may count as an act of forgiveness toward the other, and simultaneously an act of mercy toward oneself!

In 2020, a picture was posted on the Reddit website with this caption: "Kid had an old bike with no brakes and dented someone's car. A few days later the car owner surprised the kid with a new bike."[81] That is a great example of both mercy and forgiveness. The car owner's action implicitly announced forgiveness for the damage the boy caused. But he went further than that. Looking beyond the accident he saw that the boy could not afford a safe bike ... so he compassionately met that need with a surprising gift.

In the Old Testament, forgiveness is often associated with the prerequisite of a sacrificial payment. On the surface at least, a transaction is implied in which people sin against God, the people sacrifice grain or an animal to God, and consequently God forgives their sin. By the end of the Old Testament writings, however, this model has been questioned, and in the New Testament we see the earlier partial resolution of sin via sacrifice superseded by the work of Jesus. Jesus forgave sins without the need for any death or other sacrificial payment. He simply declared forgiveness to people (Matthew 9:2; Mark 2:5; Luke 5:20, 7:48) or requested his father to forgive them (Luke 23:34). After Jesus' resurrection, his followers proclaimed the same forgiveness in his name (Acts 2:38, 10:43, 13:38; 1 John 2:12).

Disrupting Mercy

Numerous New Testament passages assert that the life, death, and resurrection of Jesus add something important to the macro-story of sin and forgiveness. During the final meal with his disciples, Jesus spoke of his blood being poured out for the forgiveness of sins (Matthew 26:28). After his resurrection, Jesus explained that the intention of his suffering and resurrection was always that repentance and forgiveness would be proclaimed to everyone (Luke 24:46-47). In later theological reflection, Paul noted that even though we were dead in our sin, God made us alive with Christ (Ephesians 2:1-10). He wrote that although we all sinned, we are also all forgiven: "justified by his grace as a gift, through the redemption that is in Christ Jesus" (Romans 3:21-26).

Even prior to the writings of the New Testament, God's mercy is linked to the forgiveness of sins. Take, for instance, this verse from the Wisdom of Solomon:[82] "You are merciful to all, for you can do all things, and you overlook people's sins, so that they may repent" (Wisdom 11:23). The fascinating insight here is that it does not say "you overlook people's sins who repent" but that in mercy God overlooks their sins *so that* they may repent. That is, mercy can act preemptively, as a disruption that can promote repentance. Mercy is God's compassionate response to the underlying moral need rather than a response to a person's acknowledgment of that need!

An example of preemptive forgiveness was be seen after the tragic death of four children in Sydney in 2020. The four were walking along a suburban footpath when a drunk driver ran into them. The parents of three of those children almost immediately announced that they forgave the driver. They had been raised with this biblical understanding and embedded in a community that practiced the virtues of forgiveness and mercy. That deeply ingrained theology enabled them to react to the tragedy with forgiveness, not as a short-lived reflex but a sustained commitment. In the midst of enormous grief they have established a foundation whose aim is "to increase community awareness of the power of forgiveness to transform human relationships and to provide resilience toward human flourishing."[83]

The same automatic response was shown by an Amish community after the murder of five of their children in 2006. On that day, a man entered their small school in rural Pennsylvania with a shotgun and a handgun. He told everyone to leave except for ten young girls. An hour later, three of those girls were dead. Another two died of their wounds in hospital. Their attacker shot himself dead before the police could intervene.[84]

The Amish trace their heritage back to the sixteenth-century Anabaptists, and have always emphasized forgiveness and non-violence. Although the schoolhouse shooting was a more extreme situation than anyone in that community had ever experienced, they were still able to remain faithful to that practice of preemptive forgiveness.

What can forgiveness look like in such an extreme context? Given the deaths of both victims and attacker, there could be no repentance, no release of resentment by the immediate victims, and no reconciliation. Nevertheless, amidst grief that would be unbearable to most of us, the parents and surrounding community did not react with condemnation or malice. Instead, they prayed and cried, supported each other, and assisted the emergency teams. A grandfather helped the young boys come to grips with the trauma by saying to them, "We must not think evil of this man." The community modeled forgiveness, "determined to make sure their children did not get caught up in the cycle of hate and retribution."[85] When you hate someone, it is very difficult to feel compassion toward them.

The extensive media reporting of the events frequently voiced surprise at the Amish ability to forgive. Anyone familiar with the Anabaptist tradition would not have been so surprised. As we shall see in Dirk Willems' story, the ability to extend forgiveness and mercy to people in moments of crisis arises from a habitual posture and regular practice with smaller incidents.

More than any words could convey, the faith of the Amish was on display through the way they cared for the shooter's wife. From the very first day, the community, including the parents of the murdered girls, offered her comfort, practical support, and protected her from unwanted media attention. In an interview years later she said "It was amazing. It was one of those moments during the week where my breath was taken away, but not because of the evil. But because of the love."[86]

In the way I have been using the terms in this book, the actions toward the shooter's wife were not examples of forgiveness, but of mercy. The Amish community could forgive the shooter in the sense that they did not hold on to resentment, but there was nothing to forgive the wife since she had done them no injury. Their gift of extreme kindness to her was not in response to her guilt, but a merciful response to her own grief and to the practical hardships she faced in continuing to care for her children under intense public scrutiny.

ACCEPTING MERCY AND FORGIVING YOURSELF

One crucial component of mercy is the act of accepting it. Mercy can be thwarted by a person's inability or unwillingness to receive it. This limitation is most clearly seen in people who cannot forgive themselves. This seems to me the only sense in which mercy can be viewed as conditional. Even God cannot, or at least will not, force someone to accept mercy. God is committed to being limited by our free will. God woos but does not coerce us; God knocks but we can refuse to open the door. Consequently, even unconditional mercy can be refused and that possibility of refusal imposes a condition on mercy's efficacy.

In the normal course of childhood development, we receive mercy and forgiveness thousands of times. Through those experiences we learn both that we are loved and that we are not self-sufficient. Physically and psychologically we need a supporting community. We need friends and family who pick us up when we fall, and who forgive us when we inevitably hurt them. Underlying that experience is our individual and communal need for the multilayered kindness of God. Every good thing we have comes from God (James 1:17), including God's compassion (2 Corinthians 1:3-11 NIV). The God who cares for every sparrow (Matthew 10:31) values us enough to die for us

(John 3:16). Having received mercy and forgiveness ourselves, we become able to show mercy toward others' needs and even forgiveness to those who have hurt us.

But what happens when that formative process is broken, when someone matures without having learned to receive mercy? Some, perceiving the world to be a harsh place, toughen themselves and don't give a damn about anyone else. Another outcome can be seen in people who reach down to others from a safe distance. Unfamiliar with receiving kindness, they wrap themselves in protective superiority and take pride in needing no one. That can lead to pity for others in the Nietzschean sense: contemptuous rather than compassionate; patronizing rather than merciful.

Alternatively, people who grow up without receiving mercy and forgiveness can infer that they are of no value, unloved, and unlovable. Having internalized that belief about themselves they may be unable to see the value of others. Their self-protection mechanism may not be to feel superior but to cling tightly to everything they can gain for themselves, and consequently only ever give when they expect to profit from it. Others might not approach giving with such a transactional mentality, but with a certain type of hypocrisy that outwardly proclaims purity, virtue, even holiness, while simultaneously feeling ashamed and worthless. An inability to deal with one's own inadequacies can be projected judgmentally onto others.

On the other hand, those who have recognized their own need for help and forgiveness also recognize that they are not superior to others in need. They can offer the same help and forgiveness to others without judgment, and without the arrogance of superiority, but in humility as peers.

Jesus told his disciples that they should not expect to receive forgiveness unless they were willing to forgive others (Matthew 6:15). But the converse is equally true. In many cases, people deny forgiveness to others because of their own struggle to receive forgiveness, and to forgive themselves. Giving and receiving are inextricably linked.

A frequent reason for not being able to give or receive forgiveness is shame, which Brené Brown defines as "the intensely painful feeling or experience of believing that we are flawed and therefore unworthy of love and belonging."[87] Shame can make us unable to accept kindness from others because we feel unworthy of it. Shame can prevent us from forgiving ourselves. When shame remains hidden, it can gnaw away at us, and manifest in addiction, depression, anger, eating disorders, and aggression. We all feel shame at times. What makes us ashamed and what we do with that feeling influence our ability to feel empathy. Without empathy we cannot respond with forgiveness or mercy to the needs of others.

One initiative of the Forgiveness Project is an intensive group-based prison program, called RESTORE, which aims to explore how to heal, restore, and rehumanize people by addressing the destructive influence of shame and trauma on the lives they have lived.[88] For prisoners, shame is a recurring experience. It may have played a hand in motivating their crime. It would have been felt throughout the process of their arrest, trial, and conviction. It is driven home to them throughout their prison sentence and follows them doggedly after their release.

During RESTORE, a group of men or women serving in prison volunteer to spend four full days listening to storytellers who have either been victims of harm or served time in prison as a result of perpetrating harm. As the facilitators model their own vulnerability and strengths, they create a safe space that encourages honest, open, and mutually empathetic conversations. Participants are supported to express their feelings of hurt, pain, remorse, regret, sorrow, grief, and loss while sharing their own stories with the whole group.

Shame is the key theme of the program. RESTORE draws on Brown's Shame Resilience Theory in the belief that dealing with shame can release people to rethink and reset their life trajectory. RESTORE does not seek to resolve their difficulties but promotes a curious and enquiring approach to ask questions such as: if we had lived each other's lives could we have done what the other did?

We often hope to see signs of remorse in an accused person during their court case, but the experience of RESTORE facilitators is that remorse often becomes possible only after shame has been addressed. Offenders may need to deeply engage with their own experience as victims before they can understand the impact of their actions on the people they have harmed. Once they recognize that, prisoners may actually see positive value in their incarceration. For some, prison provides a safer place than they are used to, and within that safety they can take

Sin and Forgiveness

the inward journey through shame and victimhood to remorse and self-forgiveness.

Programs such as RESTORE use kindness as the bridge from shame to self-forgiveness. Showing offenders that they are valued and heard acts as a catalyst for personal change. Such a gift disrupts their preconceptions, creating an opportunity to make sense of their past and transform their future. Their success demonstrates how mercy can act as the antidote to shame.

What can one do for someone who is unable to accept mercy or to forgive themself? If that "someone" is yourself, perhaps start by sifting through childhood experiences to identify early examples of kindness and unkindness. Was forgiveness ever shown to you as a child? On what basis were you punished? Of what were you made to feel ashamed? Was kindness or love only given conditionally? Were there times you showed kindness and it backfired? What have significant others said about you? Have you been told you are a worthless waste of space who doesn't deserve kindness? Have you committed some unforgivable sin? Were you told that accepting mercy makes you inferior or a failure? Does receiving always make you feel in debt? Is the need to receive a sign of weakness or failure?

So many of us have suffered under guilt-driven preaching that constantly told us God loves us BUT ... But we are never good enough. But we must strive to do better. But our sin killed Jesus. But nothing imperfect can ever survive in God's presence. But all our best deeds are just filthy rags. If that has been your experience then hear the Good News of Jesus: God loves you. Full stop. No buts. God cares for every sparrow, and you are much more precious to God than sparrows. God is for you, not against you.

Psychologically that might be a difficult truth to digest, especially if your experience of church, and the attitudes projected onto you by friends and family, have been the opposite. However, there is a colorful world worth seeking on the other side of the truth that you are loved. It is a world beyond shame in which all are valued, where mercy circulates around a network of reciprocity, and where everyone has the opportunity to flourish. Jesus called it the kingdom of heaven, and asked his followers to pray for and live toward that kingdom becoming real on earth. It is a strange kingdom, nothing like any other kingdom ever seen on earth, because it has a strange king who consistently gives up power and privilege. In this kingdom there are still challenges and failures, but it is a place where God's mercy is made tangible as the challenges are faced together and the failures are covered by grace.

On the other hand, if the "someone" who is unable to accept mercy or to forgive themself is not you but another, keep disrupting their assumptions by showing mercy and forgiveness to them anyway. Be a role model for them. Show them that they are loved and valued. As Raniero Cantalamessa observed:

> *A real change of heart will take place only when, first and foremost, people discover that they are loved for themselves and are precious in the eyes of God who, in every case, will never cease loving them. Communicating this truth is the*

loftiest duty of the Church and is the best way to preach mercy.[89]

Stop being concerned about whether they deserve it or not and just be kind to them. See if they are willing to talk about their backstory to learn what hurt them so much in the past that they now fall into fight or flight modes. When they test you by doing something to hurt you, call them out and talk about what happened, but forgive them.

As Sarah Durham Wilson wrote, "The way you alchemize a soulless world is by treating everyone as if they are sacred until the sacred in them remembers."[90] Is that not what Jesus did for Zacchaeus? Zacchaeus' true nature had been shrouded by shame, but Jesus' mercy-infused intervention lifted the shroud. By affirming that Zacchaeus was a child of Abraham, and inviting himself to dinner, Jesus drew out from Zacchaeus a latent goodness that had always been there.

I am well aware that the last few paragraphs are seriously inadequate. The internal and interpersonal psychology is far too complex for such brief advice. But the first principle is to foster the recognition that we are all loved, deeply and unconditionally, by God. Because of God's love, we are able to love ourselves and others. The second principle, when someone's history has taught them they are unloved, or that mercy and forgiveness are impossible, is to demonstrate mercy and forgiveness patiently and persistently to them.

OVERCOMING THE POWER IMBALANCE

I have touched on the issue of power already, but in the context of forgiveness something further can be said. There is a kind of thinking that requires Christians to forgive as a moral necessity and consequently turns it into an imposed and burdensome law. Whereas showing mercy is usually seen as optional because it goes "above and beyond" what can be morally required, forgiveness is often seen as a special case. Indeed, Jesus himself said that if you do not forgive then you will not be forgiven (Matthew 6:15). One of the benefits of forgiveness is that it can unburden both parties: releasing the guilty party from their guilt, as well as releasing the injured party from the stress of carrying anger and hatred. Unforgiveness can eat away at you in a very destructive manner and can perpetuate a disempowered state of victimhood.

However, when forgiveness is coerced—when a person is told that they *must* forgive—forgiveness itself can become an act of self-destruction. If a person is counseled, before they are ready, that they must forgive, that counsel is itself an act of power, and one that produces further injury. The advice implies that the injured party is guilty of unforgiveness and casts them in the untenable position of being the victim of a double injury while simultaneously needing forgiveness themself.

On the other hand, withholding forgiveness can also create a power imbalance. By choosing not to forgive, the injured party can force the guilty party to remain in debt, prolonging their possible remorse and their need to repay.

Contemporary philosopher Slavoj Žižek adds to the complexity in a challenge to Christian theology that requires some response. Žižek calls himself a "Christian atheist,"[91] by which he means that he does not believe in the existence of a supreme being who created this world, but nevertheless finds something compelling in the message of Christ. He views Jesus' abandonment on the cross as a point of rupture in the very essence of God: that God is abandoned by God and hence even within the concept of God there is a fundamental lack. He writes that, "This total abandonment by God is the point at which Christ becomes FULLY human, the point at which *the radical gap that separates God from man is transposed into God himself.*"[92]

In an essay titled "Love Without Mercy," Žižek describes what he sees as a problematic power dynamic within the notion of mercy and attempts to show how a new concept of "God" is needed to surmount that problem. Of importance to me is the question of whether that problem can be surmounted without throwing away what I see as crucial to a meaningful concept of God, namely God's personhood.

In this essay, Žižek uses the term mercy, but rather than the concept of mercy I have developed in this book, he is actually referring to forgiveness: "the inexplicable gesture of undeserved pardon." He interprets traditional Christianity as affirming that "we, humans, were born in sin, we cannot ever repay our debts and redeem ourselves through our own acts—our only salvation lies in God's Mercy, in His supreme sacrifice."[93]

Disrupting Mercy

Although that may seem like a freeing act, Žižek claims that "it is precisely through NOT demanding from us the price for our sins, through paying this price for us Himself, that the Christian God of Mercy establishes itself as the supreme superego agency: 'I paid the highest price for your sins, and you are thus indebted to me FOREVER.'"[94]

For Žižek then, every expression of mercy/forgiveness is an act of power. He believes that mercy inevitably places the receiver in a position of inferiority and debt, and furthermore that this is shown absolutely by the mercy/forgiveness of God.

Neither Žižek nor I want to allow that power imbalance to be the final word. I will say a bit about how Žižek overcomes the problem and then something about my own resolution.

Recall that Žižek understands the core Christian message as undermining the traditional metaphysical conception of God; that through Christ is revealed the true nature of God as lacking, as self-divided; that God is not at one with God; and that the absolute is not an all-knowing being but inescapable unknowing. "This divine self-abandonment, this impenetrability of God to himself, thus signals God's fundamental *imperfection*."[95]

To Žižek, that is not a failing. Instead, the imperfection of God is precisely what enables a conception of love that overcomes the power imbalance of mercy/forgiveness, a "love beyond mercy":

> *Love is always love for the Other insofar as he is lacking—we love the Other BECAUSE of his limitation, helplessness,*

ordinariness even. In contrast to the pagan celebration of the Divine (or human) Perfection, the ultimate secret of the Christian love is perhaps that it is the loving attachment to the Other's imperfection. And THIS Christian legacy, often obfuscated, is today more precious than ever.[96]

Whereas a traditional view of mercy/forgiveness inevitably positions the giver as superior to the receiver, to Žižek the imperfection of God makes it possible to experience love without that power imbalance and without the ensuing debt.

It seems to me that the same outcome can be achieved without sacrificing an orthodox view of God. As discussed in Chapter 4, love and mercy arise from the Trinitarian understanding of God. God can show love to God, and subsequently mercy to the created world, because mercy is not always about guilt and forgiveness. Mercy is a caring response to compassion in the context of relationship and community.

The central insight of Christianity is not, as Žižek claims, that through Jesus we come to understand the imperfection of God, but that through Jesus we understand God's desire to be in solidarity with us. The Incarnation—God with us—reveals God's mercy as part of the network of reciprocity, within which the gift of mercy can be shared without superiority or debt.

God can, and does, walk among us in humility, so that mercy is expressed and experienced in a network of reciprocity among peers. Although equal with God, Jesus humbled himself to live among us, even to the point of death. This does not mean that Jesus gave up God-ness, but that in the incarnation Jesus gave up the divine power imbalance in order to show true God-ness.

Mercy and forgiveness are most definitely acts of power in that they seek to energize change, but always power-with rather than power-over. Rather than creating or reinforcing a dominance structure, forgiveness is a true reflection of love: a gift, given and received as part of an ongoing relationship. When we hold to the ideals of justice, mercy, and humility, forgiveness becomes a relational dance that frees both parties and promotes *shalom*.

WHAT WRONGS DO YOU FIND MOST DIFFICULT TO FORGIVE? DOES THIS CHAPTER RAISE ANY MEMORIES THAT YOU WANT TO DO SOMETHING ABOUT?

[8]

BONDAGE AND LIBERATION

An initial thought to ponder: Please watch the video by Yulia Mahr of Max Richter's piece of music, "Mercy." It is available on YouTube and elsewhere. What does mercy look like in today's world? What does it sound like? What is the touch of mercy? What is its smell?

During World War II, Maximilian Kolbe demonstrated the essence of mercy in the context of bondage.[97] Kolbe was a Catholic Franciscan priest in Warsaw when, in 1939, German military forces overran Poland. Kolbe knew that the occupation was likely to lead to his personal suffering, and he even noted to his Franciscan colleagues that Christ himself had said, "No one has greater love than this, to lay down one's life for one's friends" (John 15:13).

Kolbe set up an emergency hospital but within a month he was arrested and transported to Germany. He joked that they were lucky since the trip to Germany did not cost them a penny!

Even while in German prison camps, Kolbe showed genuine goodwill to all. Although the food rations were meagre, he would give his to prisoners suffering more than he. He was a man of peace, not out of fear but courage. He had a knack for engaging with their captors in a way that softened their hearts. In the midst of mistreatment, he would say, "All this will pass; good must win."

Within a few months the Franciscans were released and returned to Warsaw where they cared for and fed refugees, provided Christmas presents to children, and arranged a New Year celebration for local Jewish families. They provided free coffins to whoever needed them and even arranged shelter for 1,500 Germans. When a German soldier fell ill, Kolbe would visit. In 1940, Kolbe was offered German citizenship, which would have saved him, but he declined.

In 1941, Kolbe was arrested by the Gestapo along with several other priests. After a couple of months in Pawiak prison, he was transferred to Auschwitz.

Priests were a particular target of German abuse and murder in the work camps. They were given heavier loads to carry and beaten with sticks if they stopped to rest. On one occasion the guards gave Kolbe fifty lashes. Praying was forbidden in Auschwitz, though that did not stop Kolbe. At the risk of death if discovered, he heard other prisoners' confessions and led secret church services.

One Auschwitz prisoner wrote that "the struggle to conserve one's life had assumed a form so brutal that it was very rare for a prisoner to aid another."[98] Nevertheless, Kolbe continued to calmly care for everyone around him, making sure nobody was hurt trying to help him. "He intended to use every suffering that came his way, not only to show his love for God by his willingness to suffer for his faith, but to help his fellow prisoners."[99] He urged the other prisoners of faith to pardon their oppressors and return good for evil. He would give away his food and his shoes to other prisoners. He would provide spiritual comfort to the German prison doctors.

Many people did not last more than three weeks in Auschwitz. Kolbe lasted from May to the end of July when an unfortunate turn of events led to his death. After a prisoner had escaped, the whole camp went without dinner in reprisal. The six hundred prisoners who shared the accommodation block of the escaped man—including Maximilian Kolbe—stood at attention on the parade ground all the next day.

At the end of the day, the deputy camp commander, Karl Fritzsch, announced that since the fugitive had not been found, ten men would be chosen to die by starvation. One of the chosen men, Francis Gajowniczek started to sob, "My wife and my children!"

> *Suddenly, there is movement in the still ranks. A prisoner several rows back has broken out and is pushing his way toward the front. The SS guards watching this Block raise their automatic rifles, while the dogs at their heels tense for the order to spring. Fritsch and Palitsch too reach toward their holsters. The prisoner steps past the first row.*

It is Kolbe. His step is firm, his face peaceful. Angrily, the Block capo shouts at him to stop or be shot. Kolbe answers calmly, 'I want to talk to the commander,' and keeps on walking while the capo, oddly enough, neither shoots nor clubs him. Then, still at a respectful distance, Kolbe stops, his cap in his hands. Standing at attention like an officer of some sort himself, he looks Fritsch straight in the eye.

'Herr Kommandant, I wish to make a request, please,' he says politely in flawless German.

Survivors will later say it is a miracle that no one shoots him. Instead, Fritsch asks, 'What do you want?'

'I want to die in place of this prisoner,' and Kolbe points toward the sobbing Gajowniczek. He presents this audacious request without a stammer. Fritsch looks stupefied, irritated. Everyone notes how the German lord of life and death, suddenly nervous, actually steps back a pace.

The prisoner explains coolly, as if they were discussing some everyday matter, that the man over there has a family.

'I have no wife or children. Besides, I'm old and not good for anything. He's in better condition,' he adds, adroitly playing on the Nazi line that only the fit should live.

'Who are you?' Fritsch croaks.

'A Catholic priest.'

Fritsch is silent. The stunned Block, audience to this drama, expect him in usual Auschwitz fashion to show no mercy but sneer, and take both men. Instead, after a moment, the deputy-commander snaps, 'Request granted.' As if he needs

Bondage and Liberation

to expel some fury, he kicks Gajowniczek, snarling, 'Back to ranks, you!' [100]

The ten men were stripped naked and locked in a bunker containing nothing more than a bucket for relieving themselves. Kolbe led them in prayers and singing. After two weeks with neither food nor water, only four remained alive, including Kolbe. At that point, the survivors were injected in the arm with carbolic acid, killing them within ten seconds.

Francis Gajowniczek was not a friend of Kolbe's, just another fellow human. But Kolbe had compassion toward him and his family and acted on that compassion with mercy through the extreme act of sacrificing his own life. Gajowniczek survived Auschwitz and after the war travelled widely to speak of Kolbe's sacrifice.

Kolbe's act of mercy was not only transformative for Gajowniczek, but also for the other prisoners and guards who witnessed his sacrifice and the calm grace with which he faced death.

I have included the background to that final sacrifice to emphasize a crucial point: that Kolbe's act of mercy to Francis Gajowniczek was not surprising. This was not a once-in-a-lifetime act but simply the last act in a life of mercy. Mercy was deeply rooted in Kolbe's character. He was so used to being-for-others that offering to take Gajowniczek's place was as natural as giving away his food. As natural as hiding Jews from the Nazis. As natural as praying and caring for his enemies.

This repeats the pattern I have already noted about the Amish community caring for the wife of the schoolhouse gunman, and about the Bishop of Myriel in *Les Miserables* as he gives the silver candlesticks to Jean Valjean. In all these cases, extreme acts of kindness are offered by people who have trained themselves, through innumerable smaller acts, to see others' needs, to compassionately yearn for others' well-being, and to give in humility with no expectation of any repayment.

BONDAGE, IMPRISONMENT, AND SLAVERY

The biblical theme, or macro-story, of bondage is rooted in the Exodus: the Israelite's deliverance from slavery in Egypt. This identity-forming episode in Jewish history reverberates throughout the Bible. The second book of the Old Testament, aptly named Exodus, starts with the descendants of Abraham and Jacob prospering in Egypt to the point where the locals start feeling threatened by them. That led to a period of perhaps two hundred years in which the Israelites were increasingly oppressed by the Egyptians until their lives were made "bitter with hard service in mortar and brick and in every kind of field labor" (Exodus 1:14, 5:6-18). Ruthless labor exploitation was later coupled with a command from the Egyptian leader to kill all Israelite boys at birth (Exodus 1:22).

But then God intervened to free the people of Israel and to re-establish their journey toward becoming an independent nation. God saw their misery, and out of concern for their suffering acted to rescue them (Exodus 3:7-10). The narrative makes two motives of this rescue plan clear: it is a compassionate response to the people's suffering and at the same time an action that honored the covenant God previously made with Abraham (Exodus 6:1-8). As discussed in Chapter 3, there is no conflict between those two motives, and both intertwine in God's expression of mercy.

The first half of the book of Exodus documents the birth of Moses, his personal journey toward God, God's call for Moses to deliver the people from slavery, a series of confrontations between Moses and the Egyptian Pharaoh, and the dramatic escape of over a million people out of Egypt and across the Red Sea. Moses' song of praise after their escape acknowledges the enormity of this divine act of mercy (Exodus 15:1-18).

Numerous passages in the Old Testament remind Israel of the Exodus (e.g., Deuteronomy 6:21-23, 26:5-10; Psalm 78, 105). Remembering the escape from Egypt is the primary element of the annual Passover celebration. The English word "exodus" is a direct transliteration of a Greek word meaning a departure. We can see that theme in the New Testament too, when Stephen recounts the Jewish exodus story before being stoned (Acts 7), when Moses and Elijah appear to Jesus and speak about the Exodus he will achieve in Jerusalem (Luke 9:31), and when Paul refers to Jesus as the Passover lamb (1 Corinthians 5:7).

The macro-story of exodus positions human brokenness as a form of bondage. The plight of Israel in Egypt is one example, but people continue to be trapped, enslaved, chained, imprisoned, and oppressed. Many cultures still find themselves under the thumb of a foreign power. Over eleven million people are incarcerated in prisons,[101] and fifty million people are trapped in some form of modern slavery.[102] Some cults use fear, isolation, threats of violence, mystical rituals, and mandatory social conformance to brainwash members into unquestioning loyalty. Uncountable millions are trapped in destructive relationships with partners who abuse them, and who use physical and psychological constraints to make escape either impossible or unthinkable.

Just as significantly, bondage may be the result of addiction, or an inability to see ourselves having any control over our situation. Those internal chains can enforce a state of powerlessness and victimization just as much as externally imposed bondage.

As Marcus Borg notes, most of us are in bondage to cultural messages that define success, attractiveness, and gender roles. Those cultural chains constrain our ability to live well and even our ability to imagine the shape of a good life. At one time or another we have all been in bondage, enslaved or imprisoned, either internally or externally. Some are imprisoned by others, some by themselves.

What does mercy look like in the context of bondage, imprisonment, and slavery?

LIBERATION, RELEASE, AND FREEDOM

In the biblical narrative, God's response to bondage is to create the means by which we might be freed. God sees our bondage and, impelled by compassion, acts with generous kindness to alleviate our suffering. Furthermore, God calls us to engage in merciful acts so that the followers of Jesus become known as freed and freeing people. We see that most clearly in the Exodus and in the work of Jesus. Both demonstrate the liberating effect of mercy. When compassion is applied to people in bondage it breaks the chains that bind and gives people an opportunity to be free.

In my experience, bondage in all its varied forms is the most challenging context in which to show mercy. We do not always feel compassion for people constrained by bondage, especially for prisoners and addicts. Even when we do feel compassion, what expressions of kindness are likely to bring a positive change to their plight? At the best of times, helping another person is a tricky business. How do we help without making matters worse in the long term? How do we avoid the person falling into an unhealthy pattern of dependence on being rescued? How do we encourage their own abilities and agency? How do we give assistance without violating their free will?

These pitfalls are exacerbated in the context of bondage because often the physical needs are coupled with psychological barriers to being helped. Some do not recognize their situation as one of bondage, or do not want to be released. Some have been told so often that they are not worth anything that they believe it. Some are so dependent on their abuser, or on the source of their addiction, that they can no longer imagine a life without them. Consequently, many prisoners released from jail quickly reoffend to get back into jail where they feel they belong. Many people rescued from various forms of modern slavery return to their previous captors or others just like them.

Many escape an abusive relationship only to take up a new, equally abusive relationship.

What is mercy in such contexts? It is certainly not simply to remove the person from the prison, or from their abuser, or from their access to drugs. Though each of those may be an important step, thoughtful mercy must also address the deeper issues of self-worth, shame, dependence, anger, or a host of other internal chains that bind them just as surely as the externally imposed bondage. For freedom to be sustained, those released from bondage must have the will, along with practical and emotional resources, to take hold of a better alternative. This is part of why Jesus asked people, "What do you want me to do for you?" or "Do you want to be healed?"

Mercy is never coercive, and consequently we cannot use mercy to force someone to be free. Mercy can only provide an *opportunity*. Like any true gift, once mercy is given, the recipient can do whatever they like with it, including throw it away. We can show people extreme kindness, beyond what they might expect, beyond what they have been shown in their past, beyond what they might consider they deserve, but forcing someone to be free is impossible.

An exceptional book about the complexities of helping people, either individuals or in a community development context, is *When Helping Hurts*, by Steve Corbett and Brian Fickkert. One of their principles is "Do not do things for people that they can do for themselves."[103] That is an important guide for avoiding paternalism and a rescue mentality. This relates closely to Nietzsche's criticism that pity overrides the recipient's own abilities and choices, disabling rather than enabling them, taking away their dignity rather than empowering them.

I was once underground, exploring a tight cave by torchlight in Bungonia National Park when our group going one way through the cave met another group going the other way. Where we met, a vertical split about two meters wide allowed us on one side to watch their progress on the other side. They were traversing a narrow ledge that angled upwards and the space was only tall enough to crawl along. Years earlier, someone hammered a spike into the rock at the top of the crawl and there was an old rusty chain hanging down that you could hold on to. Although the traverse was reasonably safe, the possibility of falling off the ledge in the dark down the vertical slit was quite scary. In the process of crawling up that ledge, one young adventurer lost his nerve. He could not find sufficient hand holds to pull himself up nor foot holds to push himself up, and he started to panic. The group's leader was above him, sitting safely at the top of the crawl. When he saw the younger climber stuck, he crawled down a little, reached down to grasp his hand and dragged him upwards to safety.

I remember wondering at the time whether that was the best option for the leader. He kept the youth safe and thus dealt with the immediate physical need. The youth would be forever thankful that he had been saved. But was it a missed opportunity for that young man to stretch himself and learn that he was more capable than he thought he was? A better outcome would have been if the youth had found a way up himself. If the leader had spoken reassuringly to calm down the youth's panic, and given just the minimum of suggestions about moving a hand here, a foot there, would the youth have been able to save himself? Would he then have felt the thrill of achievement and a self-confidence that could propel him to even greater achievements?

In the context of bondage, the boundaries between what a person can do and what they cannot do, and between when they can choose and when they are unable to choose, become difficult to identify. In some cases, they are unable to ask for help, even unable to recognize that they need help. They may have such low self-esteem that they do not believe they are worthy of being helped. They may believe they deserve their ill-treatment. In what has become known as Stockholm Syndrome, some people become emotionally attached to their captors to the point where they will defend the abusers and refuse assistance. They may have become so accustomed to their bondage that they literally cannot conceive of a healthier scenario.

In such cases, mercy may entail removing people from their oppressive context even without their explicit permission. Even with a pure motive of compassion, that kind of action must be accompanied by extreme caution lest it turn into another form of dehumanizing abuse. That is a tricky balance to attain. To be authentically merciful, such actions need to be coupled with a commitment to nourishing the person's informed free choice. Removed from their captors, or from access to something they are addicted to, the person can look back at their bondage from a distance and understand it more truly. Beyond rescuing them from the immediate damage, mercy will also contradict the dehumanizing effect of bondage by reaffirming their inherent value. But mercy must then enable the person to make their own decisions about what to do next. Mercy cannot force the intended outcome of freedom, but only provide an opportunity for it.

If liberation from bondage is to be a true act of mercy, it must also take care not to abuse or damage *other* people. For instance, freeing people from bondage does not justify retributive violence against those who held them in bondage. Setting someone free who has been held in some form of modern slavery will no doubt annoy and inconvenience the trafficker. That might be unavoidable, but freeing one at the expense of another's freedom is neither merciful nor just, because it does not foster *shalom*.

For that reason—though this is beyond my intention here—parts of the Exodus narrative need to be carefully interpreted. Sometimes it does take extreme hardship like the ten plagues to confront people with the need to change. But did God really decide to kill the firstborn son of every Egyptian (Exodus 11:4-5)? Did the escape of Israel from slavery really necessitate the drowning of the whole Egyptian army? Does that not reinforce in a very negative way the adage that might makes right?[104]

The gospel paints a more radical picture of freedom than that. In the kingdom of God proclaimed by Jesus, mercy creates an opportunity for all to flourish rather than for some to flourish at the expense of others. Jesus, the "exact imprint of God" (Hebrews 1:3), loves even those who consider themselves to be God's enemies.

Disrupting Mercy

From the beginning of his ministry, Jesus announced release for the captive (Luke 4:16-30). Later, he noted that visiting prisoners is one of the characteristics separating the sheep whom God blesses from the goats whom God rejects (Matthew 25:31-46). Jesus did not refer only to those imprisoned unjustly and surely recognized that many prisoners are lawbreakers: thieves, murderers, terrorists, sexual abusers, etc. Why would he want his followers to visit such people? Why would he see his personal mission as promoting their release?

Central to Jesus' understanding is that mercy is to be shown to all, not just to those who seem to deserve it. Prisoners are in great need, physically, psychologically, and socially. Like us all, they need nourishment, belonging, hope, meaning. Those who have been imprisoned unfairly need justice. Those who are guilty need forgiveness. Those who are unrepentant need a new heart. All need an opportunity to recognize that they too were made in God's image, and that they too are loved. Mercy gives everyone an opportunity to reclaim their dignity and find a way to flourish.

Bondage, imprisonment, and slavery all dehumanize people. They all say, "You are worth less than your captors." That dehumanization is also caused by the metaphoric chains of addiction and coercion. By removing your freedom, they take away, or at least threaten, the free-will that is so central to the divine image in us. Because of that dehumanization, prisoners, slaves, and addicts live in survival mode with no expectation of mercy.

Bondage and Liberation

When generous and surprising acts of kindness are shown to them, the results can be transformative. Such acts may initially meet a specific, surface-level need, such as the physical release from captivity, medical care, or safety from physical or sexual abuse. But mercy can also assure people that they are valuable, that they are worth being cared for, protected, even honored. The result can be a rethinking of their identity and a step toward wholeness and *shalom*.

Such was the case with the man Jesus met in the country of the Gerasenes, on the east side of the Sea of Galilee (Mark 5:1-20, with parallels in Matthew and Luke). The man was possessed by many demons and, outcast by his people, howled day and night enchained among the tombs. Jesus released him from his enslavement by demons, and in doing so released him from the need to be bound by chains. What's more, the man could now sit before Jesus "clothed and in his right mind"—valued, cared for, and with his dignity restored. Jesus names this an act of mercy (v. 19), and it fits perfectly with the definition of mercy we have been following: a gift of extreme kindness, motivated by compassion.

Several decades later, Paul continued to show how God's mercy, expressed through Jesus' life, death, and resurrection, creates an opportunity for us to be freed from bondage. In Paul's view, we are all slaves to something—though his use of the Greek word *doulos* could equally mean a servant rather than slave. Where we were once slaves to fear (Romans 8:15), to sin (Romans 6:17), and to our passions and pleasures (Titus 3:3), the work of Jesus enables us to be slaves to righteousness (Romans 6:18), to God (Romans 6:22), and to Christ (1 Corinthians 7:22; Ephesians 6:6). We can be freed from the law of sin and death (Romans 8:2) and instead become slaves to each other (Galatians 5:13). Those new forms of slavery are motivated not by fear but love, not by coercion but by grace and choice.

Paul knew about prison from first-hand experience and knew that he could live in freedom regardless of such circumstances. While visiting Philippi, Paul was thrown in jail, along with his companion Silas (Acts 16). The story of their miraculous release is worth reading in full, but I just want to note the double act of mercy in that story. God responded to the immediate need of Paul and Silas, but that mercy overflowed to the jailer and his family as well. Paul's compassion toward the jailer averted a suicide and brought joy to the whole family. In a sense the jailer was also in jail, in bondage to fear and constrained by the magistrates. The power of God released both prisoner and jailer.

In the biblical macro-story of bondage, mercy is what creates the opportunity for liberation, release, and freedom, for oppressed and oppressor alike.

Bondage and Liberation

IN WHAT WAYS HAVE YOU BEEN OPPRESSED?
IN WHAT WAYS HAVE YOU BEEN AN OPPRESSOR?
WHAT DOES MERCY FREE YOU FROM?
WHAT ARE YOU MORE ABLE TO DO BECAUSE OF MERCY?

[9]

EXILE AND RETURN

An initial thought to ponder: Please do a web search for Martin Hudacek's statues titled "Memorial of Unborn Children." There are two, one showing a mother and child, another with a father present as well. In both pieces, the contradiction between presence and loss is overwhelming. How does anyone find their way home through such grief?

U P UNTIL TWO WEEKS BEFORE publication date, this chapter started with the moving story of a woman in prison. Removed from her home, separated from her community, and having lost any sense of where she belonged, she was effectively in exile. At the last minute I had to remove the story because of legal sensitivities.

Rather than fill this space at the last moment with other words, I draw your attention to the many people around the world in similar situations. The following page is left

Disrupting Mercy

blank to prompt us to remember all those missing in exile: the disenfranchised millions in prison, the harried millions of refugees, and the muted millions who are homeless, lost, or in hiding.

EXILE IN THE BIBLE AND IN HUMAN EXPERIENCE

In the opening chapters of Genesis, one of the consequences of the Fall was that Adam and Eve were banished from the Garden of Eden. They became exiles, refugees from the only land they had known. In a sense, humanity has wandered unhomed ever since, scattered across the earth searching for an original goodness that has been lost.[105]

Marcus Borg refers to this theme of exile as another of the major macro-stories in the Bible. There are too many examples to list, but the most important are the twin military exiles of Israel after the collapse of the unified nation. First, the northern kingdom was invaded and the people scattered by the Assyrian Empire in about 720 BCE, and basically never heard of again. Second, the southern kingdom was attacked by the Babylonian Empire several times between 605 and 587 BCE. Israelites were deported to Babylon after each attack. The Temple in Jerusalem, which had become the center of Israel's connection to God, was destroyed. "By the rivers of Babylon, there we sat down and there we wept ... How could we sing the Lord's song in a foreign land?" (Psalm 137). We read some of the spiritual reflections by the Israelites during the period in Babylon in the books of Daniel, Ezekiel, and Jeremiah.

Decades later, Babylon was itself conquered by Persia, and the Israelites were allowed to return in 538 BCE. Return to their homeland, however, did not chase away their feeling of exile. The later prophets continued to suggest that, in a spiritual sense, the people were not truly home.

This example of Israel in exile does not stand as a lone incident. In the biblical narrative it is representative of a common human experience that continues to this day. Homes are still destroyed by natural disasters, casting people onto the mercy of others. Poverty and disease continue to make millions of people outcasts from society and homeless on city streets. Political conflicts make people's country of birth so unsafe that they choose to leave. According to the United Nations High Commissioner for Refugees, "In the first half of 2021, more than 84 million individuals were forcibly displaced worldwide as a result of persecution, conflict, violence or human rights violations."[106]

Exile is not always literal banishment from one's home. In a metaphoric sense, exile is felt by migrants who yearn for their old life, by those who live at the margins of their society, and by those whose life is devoid of community. Exile is experienced by those who feel lost in the wilderness, and by those who grieve for something—a child, a marriage, good health—they have lost. Exile is seen in various forms of identity confusion and gender dysphoria.

Exile is a good way to describe the sense that we do not belong here. We find ourselves estranged from God, from each other, and from the land. We are alienated from ourselves, lost and hungry for home, yearning to grasp our true identity, and find the place where we belong. Exile is the human condition.

The history of God's people in the Old Testament, from the paradise of Eden and the Promised Land to Babylon symbolically depicts the history of all humanity. The New Testament picks up those symbols too, with Peter writing about Christians as aliens and exiles in Babylon (1 Peter 2:11, 5:13), and John describing the ultimate fall of symbolic Babylon (Revelation 18) as a precursor to the renewal of paradise on earth (Revelation 21). Since the dividing walls of tribalism have been made obsolete by the gospel (e.g., Colossians 3:11), we are all exiles together, all seeking the same homeland.

THE JOURNEY HOME

In the biblical narrative, God's merciful response to our physical, psychological, and spiritual exile is to enable the journey home. Mercy addresses the experience of exile on multiple levels. First, mercy can address some of the immediate needs of people while they are in exile, especially their needs for safety and human connection.

When a refugee arrives in a foreign land, how are they treated? Are they feared and shunned by the locals or welcomed and embraced? Mercy can be seen in the care refugees are shown: in the food, shelter, clothes, and protection they are given; in the time spent listening to their stories; in the way new roles are given to them so that in dignity they can contribute once more with the resources they already have.

Followers of the biblical God are clearly called to provide mercy in those forms. Jesus calls us to welcome strangers (Matthew 25:31-36), as does Paul (Romans 12:13). We are not to oppress the foreigners in our midst (Exodus 23:9) and not to discriminate against them (Leviticus 24:22), but to love them (Deuteronomy 10:19), treat them fairly (Jeremiah 22:3), make food available to them (Leviticus 19:10), treat them as citizens and even allocate land to them (Ezekiel 47:21-23).

The same is true for other forms of exile. Mercy is expressed in the physical and emotional care of those who are lost or unhomed, and in the development of nurturing relationships. Mercy is shown in both serving them and in enabling them to serve.

When a physical return home is not possible, safe, or desired, the appropriate form of mercy will be to help to establish a new home. Mercy might create opportunities for a new life in a new country: to learn a new language; adapt to a new culture; find a job; and become accustomed to a new community in which a new sense of belonging can grow. Such was the advice of Jeremiah to the Israeli exiles in Babylon:

> *Build houses and live in them; plant gardens and eat what they produce. Take wives and have sons and daughters; take wives for your sons, and give your daughters in marriage, that they may bear sons and daughters; multiply there, and do not decrease. But seek the welfare of the city where I have sent you into exile, and pray to the LORD on its behalf, for in its welfare you will find your welfare. (Jeremiah 29:5-7)*

The word "welfare" in that verse is literally "*shalom*." It points to the role of mercy in enabling a person or a group to flourish even in the midst of exile. Settling into Babylon may be the greatest kindness. Sometimes that results in a complete assimilation and the total loss of prior cultural identity, but that is not necessarily the case. Jeremiah's advice was not intended to encourage the disappearance of Jewish identity. On the contrary, he fully expected the people to eventually return to Jerusalem. His advice was about how to thrive while in exile: with a balance of loyalty to their temporary overlords and a subversive allegiance to their one true Lord. That balance is perfectly shown in the stories of Daniel, who cooperated with the officials in Babylon and yet engaged in non-violent resistance on issues that really mattered.

Without wishing to diminish the trauma of many people's experiences of exile, there are some cases where exile itself is an act of mercy. To be removed from a comfortable home, whether that home be literal or figurative, and forced to find a new path in a foreign place, might be exactly the challenge one needs to thrive. The discomfort of exile may produce the motivation to change that empowers growth. When birds push their young out of the nest, it is an act of mercy without which the young will never learn to fly.

Second, mercy contributes to the possibility of exiles returning home, which for many is the most obvious need. We may express mercy by rebuilding someone's house after it has been destroyed by some natural or political disaster. We may contribute to making their country of origin, or their family situation, safe to return to.

There are many examples of this return home in the Bible. Moses left Egypt aged about forty and after a further forty years in self-exile was directed by God to return to his homeland of Egypt. David fled from King Saul into exile, but eventually returned after Saul's death to become king himself (1 Samuel 21 – 2 Samuel 5). According to one of the gospel writers, Jesus was also a refugee, escaping from Herod's death threat to live in Egypt before returning to settle in Nazareth (Matthew 2:13-23).

As can be seen from Israel's experience, however, not every exile finds a way to return home. Some, like the Jews exiled by Assyria, are lost forever. Others, like the Jews exiled in Babylon, do return home only to discover that home is not what they hoped for. Although they returned to Jerusalem, they were no longer the same and nor was their homeland. They continued to be oppressed by other nations, continued to have internal conflict, continued to break their covenant with God, and were still effectively lost. The postexilic Jews started to realize that where you are is not actually so important, which is why Isaiah implies that the whole world is Babylon (e.g., Isaiah 13). The same can be true for all exiles. A physical return home does not always resolve the underlying desires for identity and belonging.

Consequently, the third level at which mercy responds to exile is to address deeper psychological needs and enable a *real* return home. Mercy is often not directed toward helping unhomed people return to a physical place but toward establishing (or re-establishing) a sense of belonging within a broader context of *shalom*.

In his life and teaching, Jesus shows God's heart for the lost and marginalized. In Luke 15, Jesus notes in three consecutive parables that God has no greater joy than when restoring the lost. Whether it be a lost sheep, a lost coin, or a lost son, God's response is to find, to restore, and to rejoice. The parable of the lost sheep is most clear about this: that the God-like shepherd will go to extreme lengths to find a lost sheep and carry it back to safety.

The brokenness in the parable of the lost son (actually two lost sons) is a combination of sin and exile. The younger son sins by demanding his inheritance ahead of his father's death and then squandering it in "dissolute living" (Luke 15:12-13). But he also finds himself in self-inflicted exile. Having forsaken his cultural heritage, he becomes lost in a foreign land, ashamed and disenfranchised. With what Pope Francis calls "overabundant mercy,"[107] the father watches the horizon, expectantly waiting for the son—and us—to return. The father, who already showed surprising kindness by giving him money and freedom, shows even more surprising kindness when the son does decide to return home. He sees the son and runs to embrace him before any words of repentance are spoken. Filled with compassion (*splagchnizomai*), he rejoices in his lost son's return (v. 20). The father's welcome is not primarily about celebrating the son's return to a physical home, but restoring to him a sense of belonging within the family.

In support of Jesus' teaching on this heart for the lost and marginalized, the Gospels also report numerous incidents to show what that attitude looks like in practice. Jesus' encounter with the woman at the well (John 4:1-40) is one example. The woman was a Samaritan drawing water at midday on her own: an outcast from an already disparaged group. Although an exile within her own community, she was the first person to whom Jesus revealed his identity as Messiah. Rather than ignoring, dismissing, or talking down to her, Jesus engaged with her in a genuine conversation. She was changed. But her change was a *result* of Jesus' kindness, not a pre-condition for it.

The simple kindness of a conversation may not seem very extreme to us, but in the context—a Jewish man and an ostracized Samaritan woman—this is a radical and highly subversive act. He surprises her with his willingness to engage with her, with his candor, with his affirmation of her inherent value, and with his supernatural knowledge of her situation.

A lot of preaching imposes moral judgment onto this story, supposing the unnamed woman to be a prostitute or adulterer. But neither Jesus nor John say a word of criticism about her. John notes the scandal of Jesus talking to a Samaritan and a woman, but doesn't raise any issue about her being sinful. Jesus does say to her, "you have had five husbands, and the one you have now is not your husband" (v. 18) but that does not cast blame on her. Perhaps she was at fault, but in the cultural context it is equally possible that she was married very young to an older man who subsequently died; that a brother was required to take on the husbandly duties (as per Deuteronomy 25:5-10); and that one or more husbands found "something objectionable" about her and chose to divorce her (as per Deuteronomy 24:1). Jesus may well have been saying to her, with compassion rather than judgment, "I know how much abuse you have suffered through five husbands, and the one you are with now is no better than the others."

Jesus does not bring her multiple partners into the conversation to accuse or shame the woman. On the contrary, Jesus names the shame that she carries so that, through being named and acknowledged, the shame can be purged.

All of this is an expression of mercy from Jesus. He saw her in exile and compassionately helped her find a way home. The effect is so affirming and energizing that she returns home as an evangelist. Furthermore, she is sufficiently respected that "Many Samaritans from that city believed in him because of the woman's testimony" (v. 39). Jesus, on the other hand, is so excited and energized by the conversation that he loses his appetite!

As we saw in Chapter 1, Zacchaeus was effectively an exile though still living in his homeland. He was morally lost and ostracized from his people. Jesus saw the outcast Zacchaeus and acted mercifully to restore his moral and cultural identity.

The healing of the woman who had been bleeding for twelve years (Luke 8:42-48) is yet another example of the same dynamic. Jesus deliberately calls the crowd's attention to the woman, not to embarrass or shame her, but to make her "cleanness" public so no one had any further excuse to shun her.

In each case, the lifting of shame is an important aspect of how Jesus expressed mercy to the marginalized. In doing so, he showed mercy's role in moving people from exile on the margins back to inclusion in their community.

The indigenous nations in Australia exemplify a more complex situation in that they live physically in their homeland and yet are dispossessed of it. They are effectively in exile within their own land. As with many dispossessed people, the restoration of their rightful land is an issue of justice rather than of mercy. They need relevant social and political recognition, altered legal status, a fair hearing, and formal treaties. It would not be an act of mercy for the descendants of colonial occupation to acknowledge that ownership of Australian land was never ceded by the traditional custodians: that would simply be fair and ethical.

Many colonizers have acted with mercy toward the indigenous people, but the more common and substantial form of mercy in the Australian context is something even more surprising: the extreme kindness and patience expressed by generations of indigenous people to their oppressors. That was evident in early examples of indigenous people showing European settlers where to find drinkable water. It continues to be evident in their ongoing restraint and willingness to engage peacefully.

That display of mercy by a disempowered minority of the current Australian population is deeply costly, uncomfortable, and disruptive. Whether the mercy will be received and understood by my own cultural peers who constitute the majority of Australia's population, and whether it is disruptive enough to transform us to pursue justice, remain open questions. Nevertheless, the establishment of *shalom* in Australia will owe its success first and foremost to that sustained mercy, and only secondarily to any legislative changes that might be inspired by that mercy. A purely legal solution might leave hearts and discriminatory attitudes unchanged. But if the mercy shown to the colonizing majority inspires a new commitment to justice for the indigenous minority, then legal changes can be crafted to encourage the true *shalom* in which all of us can flourish.

Fourth, the deepest mercy of God enables a resolution to the larger cosmological problem of exile. The ultimate resolution to exile is shown in the overall arc of the biblical narrative, which starts with our banishment from a garden paradise and ends with our citizenship in the city of God.

During the years of Jesus' life, God dwelt among us (John 1:14), which is why Jesus is sometimes given the appellation "Emmanuel," meaning "God with us" (Matthew 1:23). Through the Incarnation God reaches out to Babylon, that is, to us all in exile. Jesus left the safety and comfort of his own homeland, heaven, to live in exile with us. In his adult years, Jesus had no place to call home even on this planet, "nowhere to lay his head" (Luke 9:57-58). Homeless, but not lost, he said, "The kingdom of God is among you" (Luke 17:21). Importantly, that was said not to his disciples but to a group of questioning Pharisees. Jesus' kingdom is not an escape from here, nor contained within the church, but is to be made evident in our midst, even in the midst of people who are not his followers. At the end of his life, Jesus assured his disciples that he was going to prepare a place for them (John 14:1-7). Furthermore, he claimed to personally be the way for us to find that place, a way marked by weakness, service, and mercy.

All this guides our thinking when we read the final part of God's revelation to John (Revelation 21 - 22), which is a vision of a renewed heaven and earth, and of a renewed Jerusalem coming down to the earth. In John's vision of the new Jerusalem, God comes to live among us once more. The place prepared for us becomes manifest: a city architected by God in which we find the true home for which we have been yearning.

As noted already, during their exile in Babylon, Israel was told to make a new home and to seek the *shalom* of their new city. Those instructions did not contradict the hope of returning home but promoted a kind of dual focus that is just as relevant for followers of Jesus today. We live with an eschatological hope of future paradise where God is in our midst, where there are streets of gold, and no more crying. But that future home does not prevent or conflict with the call to be present here and now, in this world.

The dual focus is incarnated in the network of reciprocal mercy where faith, hope, and love enable all to flourish. That is the essence of the kingdom of God Jesus preached and in which his prayer, "Your kingdom come on earth as it is in heaven," is lived out in the community of his followers.

Hebrews 11 makes this dual focus abundantly clear. The consistent witness of faithful people is a commitment to doing the work of God in their present situations—saving their family from flood, finding places to live, having children and blessing them, escaping from slavery, and suffering persecution—all because of the hope of a future city whose architect and builder is God.

In the end, the biblical resolution of exile is not based on *where* we live but on *how* we live. Jesus came to show us what it would look like to live here as if this were our true home. The resolution of the deep anguish of exile is not to leave this place in order to find our real home, but to make *this* place what it was supposed to be. In the end, the vision in Revelation is not that we escape from earth to heaven, but that the city of God comes down to earth.

Disrupting Mercy

The role of mercy in that hopeful vision is multifaceted. When we live in the knowledge that mercy will dominate the future city because God will be in our midst, we build our lives around mercy now. We show mercy to all people by caring for them within their varied kinds of exile, and by helping them to find a physical place of safety and belonging. We show mercy by helping people to grapple with the existential angst and alienation they feel now, and by reassuring them that they are always loved and cared for in the embrace of God.

May mercy guide your journey home.

A SLAVE TO THE GODS

To end this chapter, I want to retell the story of a young girl from Togo in Africa. Brigitte Sossou Perenyi was a victim and survivor of modern slavery, and her story touches on many aspects of mercy.[108]

A long-standing cultural practice in parts of West Africa is to pay for past crimes by sacrificing a young girl to the gods. Through this practice of *trokosi* (slaves of the gods), the curse of the gods, which would have brought illness or suffering to the offender, is transferred onto the girl. So, when Brigitte's uncle was caught in adultery, the traditional way to atone for his crime and dispel the resulting curse was to find a female virgin in his family, typically between six and eight years old, who could be handed over to a religious shrine. Brigitte's parents told her she was going to live with her uncle so she could be educated in Togo's capital city Lomé. But in 1996, at the age of seven, she was taken by her uncle to a shrine in the neighboring country of Ghana.

Although the practice of *trokosi* is now illegal in Ghana, the problem persists. Like many others, Brigitte was required to work at the shrine, potentially for the rest of her life, and serve the priest sexually once she reached puberty. Her name was taken away, and she was banished from her community to pay for her uncle's crimes. If she left, another girl would have to be found to replace her. Her plight shows the multiple layers of abuse that comprise the global experience of modern slavery: physical hardship, exploitation, coercion, and degradation, as well as the denial of her autonomy and freedom.

What would mercy look like in Brigitte's context? It would certainly involve her rescue from that abusive situation, the provision of physical and emotional safety in which rehabilitation become possible, and opportunities for her to be reintegrated into her community. Beyond that provision of a second chance, mercy would seek apology and restitution by her abusers.

Brigitte's plight was caught on camera in a CBS news report within a year of her enslavement. As a result, an American man, working through an international development agency, travelled to Ghana and arranged for her rescue. He ended up adopting her and caring for her in the USA. That act of mercy gave Brigitte opportunities for education, health care, and material wealth far beyond what she could ever have experienced in Togo or Ghana.

However, being removed from her home country increased her estrangement from her culture and family, leaving her feeling lonely and incomplete. Brigitte's exile had several layers. She was removed from her home and forced to live in a neighboring country and another African culture. Then she was taken even further from her family to another continent with a radically different culture. As years went by, she doubted she would ever be reunited with her family. Why did they give her away? Could she forgive them or her uncle?

After turning twenty-one, Brigitte returned to Ghana several times looking for answers. During those visits, Brigitte was able to reconnect with her family, and to visit the shrine in which she had been held captive. When she met another *trokosis* who had been released from that shrine, Brigitte mused, "It is incredible that we have been given a second chance to have life." Now, Brigitte has a Master's degree in international relations and human rights, and works in Ghana as a human rights activist. After years of exile she was able to return to her home country and build a new life.

This is mercy at work. Brigitte's initial need as an abused young girl trapped in slavery was seen by someone who felt compassion, and who acted on that feeling with generous kindness. The result was life-transforming for Brigitte and she is now extending that same mercy toward others.

Whatwill you do to show mercy to those in exile (including to yourself when that is needed)?

[10]

Putting Mercy to the Test

An initial thought to ponder: Please pause for a few minutes to think about the limits of mercy. Are there people or circumstances outside the reach of mercy? How do you react to the claim that "The test of Christianity is not loving Jesus, it's loving Judas"?[109]

ALTHOUGH I HAVE INCLUDED numerous stories of mercy in action, much of the content so far has assumed without question that this conception of mercy applies to *any* need and to *any* person. Mercy most readily makes sense for people dear to us, and to people who suffer through no fault of their own. The real test of mercy, however, is whether it can apply to more offensive cases. Can this ideal of mercy as a gift of extreme kindness motivated by compassion find any traction in the contexts of horrendous wrongs or brazenly reprehensible people?

Disrupting Mercy

MERCY TOWARD ENEMIES

Dirk Willems was arrested for his Anabaptist beliefs and imprisoned in Asperen, The Netherlands, in 1569. During winter, he escaped from the prison and fled across a moat covered with a sheet of ice. Having reached solid ground, he looked back to see a "thief-catcher" who had followed him but fallen through the ice. Willems turned back to help the man, saving his life by pulling him to safety. However, the voice of a burgomaster floated across the ice demanding that the thief-catcher continue to do his duty, and so the thief-catcher seized Willems and took him back to the prison. Several months later Willems was burnt at the stake.[110]

Willems' action was a natural consequence of his desire to be like God, whom he knew was merciful even to enemies. Rescuing the thief-catcher was not a choice made in a vacuum, but a habitual ethical stance that reflects a principal component of the Anabaptist mindset. It was a gift that was not repaid, a surprising act of kindness beyond what one could morally require, expressed toward someone in need.

Dirk Willems demonstrated the sort of mercy that emerges inevitably from a non-violent, non-coercive, and non-vengeful theology. Such concepts arise naturally when Christian ethics are derived from the life of Jesus, who preached that our love, following the pattern of God's love, should be extended even to our enemies (Matthew 5:43-48, Luke 6:27-36). In Luke's account of those words of Jesus, loving enemies is specifically linked to mercy: we are instructed to be merciful just as God is merciful. Jesus demonstrated that attitude on many occasions, but most famously when, from the cross, he said, "Father, forgive them, for they do not know what they are doing" (Luke 23:34).

Jesus was not the first to advocate goodwill toward one's enemies: even amidst the violence in the Old Testament, the Israelites were called toward the same ideal (e.g., Exodus 23:4-5; 2 Kings 6:18-23; Proverbs 25:21). But Jesus moves this ideal in a new direction that undermines the very category of "enemy," prompting Paul to claim that the cross put to death enmity itself (Ephesians 2:15-16).

Love toward enemies is one of the highest forms of mercy. Such love is an extreme kindness that cannot be coerced, deserved or repaid. It is a surprise that far exceeds what can be morally required or expected. Acting nicely toward those we perceive to be our enemies can, of course, be motivated by fear or by a sense of duty. But when fear or duty are the motives, the act cannot really be labeled "loving." If our behavior is to count as loving, it will be motivated by compassion for those people *as people:* because in our hearts we see them no longer as enemies but as divine image-bearers just as we are, and as worthy of our respect. To love *as God loves* is not to love out of fear or duty, but to love out of love!

Like James Lawson, who turned aside a racial attack by asking for a handkerchief, Dirk Willems was committed to evoking the potential of all people. As we have seen in the Hebrew word *racham*, this is the posture of mercy, a posture that mirrors a pregnant mother's love for her unborn child and her hope for the child's future. Willems did not engage with his pursuer based on that man's position as thief-catcher but in the belief that there was a shared humanity beyond disputes over religious doctrines. Similarly, Lawson did not engage with his opponent based on his immediate experience of him, but on the basis of a hope that other possibilities existed beyond racial slurs and spit.

Such an attitude is inherently risky. In Lawson's case it seemed to work. In Willems' case it seemed to fail. However, we must be careful when using the language of success and failure. We do not know the full or final impact of either action on the people who witnessed it or on those who heard the stories later. In particular, we do not know the longer-term effect of Willems' mercy on the thief-catcher. Even if we did know the totality of future outcomes, whether those outcomes match the original hope is not determinative of the act of mercy. However much we hope our acts of mercy might have some positive impact, the motive for mercy, if it is to be true mercy, is always compassion rather than outcomes.

Neither Lawson nor Willems were governed by the wrong they saw in front of them, but impelled by compassion and "an imagery of infinite possibility." Displaying that posture in a moment of crisis requires deliberate will, training, and practice.

MERCY TOWARD *REALLY* BAD PEOPLE

Idealistic talk about loving one's neighbor and showing mercy to everyone is all well and good, but what about

Putting Mercy to the Test

people who have done truly horrendous things? Are we supposed to show mercy to mass murderers, rapists, pedophiles, and human traffickers? Surely some unrepentant and brutally evil people do not deserve to be forgiven. Would it not be immoral and another form of evil to let them off the hook?

I have never been personally confronted by horrendous evil, and cannot be sure how I would react if I were. Consequently, the observations I make below may be unfounded. But the pragmatism of my approach is based on this: to be prepared to show mercy in the face of such horrors, I will need to have formed a habit through long training in simpler contexts.

My first, brief, comment is that I take for granted that our primary concern in cases of horrendous evil will be to care for the victim and prevent further abuse. But showing mercy in that direction is not the focus of this section. In this section we consider whether and how mercy applies to the offender.

A second observation is that there are not many brutally evil people. We all struggle to do our best but very few people are deliberately bad or hurtful. Despite the provocative scaremongering of mass media, the overwhelming experience of humanity is that we coexist in relative peace. As Gandhi noted, the history of kings and wars and crimes makes it seem otherwise, but such history is merely "a record of every interruption of the even working of the force of love or of the soul."[111] Many deeply hurtful actions are committed for reasons of ignorance, frustration, the assimilation of unhealthy cultural values, and fear rather than calculated malevolence. I would never wish to devalue the pain of those who have experienced deliberate cruelty, but let's not use those outliers as an excuse to justify withholding mercy in general. Part of the posture of mercy is to start thinking the best of people, to hope for, pray for, and believe in the good intentions of everyone we meet.

We can certainly avoid naivety about other people's goodwill and be wary when people seek to take advantage of us. When we interact with an extreme sociopath, a deliberate manipulator, someone violently out of control, or someone pathologically unable to feel empathy, we are like a sheep among wolves, and so need to be "wise as serpents but innocent as doves" (Matthew 10:16). What wisdom can we derive from viewing mercy as the gift of extreme kindness motivated by compassion? Think of the most morally bankrupt person you can and let's see how that definition might apply.

Mercy starts with compassion, and compassion depends on being able to feel *for* someone even if they disgust us. Toward that end, an important contribution of Christian thinking is that *all* people are made in God's image and *all* are redeemable. That is what gives birth to the possibility of showing mercy to even the vilest of people.

An important step along the path to compassion is to understand the person's backstory. What has made them so deeply evil? What genetic and biological forces are at work? What abuses have they suffered themselves? What bad choices have they made along the way? Such questions are not asked in order to "go soft" on their destructive behaviors, but for the pragmatic reason that we are unlikely to change them, to enable *shalom* for either them or their victims, if we do not first understand them.

This idea of compassion for the worst of human beings returns us to the thought that justice is not about imposing deserved punishment, but about restoring *shalom*. We start by addressing what can be done to restore *shalom* to the victims. Part of the work is certainly to stop the abuses so that no one else becomes a victim, and that protective goal will often require the perpetrator to be imprisoned. Another part is assisting victims to deal with their trauma: to ensure they feel safe, to comfort them, listen to them, and in some cases to provide professional counselling. *Shalom*, however, is something more than care for victims. Since true *shalom* is a state in which *all* are whole and flourishing, we must also ask what can be done to restore holistic rightness to the perpetrator.

Compassion may be the starting point motivating us to show mercy, but it is insufficient on its own to determine the best form of help. Mercy might be motivated by compassion, but it is also informed by considerations about what form of action is most likely to address the specific need. The extreme evil we are considering here is a particular type of need. Such behaviors are symptoms of deep brokenness that cry out for help. In the face of such extreme disfunction, effective help will also be extreme. What will break the cycle of evil begetting evil? How can evil people be confronted with the reality of their own evil in a way that makes them pause, rethink, and potentially change?

Disrupting Mercy

A simple expression of the difference between restorative and retributive justice can be seen in how parents discipline their children. A relatively recent movement in child discipline encourages parents to give their children "time-in" rather than "time-out." When a child misbehaves, a time-out response removes the child from the situation and isolates them, perhaps sending them to their bedroom, or sitting in a chair facing the wall. The intention of a time-out is to punish the child, in the hope that they will learn not to repeat the unwanted behavior. In contrast, during a time-in response, an adult will sit with the child in a safe space, providing emotional coaching so the child can work through their problem and learn better ways to navigate challenging situations.

Mercy is often expressed as a time-in response, holding people within the network of reciprocity rather than expelling them. That practice assumes misbehavior is not the result of willful waywardness, but a lack of emotional, social, or problem-solving skills. Giving time-in is equally applicable to adults whose ability to self-regulate has not matured.[112]

In the context of horrendous evil, the extreme kindness of mercy might be time in prison. However, even in prison, mercy continues to hope that they will be reformed: that prison would disrupt them positively. Incarceration protects society from the evil, but can also give the offender time-in and a safe space in which to undertake the necessary inner work of reflection, self-understanding, repentance, and developing the resolution to improve.

Putting Mercy to the Test

In other cases, the extreme kindness might be the so-called "tough love" approach, where support structures are temporarily taken away so the person must face the natural consequences of their actions. This should not be confused with the manipulative abuse that sometimes perverts the label "tough love." There is a clear line between tough love and abuse. On the one side is the removal of protective mechanisms to enable someone to learn from the consequences of their actions. On the other side is contempt, shown by verbal and physical abuse, trivializing someone's injuries or fears, and damaging demands that someone behave in ways they are not capable of. Nevertheless, some people need to hit rock bottom before being able to accept real help as distinct from short-term rescue, and the merciful goal might be to accelerate that process. The extreme kindness of appropriate tough love can be given in hope, without pre- or post-conditions.

Nobody has to earn mercy, and in cases of extreme evil it might be psychologically impossible for the person to even attempt to do so. Part of the disruption for them might be to know that the giver expects nothing back: that undermines any thought of changing their behavior as part of some transaction. If mercy incurs no debt, then the recipient is more effectively forced to decide whether to change for internal reasons—because they *want* to—rather than to manipulate their way around a debt.

Like a young child with a Christmas present, the most valuable part of the gift of mercy might be the wrapping. That is, regardless of the shape of the kindness, the disruptive element of mercy might be the simple fact that someone paid attention, listened, cared, saw a person rather than a monster, and treated them with dignity rather than belittling them. The more surprising the better, because to be effective in such cases mercy must find some way to shock the person out of the story they have previously told themselves.

People Who Perpetrate Modern Slavery

The abuse, exploitation, and coercion of modern slavery provide an extreme context in which to question the reality of mercy. What would mercy look like when expressed to the people who perpetrate such horrendous wrong? I argued in Chapter 5 that mercy is not in conflict with justice, but that both are tools to create and maintain *shalom*. But how can mercy be directed toward the perpetrators of awful abuse without negating justice? I will concentrate on human traffickers because that is my recent field of research, but the principles extend to perpetrators of other atrocities as well.

During the past decade, the anti-slavery movement has understood the importance of listening to people who have been victims of horrendous abuse and exploitation, as well as to survivors of such mistreatment. We have realized it is not sufficient to rescue victims from our position of safe superiority. We have begun to recognize that the experts in modern slavery—the people with concrete knowledge and insight—are those very victims and survivors. We must hear their voices if we are to understand their real needs.

Putting Mercy to the Test

Who will sit with the people who have suffered, and listen rather than speak? Who will believe the version of the story told by, say, an unwilling prostitute? Who will step aside from their safety, superiority, and judgment, so they can reaffirm the value of those who have been told they are of no value? Who will show them mercy rather than pity, by being present within their loss, their suffering, their grief, their bondage?

We are still coming to recognize that the traffickers who abuse and exploit are also experts in this field. Who is willing to sit with them and listen? Who will take Jesus' manifesto seriously and seek freedom for them? I am not in any way suggesting that convicted traffickers should be released from prison so they avoid any consequences for their crimes. I am suggesting that even the most appalling criminal needs mercy, just like all of us do. As slaves to their own "passions and pleasures" they stand in need of liberation from the path that has dehumanized them. They need a better option than whatever led them into becoming an abuser, an exploiter, in the first place. Whatever their backstory, they need release from the bondage of their past. Otherwise, what is going to prevent them from repeating the same horrors once their prescribed punishment is over?

I have no doubt that will be a controversial position.[113] But it is a necessary part of the scandal of mercy. We *all* need mercy: the best and the worst of us. True mercy is kindness offered without consideration of whether the recipient deserves it or not. Mercy does not mean traffickers are excused or avoid the consequences of their past actions. But it does mean they are treated as people made in the image of God, people with value, moral agents who can and should be called to account for their actions, and who might still choose to be better people if given another chance.

The most merciful thing to do for a trafficker, or for other abusive offenders, might be to put them in prison. That severe mercy takes them out of normal society to protect their past and potential victims, but also gives the offender time to reconsider the significance of their abusive behavior. The "extreme kindness" of mercy in this case might confront them with the damage they have done, seeking to disrupt their own life narrative so they can start to have empathy for their victims. Then they could authentically consider how to make restitution for their past wrongs. Given the evidence that many traffickers were previously trafficked themselves, their release from bondage might involve breaking free from abuses they suffered so that they do not feel compelled to pass on their own suffering to others.

Repentance and transformation may occur spontaneously as an offender suffers through the shame of arrest and court processes, the deprivation of incarceration, and social ostracism after their release. But repentance and transformation are more likely to occur if, instead of the prison experience being constructed as punishment, it was constructed as an opportunity for rehabilitation. If abusive, exploitative, coercive people were given time-in, with appropriate, adult-grade, emotional coaching, they could learn a lot about their own emotional trauma and develop patterns of behavior that do not result in others suffering because of their own inadequate moral development. That would be an expression of both justice and mercy.

In the area of modern slavery, there are no global statistics about re-offense rates once convicted traffickers are released from prison. We expect those rates to be high because at this stage no one in the world runs rehabilitation programs for such offenders. During their imprisonment, a family member or colleague may continue running the trafficking business, and perhaps most go back to the same business after release. Furthermore, there are few programs anywhere in the world aiming to reduce people's vulnerability to becoming traffickers in the first place. Who will sit alongside vulnerable people who are considering making money off the suffering of others, and in mercy show them a better alternative?

Imagine the impact an ex-trafficker could have as an advocate for change! Suppose a convicted trafficker, transformed by a rehabilitation program while in prison, leaves prison with another chance to flourish in ways that do not require the abuse of other people. Imagine them returning to their home town and calling on their peers to forsake their abusive, exploitative practices, and showing them another way in which all can flourish.

In the current global state of modern slavery, the rescue of one victim leads, sadly and almost inevitably, to their replacement by another victim. On the other hand, when one trafficker is transformed into an ex-trafficker, every person who might have become their victim in the future is also saved. That is the same dynamic as the story of Jesus and Zacchaeus: rather than rescuing all the people Zacchaeus exploited, Jesus rescues Zacchaeus—the offender!—and in doing so indirectly rescues all Zacchaeus' past and future victims. The example in Chapter 7 of a boy given a bike with working brakes shows the same lesson: not only was he helped, but giving him a safe bike also protected the surrounding community from future accidents. Mercy not only addresses the need of the immediate recipient but often has the side-effect of saving future victims.

AFTER READING THIS CHAPTER, HAS YOUR THINKING ABOUT THE LIMITS OF MERCY CHANGED?
IF THERE ARE PEOPLE OR ACTIONS OUTSIDE THE REACH OF MERCY, IS THERE SOME OTHER HOPE FOR THEM?

[11]

OBSTRUCTIONS TO MERCY

An initial thought to ponder: In an underground shelter in Cologne, where Jews hid during World War II, these words were written on the wall:
I believe in the sun, though it be dark
I believe in God, though he be silent
I believe in neighborly love,
though it be unable to reveal itself. [114]
What might mercy have looked like in those dark days?

DESPITE THE GREAT POWER of mercy, its transformative potential is not always realized. Mercy is often withheld, or obstructed in some way, and even when mercy is offered, it can be ignored, misused, or rejected. When the intended or hoped for outcome of mercy is obstructed, does that mean mercy has failed? The question can be considered from two perspectives: from the side of those who show mercy and from the side of those who are shown mercy.

FAILURE TO LAUNCH

The largest failure of mercy is that it is so rarely offered. Although a society without mercy is unsustainable, the project of mercy often does not even get off the ground. However, this reflects a failure of imagination or will, rather than a failure of mercy itself.

My definition of mercy—a gift of extreme kindness motivated by compassion—implies several potential obstructions to the expression of mercy. Perhaps there is a lack of compassion. Perhaps a feeling of powerlessness or a lack of imagination about how to respond compassionately. Perhaps a reluctance to get involved, especially if the potential recipient is outside family or tribe.

Another reason for the scarcity of mercy is that people may not have seen compelling examples of mercy nor been taught about its value. As a result, mercy can seem naive or impractical. Even worse, many people live without ever experiencing mercy, and may be unable to conceive of the possibility of showing mercy themselves. The pervasiveness of counterexamples, teaching about rewards and punishment, and beliefs about getting what we deserve, make us ignorant as a society about the deep moral significance and interpersonal nourishment of mercy.

Coming from a different angle, there are some people who seem unable to give without strings attached. They may be moved by compassion to act kindly, but feel it is only right that the recipient do something first to deserve it, or do something later to repay it. Jonah is a biblical example, as is the elder brother in the parable of the loving father (also called the parable of the prodigal son). They are both called to join in with a celebration, but both complain against mercy. Others act with extreme kindness but feel compelled to do so out of duty. In those instances, kindness is offered to someone in need but in a way that seems to have missed the essence of mercy.

I think another barrier to many people's ability to show mercy to others is a shortage of love for themselves.[115] Mercy overflows from belovedness. From the fullness of grace and truth in Christ we have all received grace upon grace (John 1:14-16) and our gratitude for that grace overflows in mercy to others. But what of those who do not experience that grace, from God or from the significant others in their lives? When Jesus describes the commandment to love others as we love ourselves (Matthew 22:39), he assumes that we love ourselves. When that assumption is not true—when someone thinks of themselves as unloved or unlovable—both receiving and expressing mercy become all but impossible.

Shame can act in a similar way. One of the facilitators of the RESTORE program commented that "Shame is a compassion killer." Shame, especially unacknowledged shame, can quash empathy and compassion, and without compassion there can be no mercy.

A deeper understanding of our reluctance to show mercy, whether that reluctance be conscious or unconscious, comes from Richard Beck's analysis of the psychology of disgust in his 2011 book, *Unclean: Meditations on Purity, Hospitality, and Mortality.*

At the root of *Unclean* is a commentary on Jesus' interaction with some Pharisees, recounted in Matthew 9. In the context of a dispute over whether a religious teacher ought to eat with "tax-collectors and sinners," Jesus challenges the Pharisees to learn what God meant by the declaration, "I desire mercy, not sacrifice" (Hosea 6:6).[116] Beck sees in this confrontation a call to rethink the Pharisees' understanding of purity.

The academic literature on which Beck draws links the will to maintain purity with universal psychological aspects of disgust. At its core, disgust arises from violations of bodily boundaries. A simple example is the reaction to saliva: when it is in your mouth everything is fine, but if you spat it into a cup of water, would you then drink that water? We feel disgusted by bodily fluids when they are outside of our body. Saliva, blood, and urine are repulsive and dirty as soon as they leave our bodies, and anything that touches them is contaminated. Disgust motivates us to avoid such things, to push them away so that impurities do not cross the boundary into our bodies. Although disgust can sometimes protect us from real dangers, reactions based on disgust are often illogical. Would you, for instance, drink lemonade from a sterilized bedpan that had never been used before? Probably not. But why would we be reluctant to do that? Although we know intellectually that the bedpan is clean, at an emotional level the association with urine still seems to contaminate the lemonade.

Obstructions to Mercy

This core, bodily aspect of disgust frequently becomes a metaphor in other areas of life. We hear that "cleanliness is next to godliness" and conversely think of evil people as being in the gutter, dirty, and the scum of the earth. Swear words are often based on bodily functions. Our sins can be washed clean. Someone's offensive behavior makes us want to vomit.

Our reactions to bodily disgust are reflected in socio-moral contexts as well. We erect boundary protections around our tribe and feel disgust at aspects of other cultures. We may believe they smell bad, they are dirty or they don't follow basic good manners. Consequently, we have good reason to separate ourselves from them. That socio-moral sense of disgust is what drives the Pharisees' attitudes in Matthew 9. "The Pharisees, seeking purity, pull away from the sinners ... [whereas] Jesus, seeking fellowship, moves toward the sinners."[117]

> *Sacrifice—the purity impulse—marks off a zone of holiness, admitting the "clean" and expelling the "unclean." Mercy, by contrast, crosses those purity boundaries. Mercy blurs the distinction, bringing clean and unclean into contact.*[118]

Beck's central argument is that "the psychology of disgust and contamination regulates how many Christians reason with and experience notions of holiness, atonement, and sin."[119] I would add that disgust and contamination often act as barriers to mercy.

Disgust encourages us to treat certain acts and certain people with contempt. Serial killers, child abusers, drug dealers, and others are cast as unworthy monsters who do not deserve mercy. Those are extreme cases, but *whenever* we are disgusted with someone or their behavior, choosing to show them mercy becomes harder. This tendency has been noted by others in the context of sex offenders[120] and we frequently see it in people's attitudes toward human traffickers.

The focus of our anti-slavery project has been to challenge assumptions about the perpetrators of slavery within the anti-slavery movement. We hear about the extremes of abuse imposed by human traffickers on their victims: the manipulation and deliberate grooming of vulnerable children for sex, multigenerational debt bondage in rock quarries, violent indoctrination of child soldiers, young girls forced into marriage, and the savage treatment of those who try to escape. Such horrific physical, psychological, and sexual abuse rightly shocks and disgusts us.

In the absence of sufficient data about the demographics of traffickers or their personal histories, we have little understanding of the external drivers or internal motivations that lead to their actions. Since few of us meet human traffickers face-to-face or engage with them as real people, it is easy to view them as monsters.

One problem with this reaction to horrendously abusive behaviors is that our disgust can be based on significant misunderstandings. If we knew the traffickers and the survivors of their abuse as real people rather than as stereotypes, we might find that the situation is more complex. We might find backstories that help us to understand and, without reducing our condemnation of the abuse, that might reduce the extent of our disgust. We might find that the trafficker has been nominated as a scapegoat to take the fall for what is essentially a systemic social problem.

This example of modern slavery suggests two avenues for dealing with socio-moral disgust. After seeking to understand the "monsters" as real people, we may find that our visceral disgust dissolves and we become more able to show those people mercy. On the other hand, we may find that our disgust continues, in which case we face the greater challenge of finding a way to show mercy *even though* we are disgusted.

I know this example straddles a tricky boundary and I need to stress that I am not advocating that we allow or condone the kind of abuses that occur in modern slavery. Nor am I defending traffickers, minimizing their responsibility as free moral agents, whitewashing over their guilt, or ignoring the fundamental injustice of their crimes.

My point is that disgust is not a sufficient reason to suspend mercy, though in practice many people allow that to be the case. Even if someone turns out to be a moral monster, mercy can be shown to them. This is a corollary of my earlier argument that mercy does not depend on desert. We show mercy not because someone deserves it, nor because we expect them to meet any pre- or post-condition, moral or otherwise, but because it promotes the higher values of justice and *shalom*.

That higher goal of justice for all, incorporating the restoration of *shalom*, necessitates that something changes within a perpetrator of modern slavery. The injustice is not resolved by rescuing the victim and punishing the perpetrator, but by dealing with the brokenness of both parties, and by making systemic changes so that all may flourish. I am not suggesting that victims of abuse should not be rescued or that perpetrators of abuse should not be punished, but that the gospel intention of reconciling all things is something greater than what a rescue-and-punish paradigm can achieve, and mercy is the fundamental path toward that greater goal.

Can we reach a point where, as Beck writes, "the dignity of every human person is vouchsafed, embraced, and protected deep within the heart of the church"?[121] The word "every" must be interpreted as truly universal, not limited to our tribe, to good people, and to victims, but to all "others" outside our tribe, even those morally repugnant to us, even child sex abusers and human traffickers. All of us are unconditionally loved by God. All of us need mercy.

A further aspect of the psychology of disgust that can prevent people from acting mercifully is the fear of contamination. By showing mercy to someone, might we not get into some sort of trouble ourselves? That thought may have been in the mind of the priest and the Levite who passed by the beaten man in the story of the good Samaritan (Luke 10:30-32). If we show mercy to lepers, whether that leprosy be literal or metaphorical, might we not become infected with their leprosy? If we show mercy to a "sinner," might we not be seen as approving of their behavior?

As Beck notes, our beliefs about contamination display a *negativity dominance*: "When a pollutant and a pure object come into contact the pollutant is "stronger" and ruins the pure object."[122] As a result, many religious people live defensively to avoid any guilt by association. That is what the Pharisees advised Jesus in relation to eating with "tax collectors and sinners." But Jesus lived with an open-handedness that was the opposite of defensiveness. He touched lepers and dead bodies and menstruating women and allowed a "sinful woman" to wash his feet, all with apparently no fear that they were going to contaminate him with their "unholiness."

In line with the practice of Jesus, mercy refutes negativity dominance. The life-giving potential of mercy is that it can disinfect and transform sin, bondage, and exile. Rather than mercy being tainted through interactions with those varied forms of brokenness, it acts with *positivity dominance* as a catalyst for redemption.

The compassion that impels mercy can be the emotional counterpoint to disgust. Developing compassion for someone can ease our disgust at their actions. Micah's insistence on humility is also important. In humility we realize that we are not superior to the people who disgust us. When we acknowledge our own culpability and recognize our own need of mercy, we can approach disgust as peers rather than as judges or rescuers. Neither our disgust nor our fear of contamination should prevent us showing mercy. The combination of compassion and humility enables us to show mercy even in the face of personal disgust. The pharisaical drive toward purity arises from disgust and results in exclusion. In contrast, the way of Jesus puts disgust aside and shows mercy to all.

Failure to Land

Having noted that mercy too often does not even get off the ground because people are unable or unwilling to show true mercy, I now consider various ways that the trajectory of mercy, once launched, might not land where it was intended.

My definition of mercy is deliberately one-sided. Claiming that mercy is a free gift of extreme kindness motivated by compassion positions mercy as an act of the giver with no reference to the way it might or might not be received. If mercy is non-conditional, how could it be otherwise? If the definition of mercy were to imply any expectation about how the gift is received, that would become a condition. But no. We, and God, give with an attitude that is independent of any response or lack of response.

This does not mean we are unconcerned about the response to the gift of mercy. We *hope* that the gift will nourish the recipient. We *hope* that the gift will be a blessing that eases their suffering. We *hope* that the recipient's own life might be transformed by grace so that the love of God would overflow from them toward others. Beyond simply hoping, we are committed to trying our best to act authentically and helpfully through our mercy. The act of mercy, however, is independent of whether such hopes become reality. The gift is not contingent on any pre-condition, nor on any subsequent response.

That approach, however, means that in various ways the gift of mercy might not be received in the way the giver hoped.

In the first place, perhaps the giver misread the situation. The compassion motivating the gift may have been misdirected: the person being shown mercy might not be in any suffering or need at all. Such misunderstandings of the context or of the recipient, however well-intentioned, could be relationally awkward, insulting or paternalistic. Such misreadings could create a victim-rescuer dynamic that exacerbates a power imbalance or extends a form of unhealthy dependence.

In some cases, the person to whom mercy is shown may remain oblivious to the gift. They may not see the gift at all or see it but never unwrap it. They may consider what was done for them as a payment owed to them, or as something that was rightfully theirs all along—in which case they recognize the act but do not recognize it as a gift.

In other cases, the recipient may refuse the gift of mercy. Perhaps it smells like a trap: their previous experiences may have demonstrated that there is always a catch, making them suspicious of any "free gift." Perhaps accepting mercy would imply an unwelcome admission of need. As I discussed in Chapter 7, perhaps mercy is refused by a person who does not believe they are worthy of it.

In yet other cases, people may accept the gift and yet despise the giver. There is no guarantee that the receiver will respond with gratitude, as we saw in the story of Dirk Willems: although he rescued the thief-catcher who fell through the ice, the thief-catcher still arrested Willems and returned him to prison. The act of mercy toward the thief-catcher certainly did not rebound in a blessing to

Willems, though we are left wondering what the long-term effect might have been on the thief-catcher.

I am sure there are people who would soak up any gift of mercy and scheme how to get even more. People who seem to take advantage of mercy pose a huge challenge to our posture. What do we do if, after showing extreme kindness to someone, they lap it up, continue unchanged, perhaps repeating the destructive behaviors that led to their broken situation, and in the worst case actively seek further mercy? How many times can we show mercy before accepting that it is not working and giving up? Seven times?

That is exactly the question Peter asked Jesus. But Jesus replied, "Not seven, but seventy seven." It was in this context that Jesus told the so-called Parable of the Unmerciful (or Unforgiving) Servant (Matthew 18:21-35). In the parable, the massive debt of a king's servant is waived—a surprisingly generous gift arising from the king's compassion—but the servant refuses to waive the debt of a colleague that amounts to lunch money in comparison. The extravagant mercy of the king fails to land. We are not told why the servant did not respond in kind. He now owed nothing, and so it was not that he needed his colleague to pay up for any financial reason. Perhaps he was jaded, hardened, greedy, deeply insecure or just plain mean. Perhaps the king's pardon was too extravagant for him to understand.[123] He might have gone away feeling disdainful of the king's foolishness. Perhaps transactional thinking was so firmly rooted in his psyche that he could not imagine relating to others on the basis of mercy. In any case, the outcome of the servant's inability to break free from the shackles of debt-thinking was that he was handed over to be tortured until he paid his debt.

Commentators on this section of Matthew's gospel generally fail to explain how the parable supports Jesus' initial claim that we should forgive someone not seven times but seventy-seven times. What are we to make of the final torture and Jesus' conclusion that "So my heavenly Father will also do to every one of you, if you do not forgive your brother or sister from your heart"? I must admit to being a bit confused myself. How does the king's (and God's) decision to withhold forgiveness and hand over someone to torture illustrate Jesus' instructions to forgive seventy-seven times?

As with many of the parables, we must realize that the language used is hyperbolic, that is, extremely exaggerated. From the start, the idea of forgiving a person seventy-seven times (some translations even say seventy times seven) implies a huge number, beyond what one could keep track of. Then, in the parable, the servant's debt to the king is unimaginably large, a zillion dollars, 150,000 times the annual wage for a laborer. An outrageous debt that could never be repaid.

Jesus' primary reason for this use of exaggeration is that when he says we should forgive someone seventy-seven times he is not defining some fixed limit. Seventy-seven times means mercy without end. This comes as no surprise to those who know "The steadfast love *[chesed]* of the LORD never ceases, his mercies *[racham]* never come to an end; they are new every morning" (Lamentations 3:22-23).

Disrupting Mercy

New every morning! Mercy is not a transactional account-keeping of either the extent of a debt or the number of times a person is forgiven. Rather, as Matthew 18:35 shows, the important factor is that we forgive each other *from the heart.*

Nevertheless, the parable accepts that sometimes even outrageous mercy does not turn the heart of the recipient. The story spotlights a relational, compassionate, non-transactional king who is angered when the servant continues to think transactionally. Torture until an unrepayable debt is repaid is itself hyperbolic. We would do the disruptive intent of the story more justice if we imagined the voice of the king saying to the unmerciful servant: "You want to be transactional? Then let me show you the outcome of being transactional!" Transactional thinking, devoid of mercy, leads inevitably to infinite loss.

In saying that, I am not trying to explain away a difficult piece of Scripture. The torture can be very real to people who, when shown mercy, cannot soak up its scandalous intention and who consequently remain unable to show mercy to others. Mercy does triumph over judgment, but nevertheless when someone is unable to show mercy, they also become unable to receive mercy (James 2:13). By failing to be transformed by the mercy shown to them, they remain trapped in debt-thinking, bound by cynicism, and unable to flourish.

JAVERT

I was asked once, "What is the opposite of mercy?" That is a tricky question. I have already argued that mercy is not in opposition to justice. So, one should not imagine a line with mercy at one end of the continuum and justice at the other end. In fact, given such an imagined line, I cannot identify what would be at the opposite end from mercy. This one-dimensional way of thinking does not apply in any helpful way to mercy.

The first-century Roman, Seneca, proposed that the opposite of mercy was cruelty, while more recently, Raniero Cantalamessa suggested vengeance, and Jordan Peterson poetically suggested contempt. Annabella wonders if it is despair.[124] Each adds something important to the conversation. To withhold mercy is often cruel because that allows the other's pain, loss, guilt, suffering to continue. On the other hand, as Nietzsche might observe, to remove someone's suffering may be just pity, which is another form of contempt. *Not* acting to remove their suffering may sometimes be the merciful choice if it genuinely promotes their ability to overcome the challenge themself. Vengeance goes further and actively increases their suffering. To hold someone in contempt is to refuse to acknowledge their value or their dignity, to look down on them with disgust, to dismissively sneer at them because their suffering is their own fault and of no concern to me.

Those attitudes are certainly contrary to mercy, but I am not sure that any of them are mercy's opposite. Another way of thinking about the question is to consider what would be left if mercy were taken away. What would a life devoid of mercy look like? That's the context in which the dark weed of despair strangles hope.

Disrupting Mercy

The character of Javert in *Les Miserables* provides a perfect example, not only of cruelty but also of the internal disillusionment that inevitably grows when mercy is absent. Recall that Javert was the police inspector who knew Jean Valjean as a prisoner and who could never imagine him otherwise. After Valjean broke his parole and went into hiding, Javert pursued him for the rest of their lives.

Javert "was a compound of two sentiments, simple and good in themselves, but he made them almost evil by his exaggeration of them: respect for authority and hatred of rebellion. ... He had nothing but disdain for, aversion, and disgust for all who had once overstepped the bounds of the law. He was absolute, admitting no exceptions."[125] Javert was harsh and unyielding, with an absolute commitment to the simplicity and clarity of the law, regardless of whether applying the law reflected true justice.

Interestingly, Hugo tells us that Javert was born in prison and "grew up thinking himself outside of society, and despaired of ever entering it."[126] Although an officer of the law, he was, metaphorically, imprisoned by the law: the law constrained his behavior absolutely. Perhaps the young Javert was never shown mercy. He had no intention of showing mercy to anyone, including himself.

Two acts of clemency to Javert later in life disrupt his confidence: the first is an act of justice toward him—though Javert is unable to see it that way—while the second is an act of mercy. Javert's reactions to both incidents reveal the inevitable result of a life that denies mercy.

Obstructions to Mercy

In the first incident, Jean Valjean has been living under the pseudonym Madeleine, has become commercially successful, and is now the Mayor of Montreuil-sur-mer. Javert is the police inspector in that same town and comes to suspect that the mayor is in fact Valjean. He reports his suspicions to the Prefecture of Police in Paris but is told that it is impossible since Valjean has recently been arrested and is currently standing trial.

The honorable Javert admits his "fault" to the mayor (who is actually Valjean) and demands that the mayor sack him in disgrace. The mayor responds, "Javert, you are a man of honor and I esteem you. You exaggerate your fault. Besides, this is an offense that concerns only me. You deserve promotion, not disgrace. I want you to keep your job."[127]

Valjean's reaction to the mercy of Bishop Myriel has been to craft a new life that exhibits a constant posture of mercy. He feels no bitterness toward Javert and his conscience dictates that Javert deserves no retribution—even though he knows Javert would demand his death if he could prove he was indeed the escaped convict Valjean. This act of clemency in refusing to dismiss Javert is really an act of justice given that Javert was correct in his suspicion, but of course it did not look that way to Javert. Javert cannot accept the clemency ...

> *In my life I have often been severe toward others. It was just. I was right. Now if I were not severe toward myself, all I have justly done would become injustice. Should I spare myself more than others? No. You see! If I had been eager*

> only to punish others and not myself, that would have been despicable! Those who say "That scoundrel Javert" would be right. Monsieur Mayor, I do not wish you to treat me with kindness. Your kindness, when it was for others, enraged me quite enough; I do not wish it for myself. ... Such kindness disorganizes society. Good God, it is easy to be kind, the difficulty is to be just.[128]

One thing to notice about Javert is that although he is unable to give or receive mercy, he is not morally corrupt. On the contrary, he is the most respectable and principled of characters, seeking above all to be irreproachable.[129] He is the quintessential conscientious upholder of law.

Through a second major experience of mercy, Hugo shows how this moral rigidity is a flaw that leads to Javert's ultimate unravelling. The problem begins when Valjean spares Javert's life. Javert has been spying on the rebels at a makeshift barricade in the streets of Paris. When he is identified as a police officer, the rebels decide to kill him. Valjean asks to be the one to shoot him.

In a chapter headed "Jean Valjean Takes His Revenge," Valjean cuts Javert's ropes, tells him to leave, and shoots his pistol into the air so that the other rebels think Javert has been shot. Valjean does not wait for any repentance. He has no expectation of future reward, because he thinks he will die with the rebels that very night. He says simply "You are free." This free gift of life is an act of mercy: a strange form of "revenge" that resonates with Paul's advice in Romans 12:17-21.

Now things get complicated.

Obstructions to Mercy

Valjean does in fact escape from the barricade, carrying a wounded rebel who is the beloved of his adopted daughter through Paris' network of sewers. Just as he finds an exit from the sewer, he is confronted by Javert. He begs Javert to allow him time to deliver the wounded man to medical care, and to get a message to his daughter. He promises that after that he will allow Javert to arrest him.

Surprisingly, Javert agrees and even provides transport. Then, when Valjean enters the house where his daughter is asleep, Javert leaves! Having sought Valjean for so many years, and now having him in his grasp, he lets him go. Is this a change of heart in response to Valjean saving his life?

Javert walks with his head down, for the first time in his life! He was in torment: astonished that Valjean spared his life, and petrified because he, Javert, had spared Valjean. Javert's thinking had always been unidirectional: he knew what should be done and did it. There was no ambiguity and no option. He had never been lenient on either himself or others. Nor had he expected leniency. But now he had sacrificed his duty by allowing Valjean to go free.

For Javert there were now only three options. He could go back and arrest Valjean, but how could he do that to the man who had saved him? That would make him a lower man than Valjean. It would be a dishonor to himself. Alternatively, he could leave Valjean a free man. But then he would be denying the right of law that he had upheld all his life. That would also dishonor himself. He could do neither.

Javert recalled the previous kindness of Valjean and he felt an admiration for Valjean, but how can one justify admiration for a convict?

> Jean Valjean confused him. All the axioms that had served as the supports of his life crumbled away before this man. Jean Valjean's generosity toward him, Javert, overwhelmed him. ...
>
> A beneficent malefactor, a compassionate convict, kind, helpful, clement, returning good for evil, returning pardon for hatred, loving pity rather than vengeance, preferring to destroy himself rather than destroy his enemy, saving the one who had struck him, kneeling on the heights of virtue, nearer angels than men. Javert was compelled to acknowledge that this monster existed. This could not go on.[130]

Such a "monster" was anathema to all Javert had built his life on. Consequently, "His ultimate anguish was the loss of all certainty."[131] He understood that Valjean was right and he was wrong: that duty to the law was not the ultimate virtue. He understood that what he previously thought was monstrous might actually be divine. He not only recognized Valjean's kindness but also knew that he himself had now been corrupted: he had acted with kindness toward Valjean!

Since the two options of arresting Valjean or setting him free were equally impossible for Javert, he acted on the third option: he cast himself into the turmoil of the Seine in a deliberate act of suicide.

Javert's struggle illustrates some of the reasons I discussed about how mercy might fail to land. He is unable to forgive himself or be lenient to himself. He is unable to accept kindness from others when he feels he does not deserve it.

Javert's suicide bears some similarities to the death of Judas. According to Matthew's account, after betraying Jesus for thirty pieces of silver, Judas repented (that is, changed his mind) and sought absolution from the chief priests and elders (Matthew 27:3-10). When they denied him, his despair led to suicide. What Javert saw in Valjean, Judas had experienced in Jesus, and the contrast to their own behavior horrified them.

The life of Peter could have ended the same way. He too betrayed Jesus and struggled with the anguish of shame. What enabled him to survive that shame and despair long enough to hear and receive mercy from the resurrected Jesus (John 21)? What would have happened if Judas had lived a few days longer?

Suicide may seem to be the ultimate failure of mercy.[132] And yet did not Javert in the end recognize Valjean's mercy for what it really was? His excuses and pride were stripped away and he was forced to confront the truth about himself. He could no longer hide from the mercy Valjean had repeatedly shown him.

On the other side of death, would he not have found himself face-to-face with more mercy from God?

MERCY IN THE LIGHT OF FAILURE

The primary aim of this book is to encourage people, especially those who follow Jesus, to develop a posture that loves mercy. But what are we to do in the face of mercy's frequent failures to launch, and the many ways mercy can fail to land as hoped?

A risk-based calculus might weigh the costs and benefits to arrive at some utilitarian conclusion. I can imagine lengthy arguments from both sides. On the one hand mercy has a huge upside. It can bless and transform, bringing joy and nourishment to both the giver and receiver. On the other hand, it has a huge downside. Its intention can be obstructed in so many ways, it can cost the giver dearly, and in the end simply reinforce the plight of the intended recipient. So, what are the likelihood and consequence of the possible outcomes? Can the costs be contained and the risks mitigated?

In the end, however, our commitment to mercy cannot hinge on a risk calculation. Since mercy is non-conditional, mercy allows itself to misfire, to be ignored, rejected, and taken advantage of. That is the risk love takes, the risk God continually takes. Martin Luther used the term "lost love" to characterize the kind of love God has for us: a love that is "poured out in unstinting measure upon all, even those who ultimately reject it."[133]

Mercy hopes for something extraordinary: for individual transformation, for a society in which all can flourish, for true *shalom*. But the performance of mercy does not depend on achieving those outcomes. Mercy is not goal-oriented and its success cannot be measured by whether it attains any goal. Mercy is impelled by compassion, not driven by achievement.

We are merciful because of the example and instructions of Jesus, whose being-for-others was the ultimate free gift of extreme kindness, and who asked those who follow him to "Be merciful, just as your Father is merciful" (Luke 6:36). We are merciful because it is at the center of the gospel's power to transform. We are merciful because we love it: mercy has become, or at least is becoming, our default posture.

I want to emphasize this aspect of "becoming." Both my understanding of mercy and my ability to act mercifully are imperfect and under construction. Both understanding and action need, and will continue to need, improvement. Learning better ways to show mercy is an important step. Our early attempts can easily be confounded by mixed motives, misdirected by inadequate and self-centered understandings of other people, clumsy in execution, and embarrassingly patronizing. No wonder Micah coupled the love of mercy with the need for humility.

Hopefully, people will show mercy to our ill-conceived attempts at mercy!

Over time we can learn to give in a way that is truly and consistently free from conditions. We might need to listen, act with kindness, forgive, and show mercy many times before the recipient trusts our intention. We continue doing those things even if they never understand.

The best we might hope for in some contexts is that mercy confuses people! That was its chief effect on Javert.

Disrupting Mercy

But do not underestimate the value of confusion. Mercy is meant to be disruptive. It is above and beyond what is expected. It is a higher form of justice than people are used to. It is non-transactional and non-conditional. In all those aspects it is subversive, implicitly calling into question many of the accepted norms of our world.

In some cases, confusion may be mercy's primary outcome. The greatest gift may not be the way an individual act of mercy addresses the immediate contextual need, but the residual questions mercy raises about why such extreme kindness was shown, why the gift was free, whether such kindness is deserved, and what life might look like if the new relational norm was devoid of conditions and debt.

Obstructions to Mercy

HAVE YOU SEEN SITUATIONS WHERE MERCY WAS OBSTRUCTED? WHAT WAS THE OBSTRUCTION? DO THOSE SITUATIONS MAKE YOU DOUBT THE VALUE OF MERCY?

[12]

Zacchaeus, Mercy and Evangelism

An initial thought to ponder: British author Charles Williams (1886-1945) often repeated the phrase "under the mercy." His friend C. S. Lewis frequently signed off letters with the same phrase. It was an expression of faith that all things happen within the will of God. How would your life be different if it were fully lived "under the mercy"?

EVANGELISM HAS DEVELOPED a bad reputation in many circles. It has come to mean preaching a particular tribal concept of vicarious holiness through which we can be saved from our sin in order to get an entrance ticket to heaven. The word is more associated with paternalistic arrogance, judgmental dogmatism, and guilt-laden proselytism than with the justice, mercy, and humility of Jesus.

Disrupting Mercy

The source of the word, however, is the Greek *euaggelion*, which literally means "good news." As a verb, the word means to announce or to bear witness to the good news. My use of "evangelism" here is an attempt to tie together the key themes of the book to emphasize how mercy epitomizes God's good news to all humanity.

I started this book by noting the world's profound need for mercy. As one component of the ecology of love, we have seen what mercy looks like in the Old and New Testaments, and pursued the idea that, in essence, mercy is a gift of extreme kindness motivated by compassion.

As a result, we have seen the deep intentionality of mercy as it demonstrates three levels of God's love for the world. Mercy addresses the immediate needs of people, whether those needs are for physical healing, forgiveness of sins, liberation from bondage, or finding a way home from exile. Second, mercy also offers each of us disruptive opportunities for personal transformation or redemption, just as it did when Jesus called Zacchaeus down from the sycamore tree. Third, mercy is God's attempt to remove enmity between people, between people and God, and between people and the created world, so that with true and full *shalom*, all things in heaven and on earth may be reconciled in Christ.

Mercy does not "let people off the hook" as though our brokenness can be ignored, nor is mercy contrary to justice. Mercy is not an act of power wielded by a superior to rescue an inferior. Mercy is the disruption that re-orients us toward *shalom*, and the driving force that makes the Good News good news. God's mercy is infinite in scope and extent, a gift to all without condition and without regard to whether the recipient deserves it or not. Mercy is offered not just once but seventy times seven billion times!

Followers of Jesus are called to both receive and show mercy as part of the package deal that Micah called good and Jesus called abundant life. Jesus invites us into a network of reciprocity in which this giving and receiving of mercy nourishes everyone. Both receiving and showing mercy can be hard, and often fall short of its ideal, but growing in mercy is a central part of discipleship under the tutelage of the Holy Spirit. As with every element of discipleship, mercy is not an exception but a habit. We develop the ability to show extravagant mercy through frequent smaller acts that build that habit.

Although mercy is always an act rather than a feeling, it launches from a posture like the heart of God. That posture is outrageously generous, self-sacrificial, and surprising to the point of being scandalous. We model our attitudes and behavior on those of Jesus, and in doing so we imitate the character of God. We become merciful because our model is merciful.

Mercy is both part of the good news, and the primary means by which that good news is experienced. Mercy repositions our frame of reference from an economy of exchange to an ecology of love; from relational transactions to a network of reciprocity; from conditionality to gift.

Mercy is evangelistic in that it proclaims and demonstrates the good news that God acts toward us with extreme kindness motivated by compassion. Mercy is evangelistic in its desire to heal, to disrupt, to transform, to redeem, and to reconcile. Mercy is evangelistic in that it invites people into the web of mercy that is the kingdom of God.

PROACTIVE MERCY

The shape of mercy inevitably depends on the interpersonal context of the need being addressed. Mercy does not follow a rule, but flows from a desire to care for the other, from a posture of grace, and from lifelong habits of generosity and kindness. Mercy is shown when someone sacrifices a kidney to save the life of another. Mercy is equally shown in palliative care units when morphine is given to ease distress in the clear knowledge that it will also shorten the person's life. Mercy is shown by a marriage partner who lets go of personal opportunities in order to best serve their partner and the health of their relationship. Mercy is also shown in letting someone you love go when it becomes clear that your presence cannot enable their flourishing.

Mercy is not passive, nor does it amount to sweeping evil under the rug. Mercy seeks to change people: to save them from whatever sin, bondage or exile they suffer under, and to give them a new chance to flourish. It is a form of active, non-violent resistance to evil rather than either running away from evil or overcoming evil with evil.

Pope Francis conceives of God's mercy as a response: a response that is only possible when the person first moves toward God with an acknowledgement of their sin.[134] Such an attitude is well-attested in the Bible, with verses like Isaiah 55:7 declaring "Let them return to the LORD, that he may have mercy on them, and to our God, for he will abundantly pardon." There are times, however, when mercy operates proactively, that is, prior to the person in need doing anything.

Peter Rollins tells a parable of two brothers whose faith and whose life experiences took very different directions.[135] One, taking his faith very seriously, dedicated his life to serving those in need. He gave up comfort and romance for the sake of that work. The other married the woman he loved, had children, and lived in a beautiful home. He rarely thought about God and paid little attention to those who suffered around him. When the brothers died, God embraced them both and gave them an equal share in heaven. The first brother smiled deeply at the other and said "Today my joy is finally complete, for we are together again." In response, the materially prosperous brother said nothing, but began to weep over the wasted life that he had led.

By way of commentary, Rollins notes that the gift of God, and of his brother's joy, is precisely what brought the man to a place where he was finally worthy of the gift. Rather than mercy being expressed in response to any movement toward God or toward remorse, mercy was expressed proactively. Only after receiving mercy did the man change. "The gift thus retroactively creates the conditions for its justification." This is an example of the disruption of mercy. Mercy can stop people in their tracks because of its unexpectedness and its generosity, and in that moment of disruption new opportunities are created for transformation and redemption.

Do not mistakenly conclude that mercy is goal-driven. Although mercy is infused with hope, its expression does not depend on any future response. We are merciful because we follow Jesus, because Jesus is the embodiment of God, and because God desires mercy rather than sacrifice.

The great love of God, indeed the *infinite* love of God, for the entire creation, including all people, creatures and inanimate objects, results in an equally great compassion in response to creation's need. That compassion propels the gift of God's outrageous mercy: a mercy without conditions, without debt, and without regard to whether any deserve it or not; a mercy that seeks to ameliorate our immediate needs, to disrupt our transactional thinking so we can re-imagine a way of living through which all can flourish, and, ultimately, to lead creation forward until all things in heaven and on earth are reconciled in Christ.

JOINING THE GUILD OF KNOT TIERS

Nick Cave once commented that, "despite our collective state of loss, and our potential for evil, there exists a great network of goodness, knitted together by countless everyday human kindnesses."[136] Millions of everyday acts of kindness form the substrate of society, without which we are a mob rather than a society.

Mercy, it seems to me, is something more surprising. Mercy is extreme kindness, scandalously enacted beyond what anyone would expect, without regard to whether it is deserved. Mercy is when the kindness comes at great personal cost, or when it is shown to someone whom everyone else has given up on, or expressed with such generous creativity that it disrupts the normal trajectory.

If kindness knits the social fabric, mercy ties knots when threads of that fabric break. Will you join the guild of knot tiers?

Hear the good news from the stories of Chloe, Dirk Willems, Jean Valjean, Maximillian Kolbe, and others in this book. Hear the good news from Jesus, whose mercy was shown in forsaking power and status to live in exile with us, and in the surprising and extravagant kindness of giving his life for us. Remember Zacchaeus, who, though despised by his community, received mercy from Jesus in a way that redirected the whole trajectory of his life. We all need that mercy, and we can all find it in Jesus. May we also find it through the network of reciprocity that encompasses the whole world. Given the centrality of mercy to the gospel, let us seek ways to be transformed by mercy ourselves and to take the same posture as Jesus, allowing the divine well of love to overflow through mercy to all we meet.

In his letter to the church at Ephesus, Paul wrote:

> ... be kind to one another, tender-hearted, forgiving one another, as God in Christ has forgiven you. Therefore be imitators of God, as beloved children, and live in love, as Christ loved us and gave himself up for us, a fragrant offering and sacrifice to God. (Ephesians 4:32-5:2)

Paul invites all followers of Jesus to "live in love," a phrase that encompasses both knowing we are loved and showing love to others. According to that verse, love is expressed in kindness, compassion ("tender-hearted" means that visceral good feeling in our guts), and forgiveness (showing each other favor and grace). To the extent that we take Paul's advice, we join the "great cloud of witnesses" who, as imitators of Jesus, revel in the joy of acting mercifully.

Will you continue your own journey toward loving mercy? Will you cultivate compassion and express that compassion through mercy to your friends, family and neighbors, whatever their needs might be? Will you extend that mercy to people who are marginalized in our society, to those of other tribes, and to your enemies? That's absurd isn't it? Scandalous. But isn't it what Jesus asks of his followers? Will you participate in God's mission to reconcile all things in heaven and on earth by showing mercy to all?

May we all experience the mercy of God and become bearers of that wild and wondrous good news to all we meet. May we be freed from bondage, forgiven for our sin, and find the way out of exile to our true home. May we all flourish in the network of God's disruptive gift of extreme kindness, and may we be so impelled by compassion for the people around us that we surprise them with the same extravagance.

GIVEN THAT WE LIVE UNDER THE MERCY OF GOD, WHAT IS YOUR WISH FOR HOW MERCY TRANSFORMS YOU? WHAT'S NEXT IN YOUR JOURNEY TOWARDS LOVING MERCY?

PLEASE CONSIDER SHARING YOUR STORIES IN OUR COMMUNITY SPACE. DETAILS AT THIS WEBSITE: WWW.TURNINGTEARDROPSINTOJOY.COM/BOOKS

Appendix: Alternative Conceptions

CLAIMING THAT MERCY is a gift of extreme kindness motivated by compassion centers the idea in a very different location from many other understandings of mercy. Since pre-Christian times in Greek philosophy and Roman political theory, through to our contemporary English-speaking culture, many have spoken and written about mercy. In this appendix, I sift through some of the ideas that have dominated the landscape.

As is typical in Western literature, the documents and hence opinions that are available to us are nearly all written by males and reflect their perspective from a position of power. History, as often noted, is written by the victors, which makes uncovering what the marginalized majority of humanity thought about any subject difficult. Understanding the varied opinions about mercy through the published record is an important process, however, because those opinions have such an influence on how we tend to think about mercy today.

A large part of the variation in historical opinions about mercy can be attributed to the ambiguity of the word itself.

Certainly, some of the views canvassed below are in fundamental conflict with each other, but aspects of the disagreements arise because the thinkers are examining different concepts. There is no agreed definition or framework for understanding mercy as a moral virtue.

Words such as compassion, pity, and mercy do not mean the same thing. An example of mercy might not be an act of pity. Nor is a criticism of compassion automatically a criticism of mercy. Those three words mean different things to different people, and just looking them up in a dictionary does not explain the nuanced way the words are used in different contexts. As we saw on the chapters on mercy in the Old and New Testaments, when those English words are used to translate concepts in the Bible from the original Hebrew and Greek, further vagaries are added.

MERCY IN BATTLE

In Homer's *Odyssey*, Ulysses, the king of Ithaca, has been away from home for twenty years, fighting at the city of Troy and later imprisoned by Calypso. Thinking Ulysses is dead, an endless stream of suitors occupies the royal palace seeking the hand of Ulysses' wife Penelope. She, however, remains faithful and holds the persistent suitors at bay.

Ulysses eventually finds his way home and, hearing about the suitors, disguises himself as a beggar. The suitors insult and abuse Ulysses, and he is only recognized by his dog Argos and by the housekeeper Eurycleia. His identity is also possibly suspected by Penelope and, perhaps because of that suspicion, she organizes a competition to gather all her suitors to prove their worth the next day.

Appendix: Alternative Conceptions

During the competition, Ulysses tears off his disguise and, with aid from his son and a few loyal servants, attacks the gathered suitors. "Dogs, did you think that I should not come back from Troy? You have wasted my substance, have forced my women servants to lie with you, and have wooed my wife while I was still living. You have feared neither God nor man, and now you shall die." [137]

Eurymachus tries to avert Ulysses' rage by proposing that all the suitors will pay a reasonable fine. But "As eagle-beaked, crook-taloned vultures from the mountains swoop down on the smaller birds that cower in flocks upon the ground, and kill them, for they cannot either fight or fly, and lookers on enjoy the sport—even so did Ulysses and his men fall upon the suitors and smite them on every side. They made a horrible groaning as their brains were being battered in, and the ground seethed with their blood."

In the midst of the bloodshed ...

> *Leiodes then caught the knees of Ulysses and said, "Ulysses I beseech you have mercy upon me and spare me. I never wronged any of the women in your house either in word or deed, and I tried to stop the others. I saw them, but they would not listen, and now they are paying for their folly. I was their sacrificing priest; if you kill me, I shall die without having done anything to deserve it, and shall have got no thanks for all the good that I did."*
>
> *Ulysses looked sternly at him and answered, "If you were their sacrificing priest, you must have prayed many a time that it might be long before I got home again, and that you might marry my wife and have children by her. Therefore you shall die."*

Disrupting Mercy

> With these words he picked up the sword that Agelaus had dropped when he was being killed, and which was lying upon the ground. Then he struck Leiodes on the back of his neck, so that his head fell rolling in the dust while he was yet speaking.

Immediately, the minstrel Phemius likewise embraces Ulysses' knees and begs for mercy, claiming, "Your own son Telemachus will tell you that I did not want to frequent your house and sing to the suitors after their meals, but they were too many and too strong for me, so they made me." Fortunately for Phemius, Telemachus confirms his story and Ulysses spares him.

This scene became an influential portrait of mercy in the context of combat. Echoes of that scene can be heard in the 2000 movie *Gladiator*. In gladiatorial combat, Maximus (acted by Russell Crowe) knocks his opponent to the ground and the emperor signals with his thumbs down, but instead of obeying by killing his opponent, Maximus throws down his weapon. The crowd calls out, "Maximus the Merciful!"

In the original Transformers animated movie, the evil Megatron is beaten in a fight by Optimus Prime and, lying on the ground at Optimus' feet, cries out, "No more, Optimus Prime. Grant me mercy, I beg of you!"

Even in *Shrek 2*, after the ogre is bested by Puss in Boots, Puss waves his sword and demands that the ogre "beg for mercy."

One final example, from *The Lord of the Rings*. When the hero Frodo learns that the broken and twisted creature

Appendix: Alternative Conceptions

Gollum has alerted the dark lord of Mordor to the location of the One Ring, Frodo declares: "What a pity that Bilbo did not stab that vile creature, when he had a chance!" The wise wizard Gandalf disagrees:

> "Pity? It was Pity that stayed his hand. Pity, and Mercy: not to strike without need."
>
> "I am sorry,' said Frodo. "But I am frightened; and I do not feel any pity for Gollum."
>
> "You have not seen him," Gandalf broke in.
>
> "No, and I don't want to," said Frodo. "I can't understand you. ... He deserves death."
>
> "Deserves it! I daresay he does. Many that live deserve death. And some that die deserve life. Can you give it to them? Then do not be too eager to deal out death in judgement. For even the very wise cannot see all ends. I have not much hope that Gollum can be cured before he dies, but there is a chance of it. And he is bound up with the fate of the Ring. My heart tells me that he has some part to play yet, for good or ill, before the end; and when that comes, the pity of Bilbo may rule the fate of many - yours not least."[138]

Gandalf's words turn out to be accurate prophecy, for although Gollum is not "cured," his last act enables the Ring to be destroyed precisely at the moment when Frodo is unable to do so.

Disrupting Mercy

MERCY IN COURT

We have seen that a frequent setting for mercy is the battle field, or some physical striving for supremacy in combat. Just as frequently, mercy is depicted in the court room.

During World War II, Adolf Eichmann was Germany's top military administrator for Jewish affairs. Although he probably did not define any of the regime's anti-Jewish policies, he was responsible for implementing them. His actions led to the deportation of hundreds of thousands of Jews under horrendous conditions, abuses against Poles, Slovenes, and Gypsies, and to the deaths of many.

After the war, Eichmann escaped from US custody and remained free until his recapture, in Buenos Aires, during May 1960. He was tried for war crimes in Israel, convicted in December 1961, and executed by hanging six months later. Like many German military officials tried for war crimes, Eichmann argued that he had been following orders. The Israeli judges, however, concluded that he had been a key perpetrator of genocide and that he had wholeheartedly believed in the Nazi cause.

What is most interesting for our discussion are the several appeals for mercy between Eichmann's conviction and his execution. His own letter to the president of Israel a few days before his execution only became publicly available in 2016. At the end of that letter he wrote, "I am not able to recognize the court's ruling as just, and I ask, Your Honor Mr. President, to exercise your right to grant pardons, and order that the death penalty not be carried

Appendix: Alternative Conceptions

out." His request for pardon was echoed by others, including the Jewish intellectual Martin Buber.

Eichmann's own plea is based on a belief that he was not actually guilty. Is he actually asking for justice rather than mercy? From what I can gather about the other calls for Eichmann not to be executed, the petitioners were not actually asking for mercy either. They were more concerned about the morality of execution on principle, and about the future of Israel's reputation. In some cases, they even seemed to want Eichmann to suffer more through a lengthy imprisonment than taking the quick route out by hanging.

A different example of people calling for mercy in the context of the court room was the so-called Bali Nine: a group of Australian tourists who were convicted of smuggling heroin out of Indonesia in 2005. The group's leaders, Andrew Chan and Myuran Sukumaran, were sentenced to death. Six other members were sentenced to life imprisonment and the ninth member to twenty years in prison.

During the next ten years, while various legal appeals were quashed, both Chan and Sukumaran turned their lives around inside Indonesia's Kerobokan Prison. The prison governor commended them both as reformed and model prisoners. Sukuraman taught other prisoners, painted, and completed a university course in Fine Arts. Chan married, studied to become a pastor, and led church services within the prison.

Many people asked the Indonesian authorities to show clemency to Chan and Sukumaran. Australia's Foreign

Minister, Julie Bishop, pleaded in parliament for their death sentences to be commuted to prison sentences. The Australian Prime Minister, Tony Abbott, wrote to the Indonesian President, Joko Widodo, asking for mercy to be shown. The Mercy Campaign, a support group specifically formed to advocate for Chan and Sukumaran, lodged a petition requesting mercy, with 150,000 signatures.

President Widodo, however, rejected these requests and Chan and Sukumaran were executed by firing squad on 29 April 2015.[139]

What does the dictionary say?

Many contemporary definitions of mercy emphasize the power imbalance between the giver and receiver of mercy. For example, the *Merriam-Webster Dictionary* defines mercy as "compassion or forbearance shown especially to an offender or to one subject to one's power."[140]

Similarly, the *Collins English Dictionary* explains that "If someone in authority shows mercy, they choose not to harm someone they have power over, or they forgive someone they have the right to punish."[141] They note a difference in usage between British and American speakers. British speakers understand mercy as "compassionate treatment of or attitude towards an offender, adversary, etc., who is in one's power or care; clemency; pity." American speakers are more likely to understand mercy as "a refraining from harming or punishing offenders, enemies, persons in one's power, etc.; kindness in excess of what may be expected or demanded by fairness; forbearance and compassion."

Appendix: Alternative Conceptions

Images of mercy on the battle field and in the court room both highlight the power-based structure of mercy that comes across in these definitions. In both dictionaries, mercy is expressed towards someone you have power or authority over, whereas compassion may be towards anyone, independently of power relationships. Mercy is typically (though perhaps not always) directed towards someone who has committed an offense, in which case mercy involves forgiveness and probably the withholding of punishment. Compassion is typically directed towards someone's suffering rather than their offense.

Both dictionaries distinguish the *feeling* of compassion from the *action* of mercy. According to the *Merriam-Webster Dictionary*, compassion is "sympathetic consciousness of others' distress together with a desire to alleviate it."[142] Mercy, on the other hand, goes beyond a consciousness or desire. Mercy must be shown, that is, demonstrated in action.

The definition of mercy in the *Collins English Dictionary* is slightly broader, allowing for mercy to be not always an action but sometimes an attitude (at least in British usage). Nevertheless, the primary meaning implies that mercy turns compassion into action—sometimes actively alleviating suffering, and sometimes passively refraining from harm.

MERCY IN ANCIENT ROME

We are all aware of the fights between gladiators in the Roman Colosseum, but perhaps not aware of how that practice ended. Across more than three hundred years, these gladiatorial fights claimed the lives of perhaps 400,000 people and millions of animals.[143] Although some victors spared the lives of their defeated opponents, the crowd and the officiating emperor would often reject any plea for mercy and demand to be entertained by death.

These fights to the death ended during the reign of Emperor Flavius Honorius around 400 CE. According to Theodoret of Cyrus, whose account from about 450 CE has been preserved, the young emperor's decision was prompted by the martyrdom of "a certain man of the name of Telemachus."[144] More details are given much later in *Foxe's Book of Martyrs* and although Foxe's version is most likely an unfounded embellishment, it is a good story and of interest to us because of his explicit link to mercy.[145]

According to John Foxe, Honorius arranged an entertainment extravaganza in the Colosseum to celebrate a recent Roman military victory over the Goths. After many gladiators had been slain in the celebratory competition, and their dead bodies dragged away, the next combat was interrupted when a man "boldly leaped down into the arena." He was "a man of rough but imposing presence, bareheaded and with sun-browned face," recognized by some as Telemachus, a "holy man" on a pilgrimage, who had only recently arrived in Rome. "His spirit had been stirred by the sight of thousands flocking to see men slaughter one another" and after positioning himself between the two gladiators he called out to the audience, "Do not requite God's mercy in turning away the swords of your enemies by murdering each other!"

Appendix: Alternative Conceptions

His plea is reminiscent of the parable Jesus told about someone who was released from an unpayable debt by the king, but who then refused to release a colleague from a minor debt (Matthew 18:21-35). That person had been shown amazing mercy but could not show even the smallest mercy to others. Note the structural similarity in the plea by Telemachus. Telemachus draws the crowd's attention to the enormous mercy of God shown in how the Roman army had been protected from their enemy's swords. He asks whether, in the face of that great mercy, the best way to repay God is to force gladiators to kill each other. Is it not more appropriate for those shown mercy to show mercy to others?

The crowd in the Colosseum angrily called on the gladiators to continue the fight but Telemachus persists in holding them apart. People in the crowd called out, "The old customs of Rome must be observed!" and the gladiators joined together to stab Telemachus to death. In Theodora's account, it was the crowd who "stoned the peacemaker to death." But both Theodora and Foxe note that he did not die in vain, for this incident led to a change of heart, and from that day on fighting to the death as a sport ceased.

Three centuries before Telemachus' martyrdom, Julius Caesar (100-44 BCE) became famous for showing mercy to military and political enemies, although one can doubt the purity of his motives. He was skilled at winning the hearts of people, and mercy was part of his winning strategy. He supposedly said, "He conquers twice, who shows mercy to the conquered," meaning that the defeated enemy who is shown mercy is much more likely to become a compliant ally. To emphasize his own virtue, he even consecrated a temple to Clementia, the goddess of mercy.

Not long after Julius Caesar, the Roman Stoic philosopher and statesman, Lucius Annaeus Seneca the Younger (4 BCE-65 CE), expanded on that instrumental view of mercy in his advice to Emperor Nero. In the essay *De Clementia* (On Clemency), Seneca positions clemency as the "most humane of virtues" and suggests that the more power one has the more important clemency becomes. Rulers, such as Nero, can show more clemency than anyone, and they ought to do so because it makes their rule more glorious and admirable.[146] Clemency is what distinguishes kings from tyrants.[147]

Martha Nussbaum interprets this type of clemency as a way of avoiding both the mindless imposition of legal penalties and the capricious violence of retributive anger. She notes that Seneca's approach to clemency or mercy depends on a judge being aware that they are also capable of the errors they condemn in others. As a consequence, that posture allows a ruler to identify with, and have sympathy for, those they judge. While this does not mean guilt is ignored, it does mean "the punishments that one does assign will be chosen, on the whole, not for their retributive function, but for their power to improve the life of the defendant."[148]

Furthermore, Seneca observed that leaders with a reputation for showing mercy will be much safer, because it will make their subjects ashamed to do wrong. So, Nero should seize every opportunity to make his clemency

Appendix: Alternative Conceptions

widely known. Of course, there will be times when a ruler must punish, but that should be done dispassionately rather than driven by anger or fear. In most cases, mercy does more good than cruelty.

Seneca offered several definitions of mercy, admitting that none are perfect. Mercy is ...

- "a restraining of the mind from vengeance when it is in its power to avenge"
- "gentleness shown by a powerful man in fixing the punishment of a weaker one"
- "a tendency towards mildness in inflicting punishment"
- "self-restraint, which remits some part of a fine which it deserves to receive and which is due to it"
- "coming short of the penalty which might with justice be inflicted."[149]

An important aspect of these definitions is that mercy assumes an imbalance in which one person holds a position of power over another. In that context, mercy is expressed as a magnanimous act by a superior person towards an inferior. That understanding remains common today, but it is a notion I challenge throughout this book.

One consequence of this power-based, instrumental view is that mercy becomes a form of subjection. By showing mercy, one is declaring that they stand over the other: that they are superior in strength, in virtue, in righteousness, or in authority. Conversely, to accept the offer of such mercy is to acknowledge your own inferiority and enter a relationship of submission.

AUGUSTINE, ANSELM, AND AQUINAS

St Augustine (354-430), St Anselm (1033-1109), and St Aquinas (1225-1274) were all philosopher-theologians whose thinking continues to influence Western Christianity.

Although Augustine did not write a lot about mercy, one incident suggests that he positioned mercy within the service of justice. As a bishop in north Africa, Augustine was once asked whether it was right to pray for someone who had already been found guilty of a crime. Didn't justice oblige us to punish them and, if so, how could we wish or pray that they would be forgiven and go unpunished? The questioner was Macedonius, who apparently had some civil responsibility for law enforcement. Augustine responded with a lengthy letter in which he proposed a separation between the judgment God brings about through the state, and the mercy God brings about through the church. According to Augustine, it is right that Macedonius, as law enforcer, should impose the just punishment. But it is also right that Augustine, as a priest, should hope for mercy. Justice requires them both, and both may change the heart of the guilty one. "There is good, then, in your severity which works to secure our tranquility, and there is good in our intercession which works to restrain your severity. Do not be displeased at being petitioned by the good, because the good are not displeased that you are feared by the wicked."[150]

In relation to divine action, however, Augustine painted a different picture in which God's sovereignty allows God

Appendix: Alternative Conceptions

the freedom to choose between mercy and justice. Describing his view on predestination, Augustine wrote that God could certainly turn the wills of evil people to good, but whether that happens or not is purely God's prerogative. When God does so, it is an expression of mercy; when God chooses not to, it is an expression of justice.[151] Justice would leave us in our evil state, while God's mercy—shown in the overthrowing of our will!—is reserved for those to whom God chooses to show it. That makes mercy a type of coercion, and makes mercy and justice seem mutually exclusive.

Anselm, Archbishop of Canterbury from 1093 to 1109, was troubled by that apparent conflict within the concept of God. He saw mercy and justice as opposed to each other but also acknowledged that both were found in God, which struck him as logically problematic. If God were perfect and without inconsistency, how could justice and mercy be opposed to each other and yet both be attributes of God?

In Anselm's early writings, he attempted to account for the conflict between justice and mercy by making them both subservient to God's goodness. It is good to act justly, he writes, just as it is good to act mercifully. As the Supreme Good, God is good to both the good and to the wicked, and can both justly punish and spare from punishment. Furthermore, Anselm tentatively ponders whether the core of God's justice is not a response to our wrongdoing, but a reflection of fidelity to God's own goodness. In that scenario, acting justly (faithfully?) towards God's supreme goodness might account for how God can act mercifully towards wrong doers.

Don't be surprised if that sounds confused!

In Anselm's later writing he seems to admit that this model failed. Instead, he moved away from the legal approach in which justice is about receiving the reward or punishment that we deserve and focused on justice as the outcome of good governance. In a governance model, justice is about establishing and maintaining a society that is rightly ordered: in which everything has its proper place and works harmoniously together. To maintain right order, a good governor may impose laws, and punish violations of those laws, but law enforcement is a means towards the well-ordered society, not an end in itself. A good governor may also deal kindly with a person who has been hurt or lost their way in order to restore that person's own "right order." With that understanding, there is no conflict between justice and mercy. Both laws and mercy are means towards the larger goal of true justice.[152]

Writing in the century after Anselm's death, Thomas Aquinas seemed less troubled by Anselm's philosophical dilemma. To Aquinas, "God acts mercifully, not indeed by going against His justice, but by doing something more than justice." In fact, every work of God demonstrates both justice and mercy.[153]

Aquinas approved of Augustine's view that "mercy is heartfelt sympathy for another's distress, impelling us to succor him if we can."[154] Rather than being restricted to the legal world of guilt and punishment, mercy is a form of charity (in the old sense of that word as love) that we can and ought to show to all people including our enemies. Although we cannot be everyone's benefactor, we do have

Appendix: Alternative Conceptions

an obligation to show charity and mercy to those close to us. What's more, it is not sufficient to feel sympathetic towards someone's need: mercy must be enacted rather than simply felt.[155]

So, we see quite a diversity in these three influential thinkers. Augustine positioned mercy in the service of justice; Anselm struggled to account for the apparent opposition between mercy and justice; while Aquinas thought that mercy surpasses justice.

In my own opinion, the supposed conflict between justice and mercy is a result of a misconstrual of both concepts. The conflict only arises when justice is understood as getting what you deserve, especially in the form of punishment for wrongdoing, and mercy is seen as being let off from that deserved punishment. In a similar way to Anselm's later model, my argument in this book depends on moving away from a view of justice based on people getting what they deserve, to one based on communal *shalom*. Having made that shift, a radically different view of mercy emerges.

NIETZSCHE

In the history of Western thought, Christianity's boldest critic was probably the German Friedrich Nietzsche (1844–1900). Nietzsche considered Christianity to be based fundamentally on pity, and he picked up a distaste for pity from his reading of the Greek and Roman Stoics such as Seneca.

For Nietzsche, "To offer pity is as good as to offer contempt."[156] Pity demeans the receiver by implying that they are not able to deal with their own suffering. To show pity takes away the possibility of the sufferer learning and growing through their suffering. Hardship is part of life, and a child with a perpetually runny nose needs to learn to wipe their own nose! In a perverse way, but one that makes sense from a Stoic perspective, Nietzsche argues that pity demeans the giver too, that pity is neither virtuous nor altruistic, that pity is closely related to revenge and increases the overall amount of suffering.

Despite his criticism of pity, however, Nietzsche noted that mercy is different from pity. Like Seneca, he understood pity as being a response to suffering that is not the person's fault, whereas mercy is a response to someone's guilt. Pity says, "You poor thing! I'm sorry that bad experience happened to you. Let me fix it for you." But mercy assumes the person is at fault and says, "You did something wrong, but I will waive or lessen your deserved punishment." Mercy refuses to let the person off the hook: it mitigates the sentence rather than declaring them not guilty.

In an important passage in his book *On the Genealogy of Morals*,[157] Nietzsche praises mercy but condemns pity. When someone (or a community) is strong, they can put aside any feelings of revenge and have nothing to fear by being merciful. If a guilty party is not punished, or not punished to the full extent, what harm could that do to the strong? Not showing mercy is a sign that you are still weak and fearful. Once you are strong and secure enough not to fear another's wrongdoing, then you can decide to act in ways that bring about healing rather than retribution. In that way, the justice that first demands punishment overcomes itself in mercy.

Nietzsche's observations are important in the way they apply to God. Is it because God is supremely strong and secure that God shows mercy rather than pity? Would that enable God's people to also express a justice that overcomes itself in mercy? Or is this way of thinking about mercy too dependent on a worldview dominated by superior-inferior power dynamics? These questions are not the direction Nietzsche—who is perhaps most famous for declaring that God is dead—would take. Nevertheless, his understanding is insightful and provides helpful fertilizer for growing a more robust tree of mercy.

MERCY IN ISLAM

Bismillah ir-Rahman ir-Rahim is proclaimed at the start of 113 of the 114 chapters of the Qur'an: "In the name of God, the All-merciful, the Ever-merciful." Although the *bismillah* has been translated into English in varied ways that affect its implications—"most gracious, most merciful," "most benevolent, ever merciful," "the all-gracious, the all-compassionate"—mercy is indisputably at the center of Islamic theology. The *bismillah* preface sets the scene of all Qur'anic readings, acting as an invocation of a God in whose name all truth is revealed. This God is fundamentally merciful and all understandings of the text must flow from that understanding of God.

The two words *rahman* and *rahim* share a linguistic heritage with the Hebrew *racham* which plays a central role in the Old Testament's portrayal of mercy. In the context of the *bismillah*, the difference between the two is subtle but important. *Rahman* and *rahim* are the first two of the ninety-nine names of God. According to Omar's *Dictionary of the Holy Quran, rahman* "conveys the idea of fullness and extensiveness and indicates the greatest preponderance of the quality of love and mercy which comprehends the entire universe without regard to our effort and asking even before we are born."[158] On the other hand, *rahim* "denotes the idea of constant repetition and giving of liberal reward to those who deserve it and seek of it." Whereas *rahman* describes God's fundamental character and willingness to show mercy, *rahim* describes the expression of that mercy in specific cases. The prophet Muhammad also noted that *rahman* generally pertains to this life but *rahim* to the life to come. "Allah is to *all people* most surely full of kindness, Most Merciful" (Qur'an 2:143, see also 21:107), although there is also a sense in which he shows mercy *(rahim)* only to Believers (e.g., Qur'an 33:43, 2:161).

Alongside the Qur'an, Muslims hold profound respect for various documents, Hadith, that record the words of Muhammad. One of those recorded sayings is that "when God created mercy, he created it in one hundred parts. He kept ninety-nine parts with himself and sent one part into the world."[159] In other words, the mercy we see on earth is only a tiny fraction of what God's mercy is like.

Around the same time as Anselm and Aquinas, the Islamic philosopher Ibn 'Arabî (1165–1240) asserted that existence is synonymous with mercy, which is why Allah can say, "My mercy embraces everything" (Qur'an 7:156).

Appendix: Alternative Conceptions

Because "mercy pertains to the very stuff of reality," Allah cannot be unmerciful without denying reality.[160] Ibn 'Arabî's mystical Sufism is a minority position within the various schools of Islamic theology, but nevertheless his approach to mercy is broadly influential.

Ibn 'Arabî is one in a long line of Islamic scholars who discuss the symbolic meaning of the two hands of God: the left hand representing concepts such as fear, majesty, fire, awe, and wrath; the right hand representing hope, beauty, pleasure, paradise, intimacy, and mercy. Of all that Allah created, only humans were created with both hands (Qur'an 38:75), and so "we fear His wrath and hope for His good pleasure."[161]

Despite this emphasis on the differences between God's left and right hands, there is a hadith in which Muhammad says "both hands of God are right hands" and another that assures us that Allah's mercy takes precedence over his wrath.[162] This can be understood as implying that from God's point of view, both wrath and pleasure are good and right, and only from the human point of view is the left hand to be feared.[163] Another explanation is that Allah expresses two types of mercy: a fundamental form related to *rahman* that permeates all things, flowing from God to both paradise and to hell; and a secondary form related to *rahim* that is the opposite of wrath and restricted to the faithful.[164] With that understanding, one form of mercy is free and unconditional, while another form is conditional.

When Islamic principles are applied to personal and communal ethics, actions are categorized under five *ahkam* (rulings): those that are compulsory, recommended, morally neutral, disliked, and forbidden. Significant theological and legal effort is spent determining in which category specific acts lie. Although true believers are instructed to be merciful among themselves (Qur'an 48:29) and compassionate (Qur'an 90:12-17), the ethical classification depends on the specific act. Doing good to parents, relatives, those in need, and even slaves, is prescribed in the Qur'an (4:36) and hence considered *compulsory*. On the other hand, allowing compassion to prevent the physical punishment of an adultery is *forbidden* (Qur'an 24:2).

One of the five pillars that guide adherents to Islam is the practice of *zakat*. Zakat is the contribution of 2.5 percent of one's wealth (though the exact calculation is ambiguous) to approved charitable purposes. This defines a *compulsory* expression of "mercy" for all Moslems, leaving additional charitable giving *(sadaqat)* as optional. Forgiving a financial debt if the person is having trouble paying is *recommended* (Qur'an 2:280). When someone has been wronged, the ordained punishment is to extract an eye for an eye or life for a life. Relinquishing that requirement is recognized as a virtuous act of mercy but is not obligatory (Qur'an 2:178, 5:45).[165]

MERCY IN JUDAISM

Much of the Jewish understanding of mercy matches that of the Christian tradition and so I will not repeat those aspects here. I discussed one contemporary Jewish understanding of mercy's relationship to justice in Chapter 5. Here, I will mention two other distinctive approaches to

Appendix: Alternative Conceptions

mercy within Jewish thinking, both summarized from secondary sources.

During the month preceding the Jewish New Year (Rosh Hashanah), as well as on other holy days, Jewish communities gather to recite *selichot*, prayers for forgiveness. The *selichot* liturgy varies across traditions and countries, but the gatherings are typically just before morning and encourage worshippers to turn their hearts and minds towards repentance.

Within that liturgical context, a core element is the repeated recitation of the thirteen attributes of mercy, derived from a passage in Exodus. After the golden calf incident, and after Moses begged God not to destroy the Israelites for their idolatry, Moses threw the stone tablets containing the ten commandments to the ground and broke them. After a heart-to-heart discussion between God and Moses, Moses saw God and heard the words:

> *The LORD, the LORD, a God merciful and gracious, slow to anger, and abounding in steadfast love and faithfulness, keeping steadfast love for the thousandth generation, forgiving iniquity and transgression and sin, yet by no means clearing the guilty. (Exodus 34:6-7)*

Jewish theologians derive thirteen attributes of God's mercy from those two verses, though the exact attributes vary between different traditions. One list is as follows:

- **The Lord!** —God is merciful before a person sins
- **The Lord!** —God is merciful after the sinner has gone astray

- **God**—ruler over nature and humanity, giving to all creatures according to their need
- **Compassionate** ("merciful" in the NRSV)—God is filled with loving sympathy for human frailty, does not put people into situations of extreme temptation, and eases the punishment of the guilty
- **Gracious**—God shows mercy even to those who do not deserve it, consoling the afflicted and raising up the oppressed
- **Slow to anger**—God gives the sinner ample time to reflect, improve, and repent
- **Abundant in kindness** ("steadfast love" in the NRSV)—God is kind toward those who lack personal merits, providing more gifts and blessings than they deserve
- **Truth** ("faithfulness" in the NRSV)—God never reneges on the promise to reward those who serve God
- **Preserver of kindness for thousands of generations**—God remembers the deeds of the righteous for the benefit of their less virtuous generations of offspring
- **Forgiver of iniquity**—God forgives intentional sin resulting from an evil disposition, as long as the sinner repents
- **Forgiver of willful sin** (transgression in the NRSV)—God allows even those who commit a sin with the malicious intent of rebelling against and angering God the opportunity to repent
- **Forgiver of error** (sin in the NRSV)—God forgives sin committed out of carelessness, thoughtlessness, or apathy

Appendix: Alternative Conceptions

- **Who cleanses**—God pardons, wiping away the sins of those who truly repent; however, if one does not repent, God does not cleanse. This interesting interpretation of the original Hebrew phrase drops off the last part of verse 7, "yet by no means clearing the guilty."[166]

In Jewish mysticism, the number thirteen is associated with the infinite. So, listing thirteen attributes of mercy is also an observation that God's mercy is without limit.

The second distinctively Jewish idea about mercy I want to highlight also comes from the mystical tradition of Jewish kabbalah: the concept of *zimzum* and its relationship to mercy. The Arizal, a leading sixteenth-century rabbi, radically shifted kabbalistic thinking about the process of creation. His complex cosmology cannot be adequately summarized here, but he noted that before creation the infinite God occupied all conceptual space. Any creation would have been impossible because there was nowhere for creation to *be*. Through the process of *zimzum*, however, God withdrew, or contracted, to make space for something other than God. God concentrated all the power of judgment to leave a point of unoccupied, primordial space. *Zimzum* was an act of judgment, devoid of mercy. Once space was created, God sent a single symbol of power into that space to commence creation, and that power of formation and organization belonged to God's attribute of overflowing mercy.[167]

In kabbalistic thought, judgment and mercy are opposing forces, or contradictory tendencies. Yet both were needed in the act of creation. According to the Tanya, an eighteenth-century work of Jewish mystical philosophy:

Disrupting Mercy

"The original plan for creation, therefore, was that it should be dominated by the attribute of stern judgment. When, however, G-d saw that if He created the world in this manner it could not endure, He tempered it by the attribute of mercy."[168]

Christian theologian Jürgen Moltmann relates *zimzum* to the concept of mercy as womb-love *(racham)* in a helpful way:

> *The idea of zimzum probably goes back to the contraction of the womb at the birth of a child, just as the Hebrew word racham means the birth pangs, and is only inadequately rendered as compassion or mercy. Where God withdraws into himself he can create something whose essence is not divine, can let it co-exist with himself, give it space, and redeem it.*[169]

MERCY IN AUSTRALIAN INDIGENOUS CULTURE

Ginyiwanga, an elder of the Yolŋu people of north-eastern Northern Territory, Australia, told me of a Japanese airman whose plane was shot down near the Wessel Islands during World War II. A local Yolŋu man was fishing nearby when he heard the noise and saw the plane land in the water. Investigating, he found a man who, though badly hurt, had managed to swim to shore. They could not understand each other, but it was clear the airman needed help, so the Yolŋu man cared for him for several days. When the airman was well enough to travel, he took him to the mission station at Galiwin'ku—that's perhaps 80km away, paddling all the way in a dugout canoe!

Appendix: Alternative Conceptions

Even though the airman was an enemy who had been bombing Yolŋu country, the Yolŋu man had no hesitation to show mercy.

In the local language, kindness is *maŋutji-wuyun*: a feeling of compassion that springs from one's inner being. The prefix *maŋutji* indicates that mercy is in response to what one has seen. Mercy, *ŋayaŋu-wuyun*, springs from kindness. Being a verb, *ŋayaŋu-wuyun* marks mercy as an action rather than a feeling. That action arises from what one has seen, motivated by deeply rooted compassion.

According to Ginyiwanga, mercy is like a network of umbilical cords connecting everyone. It is not something added later, but always already there within the relationships that form the essence of indigenous Australian cultures. This is challenging to my Western culture because we do not have the same sense of relational connection outside our immediate family. I have a mother, a father, a sister, a couple of aunts, uncles, and cousins, but for Australian indigenous people everyone is related and mercy is just one aspect of that relatedness. Without that essential connectedness to each other, mercy can seem to us as an optional extra.

Yolŋu culture promotes an expectation that you will live in peace with everyone. In reality of course, that does not always happen and so there are ceremonial approaches to healing damaged relationships. I asked Ginyiwanga how justice and mercy interacted in situations where some wrong has been done. She looked a bit quizzical at that question and told another story to show that justice and mercy are not connected.

Ginyiwanga spoke of a horrible incident in which her husband's grand-daughter was attacked by a young man with a machete. Her injuries brought her close to death and a friend took her to hospital as well as contacting the police.

Naturally, the young man was a relative and so the attack was not only a personal evil against the girl but also an offense with relational implications for the larger family. Consequently, that boy's great-grandfather, who is in the same family group as Ginyiwanga, took up the responsibility of addressing the relational damage. The great-grandfather travelled a long way to see Ginyiwanga and her husband. He sang a traditional song of peace, then described what had happened, and expressed sorrow for his great-grandson's violence. He said, "Now, if you want to do anything to him, you do it to me."

In this context, the issue was not how to bring justice to bear on the young man. Justice and legal consequences are one thing, but mercy operates quite separately, at a different level and with different intentions. Like many Australian indigenous cultures, Yolŋu people emphasize shame and honor more than guilt and innocence. So the issue was how to heal and restore the people and the interconnected relationships between them all.

Ginyiwanga says that if the great-grandfather had not followed that ceremonial act of reconciliation, if he had not sung that song and stood as a representative of the young man, she would have been in a great rage. But this relational process itself was an act of mercy, arising from the inner being of all the people involved.

Appendix: Alternative Conceptions

This vicarious apology did not mean that the young man escaped any consequences for his actions. He was subject to both Yolŋu and *balanda* (white people's) law. Under the first, he was physically punished and publicly shamed by his father, although more correctly he should have been punished by Ginyiwanga's husband, the elder of the girl's clan. In this case, Ginyiwanga's husband bears some shame for not carrying out that punishment, but the punishment by the boy's father allowed Ginyiwanga's husband to show mercy.

The girl is now doing well, though still bearing the scars of the attack. The boy who attacked her, having completed the punishment of both Yolŋu and *balanda* cultures, still has a place in his community where he quietly participates in the important Yolŋu ceremonies.

THE ECOLOGY OF LOVE IN ROMAN CATHOLIC THEOLOGY

In writings on mercy within the Roman Catholic tradition, the term typically encompasses the whole ecology of love: that complex suite of interacting virtues that include pity, compassion, kindness, forgiveness, grace, clemency, justice, humility, empathy, generosity, and love. In the 2013 book *Mercy* by Cardinal Walter Kasper for instance, there is no explicit definition of mercy, but his target can be inferred from references to the *corporal works of mercy*—feed the hungry, give drink to the thirsty, clothe the naked, shelter the homeless, visit the sick, ransom captives, and bury the dead—and the *spiritual works of mercy*—instruct the ignorant, counsel the doubtful, comfort the sorrowful, admonish the sinner, gladly forgive injuries, bear wrongs patiently, pray for the living and the dead.[170] In this, and across the whole book, Kasper applies the term mercy to a wide range of actions and motivations. Mercy is integral to God's nature and expressed to us through all the nuanced forms of love.

Kasper's understanding follows on from earlier Catholic documents, significantly the encyclical *Dives in Misericordia* ("rich in mercy") in which Pope John Paul II associates mercy so closely with love that he repeatedly uses the hyphenated form "love-mercy." In his understanding of biblical language, mercy is the mode in which love expresses itself.[171] Mercy is "love's second name."[172]

Like Kasper and Pope John Paul II, Pope Francis believes mercy is not only part of the message of Jesus, "it is the Lord's strongest message,"[173] which is why one of his first acts as pope was to declare a year of mercy. In his announcement of that "extraordinary jubilee of mercy" he wrote that "the mercy of God is not an abstract idea, but a concrete reality with which he reveals his love as that of a father or a mother, moved to the very depths out of love for their child."[174] Like Kasper, he recommends that the church demonstrate God's love-mercy through the traditional list of corporal and spiritual acts of mercy.[175]

Appendix: Alternative Conceptions

Pope Francis' usage of "mercy," however, often shows a more restricted meaning than those other writers. In *The Name of God is Mercy*, Pope Francis writes:

> Etymologically, "mercy" derives from *misericordis*, which means opening one's heart to wretchedness. And straight away we go to the Lord: mercy is the divine attitude which embraces, it is God's giving himself to us, accepting and bowing to forgive.[176]

Jesus "goes beyond the law and forgives by caressing the wounds of our sins."[177] Our sins are erased by forgiveness, "but mercy is the way in which God forgives."[178] To Pope Francis then, mercy is not primarily a response to our suffering but to our sin. "Pardoning offences becomes the clearest expression of merciful love."[179] In that context, the "medicine of mercy" is readily available "if only we take a step towards God ... or even just have a desire to take that step."[180]

Joseph Nassal's book *Premeditated Mercy: A Spirituality of Reconciliation* is another Catholic take on the theme, this time inspired by Jesus' advice that people who wish to worship God should first make sure they are reconciled with their brothers and sisters (Matthew 5:21-24). He writes that "Premeditated mercy implies a deliberate, thoughtful, and willful act to forgive, to be reconciled, to live at peace with others, even those who have betrayed us, forsaken us, abandoned us, threatened us."[181] That is as close to a definition as I can find in Nassal's book, and shows that his use of "mercy" covers a broad landscape. His call is for those in the church to engage more fully in the process of discipleship, that is, to take more seriously Jesus' example and instructions to embody the reconciliatory posture of God. We are to "stand before the world and shout with our lives that Jesus, who suffered, died and was buried, is now alive in the action of our becoming a new creation, a minister of reconciliation."[182]

These authors have passed on amazing insights into the nature and mission of God, and the ways each follower of Jesus is called to engage in loving action. They have called the church to embed those expressions of love into the foundations of its identity, structure, and operations. And yet to me, something about those approaches seems inadequate. Yes, mercy relates to forgiveness, but they are not the same thing. Yes, mercy is part of the ecology of love, but it is not the whole of that ecology: that conceptualization of mercy is too broad and more accurately covered by the concept of love.

Among contemporary Catholic writings, the one closest to the focus of this book is perhaps Mathew N. Schmalz's *Mercy Matters*: a book that relates mercy to other concepts in the ecology of love through a rich series of personal stories. Although Schmalz deliberately avoids locking in a definition of mercy, he gets close with this: "Mercy is love that responds to human need in an unexpected or unmerited way."[183] Implied in that statement is an understanding that mercy is one way for love to be expressed rather than the whole ecology. Mercy goes beyond normal acts of kindness. Mercy is typically not deserved. On all those points, I agree wholeheartedly with him.

Appendix: Alternative Conceptions

THREE FORMS OF MERCY IN REFORMED THEOLOGY

While doing research for this book I was pleasantly surprised to find a series of 26 articles on mercy published in 2019 by the Missouri Synod of the Lutheran Church in the USA.[184] I also read the book *Ministries of Mercy: Learning to Care Like Jesus*, written by the Presbyterian minister Timothy Keller. From those sources of Reformed scholarship, mercy is described in three contexts, which, if not inconsistent with each other, are at least not clearly in unison.[185]

First, Reformed theologians depict mercy as the source of creation. Martin Luther asserted that the act of creation itself springs from God's goodness and mercy, by which he was primarily emphasizing that we were created prior to any merit or worthiness of our own.[186] All people experience and benefit from God's mercy, because their very creation is the first work of God's mercy.

Second, the principal understanding of mercy in Reformed writings is always in the context of sin and salvation. According to one Lutheran scholar:

> *What is the nature and shape of this mercy? Mercy is the Lord's compassionate action toward sinful human beings in that He does not leave us alone with our sin, forsaking us to death and condemnation, but instead rescues us by His death and resurrection to live with Him.*[187]

In Luther's own words: "This is the highest article of our faith, ... that He might be merciful and that He desires to pardon sins for His Son's sake and to save."[188] Thus, the true or greatest form of mercy is evangelism,[189] for only when the gospel is preached can people hear, repent, and be saved.

In the standard Reformed interpretation of the gospel, which is mirrored in much of today's Evangelicalism, mercy is fundamentally shown in our spiritual salvation, achieved through the sacrifice of Christ. God's mercy is shown in the unearned "happy exchange" through which Christ bestows righteousness on us. Keller expresses that belief when he writes:

> *And the mercy of God is simply this. We must see that all of us are spiritually poor and bankrupt before God (Matt. 5.3), and even when we put on our best moral efforts for God, we appear as beggars clothed in filthy rags (Isa. 64.6). Yet in Jesus Christ, God provided a righteousness for us (Rom. 3:21-22), a wealth straight from the account of the Son of God, who impoverished himself through suffering and death that we might receive it (2 Cor. 8.9).[190]*

One might ask then, from what does mercy save us? That becomes clear, in Reformed logic, when we follow the thread of Oswald Bayer's view that "God's mercy stands opposite God's wrath."[191] In the same way another Lutheran scholar opposed mercy and justice as follows:

> *Thus, justice and mercy, the two hands of God, work on the same fallen, sinful being. After the one strikes, the other binds up the wounds made by the first. ... Men for their part become either children of God's mercy or people of His avenging hand.[192]*

Appendix: Alternative Conceptions

In other words, what mercy saves us from is the wrath of God. Although I certainly believe the epitome of mercy is shown is the life and death of Jesus, the rest of this book paints a radically different picture of the dynamics of that mercy.

Third, Reformed authors write of our responsibility to show mercy in the form of almsgiving and welfare services. Notwithstanding the centrality of spiritual salvation in Reformed thinking, there is still a role for individual Christians and church congregations to assist people with physical needs. Standing beside the ministers of the Word in the Lutheran church are those of the deaconate whose office is bodily mercy through acts of service such as feeding the hungry, clothing the naked, and visiting the sick. This is very similar to the Islamic obligation of *zakat* described in Chapter 3.

We are instructed to provide such care in the Old Testament (e.g., Exodus 23:4; Deuteronomy 24:19-21), by Jesus (Matthew 10:8; Luke 10:29-37), Paul (1 Timothy 5:3-5), and warned that the final judgment may depend on whether we have done so (Matthew 25:31-46). This gives some guidance to individuals, but the Bible also illustrates congregational programs of care such as feeding widows (Acts 6:1-7) and taking up financial collections for other churches in need (Acts 11:27-30; 2 Corinthians 8).

From early in church history, individuals have given money into a congregational chest so that the money can be distributed to those in need. Martin Luther gave specific instructions about how such funds should be managed[193] and the practice continues to be an important characteristic of the Lutheran and Reformed traditions. Keller's book is primarily a manual for how churches can manage welfare programs using such funds.

These three contexts for mercy imply a significant difference between God's mercy and ours. God's mercy is revealed in the extraordinary gifts of creation and atonement that aim to reconcile all things in Christ; ours is shown in quite ordinary acts of service to help the poor and needy, especially those who are fellow believers. Reformed thinking tends to separate spiritual from physical needs and to elevate the importance of the former above the latter. That dualism inevitably concludes that the mercy of forgiveness is fundamental and that mercy towards other needs is secondary.

Several Reformed writers bemoan the difficulty they have convincing their congregations to engage with the third context for mercy. I expect that resistance arises from their own preaching about the primacy of mercy-as-salvation. If God's ultimate mercy is directed towards eternal life after death, then any mercy directed towards the sufferings of this life is necessarily secondary and easily seen as optional.

In my view, the biblical concept of mercy is much more integrated and holistic than these Reformed views. Compassion towards spiritual and physical needs have equal importance in both the mission of God and consequently in the mission of the church. Our mercy is to imitate the mercy of God, which is freely given to all. The mercy we are called to love goes beyond patronizing handouts, and beyond the instrumental approach inherent in Reformed practice. Mercy towards people's physical needs is not a technique to get them in through the side door of the church so that they can then be saved through effective preaching.

Notes

[1] This is a quote from Nick Cave's journal of correspondence with his fans, *The Red Hand Files #109*. https://www.theredhandfiles.com/what-is-mercy-for-you (accessed 10 March 2022).
[2] Pope John Paul II, "Dives in Misericordia," 4.
[3] Pope Francis, "Misericordiae Vultus," 2.
[4] According to the 2022 "Global Estimates of Modern Slavery," the likely number is 49.6 million, an increase of 9.3 million over the previous estimate from 2017.
[5] Unless otherwise noted, biblical references are from the New Revised Standard Version. At the risk of disrupting the flow of many sentences, I cite virtually every reference and allusion to biblical ideas. This is not because I am a fan of so-called prooftexting. Quoting a verse does little to prove anything. Rather, I am aware that many readers may not have extensive knowledge of the Bible and I want to provide clear pointers if they wish to dig more deeply.
[6] Bailey, *Jesus through Middle Eastern Eyes*.
[7] Bailey, 175–85.
[8] Lodging overnight is implied by Luke's use of *katalysai* in 19:7 (Bailey, 180).

[9] Perhaps it is necessary to note that asking someone to help does not always signify the same thing. In other contexts, such a request could be inadvertently or deliberately oppressive. It could embarrass the other if they are unable to comply. It could be an act of power, merely forcing the other to do one's bidding.
[10] Early readers of this book noted that my two cases are not exhaustive. We cannot simply assume that the second person, who charges the refugees for the water, does so because of greed. They may do so out of a desire to ensure that their ongoing contribution can be sustained rather than exhausted after the first day. Alternatively, if they are well-trained in developmental principles and wish to avoid the power imbalance of a rescue operation, their motivation in charging for the water may be to avoid future dependency. But the point of the thought experiment remains unchanged: whether an act can be characterized as mercy depends (among other things) on the giver's motivation.
[11] Nietzsche discussed pity in various places, but I have taken the idea primarily from Martha Nussbaum's analysis in "Pity and Mercy."
[12] Derrida, *Given Time*.
[13] Caputo and Scanlon, *God, the Gift, and Postmodernism* loc. 56.
[14] By "asymptotically," I am drawing on my background in mathematics in a way that might help you if you know maths, but which you can just skip over otherwise. In maths, the function $f(x)=1/x$ has a horizontal asymptote at zero, meaning that as x gets bigger and bigger, $f(x)$ gets closer and closer to zero, though it never reaches zero. If you consider zero as the ideal or ultimate value, then no value of this function ever reaches the ideal. But for any difference you point out between

an f(x) value and the ideal of zero, I could show you an example of f(x) that is closer to zero. (Aaah, fond memories of epsilon-delta proofs back at Newcastle University in 1980!) For all practical purposes, you can find examples of the f(x)=1/x function that are as close to the ideal as you could ever want. The same is true of gifts, including the gift of mercy: even if they never attain the asymptote of purity, they can come as close as you could ever wish.

[15] https://www.nationalgeographic.org/projects/out-of-eden-walk/articles/2016-12-cocoon-days/ (accessed 11 June 2022)

[16] See the discussion between Derrida and Marion in the chapter "On the Gift" in Caputo and Scanlon, *God, the Gift, and Postmodernism*.

[17] Vaughan, *For-Giving*. For readers interested in understanding an economy of gift, I'd suggest first of all reading or listening to the essay by Robin Wall Kimmerer "The Serviceberry." The website noted in the Bibliography includes an audio recording of Kimmerer reading the essay herself. I find this essay nothing short of amazing, rich in both intellectual clarity and inspirational imagery.

[18] Vaughan, *Homo Donans*.

[19] Kashtan, "Deserving, Gifting, and Needs," 102.

[20] e.g., Bregman's book *Humankind: A Hopeful History*, Aronson's *HumanKind: Changing the World One Small Act at a Time*, Abel's *The Compassion Project: A Case For Hope & Humankindness from the Town that Beat Loneliness*, Zaki's *The War for Kindness: Building Empathy in a Fractured World*, Kraft's *Deep Kindness: A Revolutionary Guide for the Way We Think, Talk, and Act in Kindness*, Santomero and Chopra's *Radical Kindness: The Life-Changing Power of Giving and Receiving*, Lovasik's *The Hidden Power of*

Kindness: A Practical Handbook for Souls Who Dare to Transform the World, One Deed at a Time, Ferrucci and the Dalai Lama's *The Power of Kindness: The Unexpected Benefits of Leading a Compassionate Life*, and Mackay's *The Kindness Revolution: How We Can Restore Hope, Rebuild Trust and Inspire Optimism*.

In particular, I think Matthew Friedman is correct to argue in his book *Be the Hero: Be the Change* that the world needs a million small acts of kindness rather than single heroic acts. Significant and sustainable global improvements in areas such as climate change, modern slavery, poverty, and refugees, will not occur because of a few dynamic leaders but by the "collective actions of ordinary people."

[21] Although that parable is my own invention, the idea came from Soren Kierkegaard's essay "Mercy, a work of love, even if it can give nothing and can do nothing" (Kierkegaard, *Works of Love*, chap. VII).

[22] On Talmudic opinion, see Sotah 47a, https://www.sefaria.org/Sotah.47a.5 (accessed 11 June 2022). For an early example of the claim that the bear attack was just, see Tertullian, "Adversus Marcionem," chap. IV.XXIII.

[23] Pope John Paul II, "Dives in Misericordia" footnote 52.

[24] *Rabbi Tovia Singer Explains Why 'Rachem' in Hebrew Means Both 'Mercy' and 'Womb'? What is Mercy?* at https://www.youtube.com/watch?v=nu7Pr4RmbV0 (accessed 11 June 2022).

[25] For a thorough analysis of the relationship between *kapporeth*, the Greek translation *hilastērion*, and the English mercy-seat, see Belousek, *Atonement, Justice, and Peace*, chap. 14.

[26] Strangely, the New International Version mostly uses the translation "adulterer" rather than "prostitute," though it has to use "prostitute" when both terms are used in the same verse (e.g., 4:14). Also strangely, the NIV translates *racham* as love rather than mercy (e.g., in 1:6 and 2:4).

[27] Kasper, *Mercy*, 51.

[28] Brueggemann, *Materiality as Resistance*, 92.

[29] I have quoted the New International Version here because it translates the Hebrew *chesed* as "mercy" whereas the New Revised Standard Version uses "kindness." As we have seen, both mercy and kindness are aspects of *chesed*, and the difference in those two English versions simply reflects the normal translational challenge when there is no one-to-one correspondence between words in two languages. In this case, the translation of *chesed* to mercy may be justified by the fact that the Septuagint uses *eleos*.

[30] Kasper, *Mercy*, 42.

[31] "Joint Declaration on the Doctrine of Justification."

[32] Pope John Paul II, "Dives in Misericordia," 8.

[33] The inspiration for this paragraph comes from John Paul Lederach's commentary on Psalm 85 in *The Journey toward Reconciliation*, chap. 4.

[34] Pope John Paul II, "Dives in Misericordia," 25.

[35] For a more extensive discussion and criticism of the supererogatory view of mercy, see Floyd, "Aquinas and the Obligations of Mercy."

In this section I am trying to avoid conflict with a notion that the Anglican Church dismisses as "arrogancy and impiety" ("Thirty Nine Articles of Religion," sec. XIV). That Article warns against the view that we can do more for God beyond what God asks, as though we were adding to our stature by pious works. I'm not suggesting that by showing mercy we are doing any more than God's requirement as part of the good life Micah envisages, but rather that mercy is always beyond any statute and beyond any cultural obligation.

[36] Vine, *An Expository Dictionary of New Testament Words.*
[37] Bayer, "Mercy from the Heart," 4.
[38] Löhe, "On Mercy. Volume 1."
[39] Keller, *Ministries of Mercy*, 19.
[40] Moloney, "What Mercy Is."
[41] Barclay, *Paul and the Power of Grace* as well as personal communications.
[42] Although the informal tone of my claim that "mercy can only be expressed once one has seen someone in need" makes the relationship between mercy and need seem temporal, I hope to avoid taking sides in the ongoing philosophical debates about whether God, or God's knowledge, is limited by linear time. To say that mercy is always in response to a need does not have to imply that mercy temporally precedes the need. If God has perfect future knowledge then God could act in anticipation of a future need. My point is not about whether mercy can precede need in time, but that mercy cannot be a necessary attribute of God since it is contingent upon some (human) need.
[43] Pope John Paul II, "Dives in Misericordia," 3.
[44] Harnack, *The Mission and Expansion of Christianity in the First Three Centuries, Volume 1*, 148.
[45] This observation comes from Cantalamessa, *The Gaze of Mercy*, 56.
[46] Bolt and Harrison, *Justice, Mercy, and Well-Being*, 64.
[47] Pope John Paul II, "Dives in Misericordia," 12.
[48] Like mercy, grace is a word whose meaning is generally kept vague so that it can evoke sympathetic reactions rather than

define anything specific. I never liked the aphorism that God's mercy is not giving sinners what they deserve, while God's grace is giving sinners what they do not deserve.

Don Carson's approach is better. "What is mercy?" he asks, and "How does it differ from grace? The two terms are frequently synonymous, but where there is a distinction between the two, it appears that grace is a loving response when love is undeserved, and mercy is a loving response prompted by the misery and helplessness of the one on whom the love is to be showered. Grace answers to the undeserving; mercy answers to the miserable." (*The Sermon on the Mount*, 23f.)

But I think Barclay's distinction is even better: that grace is a stance or posture or propensity, while mercy is an outworking or expression of that posture.

[49] Barclay, *Paul and the Power of Grace* loc. 485-545.
[50] Barclay loc. 2772.
[51] Barclay loc. 1178.
[52] Barclay loc. 1769.
[53] Barclay loc. 3454.
[54] It might be worth noting one finer nuance about hopes and expectations. Suppose a person were considering acting mercifully to another, and somehow knew with 100% certainty that the intended effect was not going to be achieved. They planned to give one of their kidneys to someone but somehow knew the transplant would fail. Or they planned to bail someone out of financial trouble in the hope that the person would see the light and give up gambling, but somehow they knew the person would not change. With such sure future knowledge, would the giver bother to show mercy at all? If choosing whether to act or not would be affected by your

knowledge of whether the hoped-for outcome is achieved, then isn't the outcome a condition of the action?

Showing mercy requires experience and wisdom, since there are many times when actions intended to be helpful are not. Even in the absence of sure future knowledge, we should take note of the outcomes and learn how to show mercy effectively. If the hoped-for outcome does not eventuate, that should not cause us to withhold mercy, but it might inform our choice about the appropriate form of our mercy. In this way, our hopes and expectations guide our execution of mercy without being a post-condition for whether we show mercy or not.

[55] Barclay, *Paul and the Power of Grace* loc. 2911.

[56] The concept of being saved, especially saved by God, is so common in both the Old and New Testaments that a full analysis is impossible here. I already noted three senses of the Greek root *sózó* in Chapter 1. But in the gospels we see other meanings as well: an angel announces that Jesus "will save his people from their sins" (Matthew 1:21), Zechariah prophesied that God would save us from our enemies (Luke 1:71), a twelve-year-old girl is saved from death (Luke 8:49-56), Peter is saved from drowning (Matthew 14:30), a man is saved from blindness (Luke 18: 35-43), and Jesus is taunted about not saving himself from the cross (Matthew 27:40-42, Mark 15:30-31, Luke 23:35-37). Paul writes that women can be kept safe through childbirth (1 Timothy 2:15), and he has confidence that he will be saved from prison (Philippians 1:19).

Paul also suggests that through Jesus we can be saved from the wrath of God (Romans 5:9). Not being a Greek scholar, I will only say this with humility, and in a footnote, but although most English translations of Romans 5:9 (and Romans 12:19 as well) say the "wrath of God," the original Greek merely says the "wrath." Is God being blamed for something here that Paul did not intend?

In other parts of the New Testament, we read that sailors are saved from a shipwreck (Acts 27), God could have saved Jesus from death (Hebrews 5:7), God saves the physically sick (James 5:15), Noah and his family were saved from the deluge (Hebrews 11:7; 1 Peter 3:20; 2 Peter 2:5), and God saved Israel from bondage in Egypt (Jude 1:5).

So, the scope of what we may be saved from is quite broad. Being saved in the New Testament does not mean simply going to heaven rather than hell after we die.

[57] The details in this section come from personal communications with Chloe and others involved with her.

[58] See the lecture "Rabbi Dr. David Gottlieb - Jewish Philosophy: Mercy" at https://www.youtube.com/watch?v=Evw4XnmEIC4 (accessed 11 June 2022).

[59] These couple of paragraphs are based on chapter 3 of Yoder, *Shalom: The Bible's Word for Salvation, Justice and Peace*.

There is no space in this book to make a detailed case for the restorative and *shalom*-oriented form of justice that dominates the biblical story. To understand the centrality of *shalom* to the biblical picture, Yoder's book is a good starting point. For a comprehensive account of restorative justice, see Marshall, *Beyond Retribution* or, for a quicker read of the key ideas, try Marshall, *The Little Book of Biblical Justice*.

[60] Marshall, *The Little Book of Biblical Justice*, 37.

[61] For more details, see the articles in the *Stanford Encyclopedia of Philosophy* (https://plato.stanford.edu/entries/desert) and the *Internet*

Encyclopedia of Philosophy (https://iep.utm.edu/desert) (both accessed 11 June 2022).

[62] I understand that for some readers this might be the most confronting claim of this book. To question the common Evangelical rendition of sin, deserved punishment, and substitutionary atonement can seem like a heretical rejection of the whole gospel. In many churches it is not possible to question this prevailing interpretation. Nevertheless, many Christians with high views of scripture believe otherwise. If you have been brought up thinking there is only one way to interpret the Bible, I recommend Peter Enns' book *How the Bible Actually Works*. To understand alternatives to the gospel of retribution, try Zahnd and Young's *Sinners in the Hands of a Loving God: the scandalous truth of the very good news*, or Jersak's *A More Christlike God: a more beautiful gospel*. For those of a more academic inclination, a thorough reexamination of the atonement can be found in the essays in Jersak and Hardin's *Stricken by God?: nonviolent identification and the victory of Christ*, and in Belousek, *Atonement, Justice, and Peace*. A more visual explanation from an Orthodox perspective is in the video at https://www.youtube.com/watch?v=WosgwLekgn8 (accessed 11 June 2022), where Steve Robinson uses black and white chairs to depict the relationship between God and humanity.

[63] Belousek, 34.

[64] Bolt and Harrison, *Justice, Mercy, and Well-Being*, 26.

[65] Globally, about 143 people out of every 100,000 are in prison. But the USA currently holds over 2,100,000 people in prison—roughly 639 per 100,000 of the population. (Data from the World Prison Brief website

https://www.prisonstudies.org/highest-to-lowest/prison-population-total, accessed 17 September 2021.)

[66] Fins, "Death Row U.S.A."

[67] Stevenson, *Just Mercy* loc. 4859.

[68] Stevenson loc. 4867.

[69] Rosendale, "Aboriginal Stories and Customs: Resources for Gospel Preaching," 18.

[70] Stevenson, *Just Mercy* loc. 4648.

[71] Hugo, *Les Misérables*, 89–90.

[72] Hugo, 105–6.

[73] This name, and some others in the book have been changed to protect the respective people.

[74] Borg, *Meeting Jesus Again for the First Time*, chap. 6, but also neatly summarized in Borg, *The Heart of Christianity: Rediscovering a Life of Faith*, 176.

[75] Dark, "Can I Get a Witness?" See also his verbal retelling of this incident in the last five minutes of his 2020 talk *Beloved Community and Guilty Pleasures and Robot Soft Exorcism* at the Collaborators Conference in 2020, available at https://www.youtube.com/watch?v=H3DDjhv2nL0 (accessed 11 June 2022).

[76] Plantinga, *Not the Way It's Supposed to Be*.

[77] LeBaron et al., "Confronting Root Causes: Forced Labour in Global Supply Chains."

[78] Augsburger, *The Freedom of Forgiveness*, chap. 2; Murphy and Hampton, *Forgiveness and Mercy*, chap. 2.

[79] This comes from Jeffrie G. Murphy in Murphy and Hampton, *Forgiveness and Mercy*, 34. In a similar vein, Jean Hampton comments in the same book: "Whereas forgiveness is a change of heart toward a wrongdoer that arises out of our decision to see him as morally decent rather than bad, *mercy is the*

suspension or mitigation of a punishment that would otherwise be deserved as retribution, and which is granted out of pity and compassion for the wrongdoer" (158). While there is plenty in that book at odds with my approach, and while I am more aligned to Hampton's contributions than to Murphy's, both bring deep insights to this topic.

[80] One of the most powerful discussions of who has the right or the relevant standing to forgive is in Wiesenthal, *The Sunflower*. In that book, Wiesenthal, a Jew, is asked by a dying Nazi SS soldier to forgive him. The soldier had done nothing to Wiesenthal, but was asking forgiveness for his involvement in murdering other Jews. In later editions of the book we read not only Wiesenthal's response to that request, but the subsequent commentary of 53 other people.

[81] Posted by user u/schefar at https://www.reddit.com/r/aww/comments/iwaoy1/kid_had_an_old_bike_with_no_brakes_and_dented (accessed 8 June 2022)

[82] The Wisdom of Solomon is included in the Bibles used by Roman Catholic and Orthodox churches, though only referenced as part of the Apocrypha in Protestant churches. In the Anglican Communion, it is one of those books that "the Church doth read for example of life and instruction of manners; but yet doth it not apply them to establish any doctrine" ("Thirty Nine Articles of Religion").

[83] From https://www.i4give.com (accessed 17 August 2022).

[84] Details are drawn from Beiler and Smucker, *Think No Evil*. Capturing the horror of this tragedy and the heart of the community's response is impossible in such a short summary. I hope some readers will delve into the story through Beiler and Smucker's book.

[85] Beiler and Smucker, 119.

86 Folmer, Singh, and Clarke, "Amish School Shooter's Widow, Marie Monville, Speaks Out."

87 Brown, *Daring Greatly*.

88 See https://www.theforgivenessproject.com/restore-programme (accessed 6 June 2022) and the report by Barefoot and Chitty, "Exploring Shame Resilience Theory (SRT) and Its Potential for Understanding How Shame Affects the Behaviours of Women with Lived Experience of Imprisonment." Some of the thoughts in this section also come from "The Prison Chronicles," a series of six video interviews also produced by the Forgiveness Project.

89 Cantalamessa, *The Gaze of Mercy*, 72.

90 In internet memes, this quotation has been attributed to various people, but in email conversation I have confirmed with Sarah that she is the originator. Although I do not know enough about her work to endorse her broader position, this poetic aphorism shows deep wisdom.

91 Žižek, *Pandemic*, 1.

92 Žižek, "Love Without Mercy," 198. Emphasis in the original.

93 Žižek, 197.

94 Žižek, 198.

95 Žižek, 199. Emphasis in the original.

96 Žižek, 199. Emphasis in the original.

97 Details in this section are from Treece, *A Man for Others*.

98 Treece, 145.

99 Treece, 145.

100 Treece, 170–71.

101 "Global Prison Trends 2021."

102 The prevalence of modern slavery is extremely difficult to measure. Even defining what forms of abuse to include in the categories "modern slavery" or "human trafficking" is

controversial. Nevertheless, the most detailed estimate we have is 49.6 million people worldwide—from the report "Global Estimates of Modern Slavery."

[103] Corbett and Fikkert, *When Helping Hurts*, 109.

[104] For a detailed discussion about how to read the violence in the Bible, see Flood, *Disarming Scripture*.

[105] For readers interested in understanding more about this theme of exile, and its centrality in the biblical narrative, I recommend the series of podcasts and related material by Timothy Mackie and Jonathan Collins at the Bible Project: https://bibleproject.com/podcast/series/exile-series (accessed 1 June 2022).

[106] From https://www.unrefugees.org/refugee-facts/statistics (accessed 7 May 2022).

[107] Pope Francis, *The Name of God Is Mercy*, 43.

[108] Most of the details in this section are taken from the Forgiveness Project https://www.theforgivenessproject.com/stories-library/brigitte-sossou-perenyi (accessed 11 June 2022) and the 2018 BBC documentary *My Stolen Childhood; Understanding the Trokosi System* (available on YouTube). For more information about the practice of *trokosi*, see Boaten, "The Trokosi System in Ghana."

[109] I saw this quote on the Internet, attributed to the Rev. George C. Woodruff, pastor of Columbus Avenue A.M.E. Zion Church in Boston, Massachusetts. I tried to contact him to confirm that attribution but received no reply.

[110] The primary source for this story is van Braght, *Martyrs Mirror*. but further details have been reported (or perhaps imagined) in Mathias, *The Story of Dirk Willems*.

[111] Gandhi, *Non-Violent Resistance (Satyagraha)*, 16.

[112] For a thorough description and academic justification of how the "time-in" concept can be applied to both children and adults, see the Collaborative Problem Solving approach in Ablon, *Changeable*.

[113] I won't argue the full case here, but for reasons both theological and pragmatic I have promoted the idea elsewhere that we will never end the blight of modern slavery unless we engage with traffickers in ways that change their behaviors. For more detail about the foundations of that claim, see Clarke, "Perpetrator-Centric Strategies for Addressing Modern Slavery"; Clarke, "Four Theological Schemas for Actively Responding to Modern Slavery."

[114] These words inspired the beautiful and haunting choral piece "Even when He is Silent" by Kim André Arnesen, which is worth listening to online. For a detailed analysis of the provenance of those words, see https://humanistseminarian.com/2017/03/19/i-believe-in-the-sun-part-i-look-away (accessed 22 August 2022).

[115] My thoughts here reflect the relational theology of Albert Nolan, especially the chapters "One with Ourselves" and "One with Other Human Beings" in his book *Jesus Today*.

[116] Beck quotes the NIV rendition of this verse, in which *chesed* has been translated as "mercy" rather than the NRSV's "steadfast love." As we saw in Chapter 3, there is considerable breadth in the meaning of *chesed*.

[117] Beck, *Unclean* loc. 913.

[118] Beck, loc. 80.

[119] Beck, loc. 102.

[120] e.g., Schultz, *Not Monsters*.

[121] Beck, *Unclean* loc. 2437.

[122] Beck, loc. 489.

123 Suggested by Nassal, *Premeditated Mercy*, 129.
124 Seneca, "De Clementia," bk. 2 chap. 4; Cantalamessa, *The Gaze of Mercy*, 178; Peterson, *A Wing and a Prayer* at https://www.youtube.com/watch?v=PcM3Y8kACo4 (accessed 11 June 2022). The suggestion of despair being the opposite of mercy arises from our reading of Stephen Donaldson's fantasy series *The Chronicles of Thomas Covenant*, which I consider the deepest analysis of despair ever written.
125 Hugo, *Les Misérables*, 171.
126 Hugo, 170.
127 Hugo, 210.
128 Hugo, 210.
129 Hugo, 1324.
130 Hugo, 1322.
131 Hugo, 1323.
132 Another literary example in which a character cannot accept the mercy shown to them is Ralph Nickleby in Charles Dickens' *The Life and Adventures of Nicholas Nickleby*. In that novel, Nicholas' uncle Ralph is a scoundrel. He refuses to care for his dead brother's family, gains financially from others' misfortune, misuses his niece Kate, and turns away from the son he fathered in his youth. Although he is shown mercy by Nicholas and others, he commits suicide after learning who his son is, partly in remorse and partly in a deliberate attempt to spite the kindness shown to him. He has experienced mercy, and recognizes the call for a change of heart, but is unwilling to allow his own personal transformation.
133 Preus III, "The Vocation of Every Christian: Life in Christ as a Holy Calling," 15.
134 Pope Francis, *The Name of God Is Mercy*, 53–54. He does accept, however, that this acknowledgment only needs to be a

small step or even just "the desire to take that step" (xviii as well as 49).

[135] Rollins, "The Reward of a Good Life," *The Orthodox Heretic*, chap. 32.

[136] The *Red Hand Files* #204 https://www.theredhandfiles.com/what-is-the-point-in-life/ (accessed 4 October 2022).

[137] This, and subsequent quotes, taken from Samuel Butler's translation of *The Odyssey*, available at http://classics.mit.edu/Homer/odyssey.html (accessed 11 June 2022).

[138] This quote is from *The Fellowship of the Ring*, but see also some commentary by Tolkien in *The Letters of J.R.R. Tolkien*. He notes that Frodo and the Cause "were saved – by Mercy: by the supreme value and efficacy of Pity and forgiveness of injury" (p. 251-52) and "his [Frodo's] exercise of patience and mercy towards Gollum gained him [Frodo] Mercy" at the time of his own failure (p. 326).

[139] Details of the Bali Nine were pieced together from multiple news reports and the Mercy Campaign website which is archived at https://web.archive.org/web/20150205230631/https://mercycampaign.org/ (accessed 13 June 2022).

[140] https://www.merriam-webster.com/dictionary/mercy (accessed 1 October 2021)

[141] https://www.collinsdictionary.com/dictionary/english/mercy (accessed 1 October 2021)

[142] https://www.merriam-webster.com/dictionary/compassion (accessed 1 October 2021)

[143] From the official Colosseum website https://www.thecolosseum.org/facts (accessed 27 July 2021)

[144] Theodoret of Cyrus, *The Ecclesiastical History*, chap. 26.
[145] Foxe, *Foxe's Book of Martyrs*, chap. 3.
[146] Seneca, "De Clementia," bk. 1, chap. 3.
[147] Seneca, bk. 1, chap. 12.
[148] Nussbaum, "Equity and Mercy," 102–3.
[149] Seneca, "De Clementia," bk. 2, chap. 3.
[150] Augustine, *Saint Augustine: Letters, Volume III*, letters 152-153.
[151] Augustine, *Enchiridion on Faith, Hope and Love*, chap. XXV.
[152] I take this reading of Anselm from Moloney, "The Mirror of Justice: Anselm's Solution to (His Own) Paradoxes of Justice and Mercy."
[153] Aquinas, *Summa Theologica*, pt. I, Q. 21.
[154] Aquinas, pt. II–II, Q. 30.
[155] Much of this paragraph comes from Floyd, "Aquinas and the Obligations of Mercy."
[156] Nietzsche's words, quoted in Nussbaum, "Pity and Mercy," 150. Most of the thoughts in this section on Nietzsche come from that essay.
[157] *Genealogy of Morals*, II:10, but once again I am drawing from Nussbaum here, p. 155.
[158] Several quotes in this paragraph come from Omar, *Dictionary of the Holy Quran*.
[159] Chittick, "The Islamic Notion of Mercy."
[160] Chittick, "The Anthropology of Compassion."
[161] Murata, *The Tao of Islam*, 91, 82.
[162] Murata, 82.
[163] Murata, 84.
[164] Murata, 55, 107.

[165] I am grateful to Stack Exchange user UmH for pointing me to those examples.
[166] This list, along with additional commentary, can be found at https://www.myjewishlearning.com/article/the-13-attributes-of-mercy. See also https://www.chabad.org/parshah/article_cdo/aid/3609722/jewish/What-Are-the-13-Attributes-of-Mercy.htm (both accessed 17 February 2022).
[167] Scholem, *Kabbalah*, 130.
[168] From a commentary on *The Tanya* by Manis Friedman, at https://www.chabad.org/library/tanya/tanya_cdo/aid/460076/jewish/Chapter-5.htm (accessed 17 February 2022).
[169] From Moltmann's book *Science and Wisdom*, and quoted by Wyatt Houtz at https://postbarthian.com/2018/03/08/zimzum-jurgen-moltmann-gods-self-contraction-make-space-life (accessed 17 February 2022).
[170] Kasper, *Mercy*, 142.
[171] Pope John Paul II, "Dives in Misericordia," 5.
[172] Pope John Paul II, 14.
[173] Pope Francis, *The Name of God Is Mercy*, ix.
[174] Pope Francis, "Misericordiae Vultus."
[175] Just in case some readers view this Catholic approach as a works-based strategy for gaining God's favor, I should note that senior Catholic clergy very clearly deny that understanding. The official preacher to the papal household, Raniero Cantalamessa, for instance, emphasizes that "Pious practices, like all 'good works,' are righteous and holy if they are seen as a response to grace and not its cause." (Cantalamessa, *The Gaze of Mercy*, 136.) We are to participate in works of corporal and spiritual mercy out of gratitude for

what we have already received, not in order to earn God's mercy.

[176] Pope Francis, *The Name of God Is Mercy*, 6.
[177] Pope Francis, xiii.
[178] Pope Francis, xvi.
[179] Pope Francis, "Misericordiae Vultus."
[180] Pope Francis, *The Name of God Is Mercy*, xviii.
[181] Nassal, *Premeditated Mercy*, 10.
[182] Nassal, 59.
[183] Schmalz, *Mercy Matters*, 9.
[184] Available from https://reporter.lcms.org/2018/mercy-essays-feature-lutheran-theologians-from-reformation-to-today
[185] For a more detailed description and critique of Reformed views on mercy, see my essay *Mercy in the Reformed Tradition* at https://mattsopus.xyz/christian/mercy-in-the-reformed-tradition/
[186] Bayer, *Martin Luther's Theology*, 95.
[187] Pless, "Answering the Why Question," 10.
[188] Quoted in Preus, "Clergy Mental Health and the Doctrine of Justification," 4.
[189] Löhe, "On Mercy. Volume 1," 27.
[190] Keller, *Ministries of Mercy*, 14.
[191] Bayer, *Martin Luther's Theology*, 228.
[192] Löhe, "On Mercy. Volume 1," 6.
[193] Luther, "Ordinance of a Common Chest."

Bibliography

Ablon, J. Stuart. *Changeable: The Surprising Science behind Helping Anyone Change*. 1st edition. New York: Tarcher, 2018.

Aquinas, Thomas. *Summa Theologica*, n.d. http://summa-theologiae.org/.

Augsburger, David W. *The Freedom of Forgiveness*. Chicago: Moody Press, 1988.

Augustine. *Enchiridion on Faith, Hope and Love*. Translated by Albert C. Outler, n.d. https://www.ccel.org/ccel/augustine/enchiridion.html.

———. *Saint Augustine: Letters, Volume III*. Translated by Sister Wilfrid Parsons. Vol. 20. The Fathers of the Church. Fathers of the Church, Inc., 1953. http://archive.org/details/letters0020augu.

Bailey, Kenneth E. *Jesus through Middle Eastern Eyes: Cultural Studies in the Gospels*. Downers Grove, Ill: IVP Academic, 2008.

Barclay, John M. G. *Paul and the Power of Grace*. Grand Rapids, Michigan: Eerdmans Publishing, 2020.

Barefoot, Sandra, and Ruth Chitty. "Exploring Shame Resilience Theory (SRT) and Its Potential for Understanding How Shame Affects the Behaviours of Women with Lived Experience of Imprisonment." The Griffins Society, 2019. https://www.thegriffinssociety.org/exploring-shame-resilience-theory-srt-and-its-potential-understanding-how-shame-affects-behaviours.

Bayer, Oswald. *Martin Luther's Theology: A Contemporary Interpretation*. Grand Rapids, Michigan: W.B. Eerdmans, 2008. http://archive.org/details/martinluthersthe0000baye.

———. "Mercy from the Heart." Translated by Jonathan Mumme. Mercy Booklet Series. The Lutheran Church, Missouri Synod, 2019. https://reporter.lcms.org/2018/mercy-essays-feature-lutheran-theologians-from-reformation-to-today/.

Beck, Richard Allan. *Unclean: Meditations on Purity, Hospitality, and Morality*. Eugene, OR: Cascade Books, 2011.

Beiler, Jonas, and Shawn Smucker. *Think No Evil: Inside the Story of the Amish Schoolhouse Shooting-- and Beyond*. New York: Howard Books, 2009.

Belousek, Darrin W. Snyder. *Atonement, Justice, and Peace: The Message of the Cross and the Mission of the Church*. Grand Rapids, Michigan: William B. Eerdmans, 2012.

Boaten, Abayie B. "The Trokosi System in Ghana: Discrimination Against Women and Children." In *African Women and Children: Crisis and Response*, edited by Apollo Rwomire, 91–103. Greenwood Publishing Group, 2001.

Bolt, Peter, and James R Harrison. *Justice, Mercy, and Well-Being: Interdisciplinary Perspectives*, 2020. http://public.eblib.com/choice/PublicFullRecord.aspx?p=6211513.

Borg, Marcus. *Meeting Jesus Again for the First Time: The Historical Jesus & the Heart of Contemporary Faith*. San Francisco, CA: Harper, 1994. http://archive.org/details/meetingjesusagai00borg.

———. *The Heart of Christianity: Rediscovering a Life of Faith.* 1st HarperCollins pbk. edn. New York NY: HarperSanFrancisco, 2004.

Braght, Thieleman J. van. *The Bloody Theatre or Martyrs Mirror of the Defenceless Christians Who Baptized Only Upon Confession of Faith, and Who Suffered and Died for the Testimony of Jesus, Their Saviour, From the Time of Christ to the Year A.D. 1660.* Translated by Joseph F. Sohm, 1886. https://www.homecomers.org/mirror/head.htm.

Brown, Brené. *Daring Greatly: How the Courage to Be Vulnerable Transforms the Way We Live, Love, Parent, and Lead.* First trade paperback printing. New York, NY: Avery, 2012.

Brueggemann, Walter. *Materiality as Resistance: Five Elements for Moral Action in the Real World.* First edition. Louisville, KY: Westminster John Knox Press, 2020.

Cantalamessa, Raniero. *The Gaze of Mercy: A Commentary on Divine and Human Mercy.* Translated by Marsha Daigle-Williamson. Frederick, MD: Word Among Us Press, 2015.

Caputo, John D., and Michael J. Scanlon, eds. *God, the Gift, and Postmodernism.* New Ed Kindle edition. The Indiana Series in the Philosophy of Religion. Indiana University Press, 1999.

Carson, D. A. *The Sermon on the Mount: An Evangelical Exposition of Matthew 5-7.* Grand Rapids, Michigan: Baker Book House, 1982. http://archive.org/details/sermononmounteva0000cars.

Chittick, William C. "The Anthropology of Compassion." *Journal of the Muhyiddin Ibn Arabi Society* 48 (2010). https://ibnarabisociety.org/the-anthropology-of-compassion-william-chittick/.

———. "The Islamic Notion of Mercy." *HuffPost*, December 14, 2010, sec. Religion. https://www.huffpost.com/entry/the-islamic-notion-of-mer_b_795275.

Clarke, Matthew C. "Four Theological Schemas for Actively Responding to Modern Slavery." *Journal of Sociology and Christianity* 12, no. 1 (2022): 10–32.

———. "Perpetrator-Centric Strategies for Addressing Modern Slavery." *Journal of Human Rights Practice*, 2022. https://doi.org/10.1093/jhuman/huab036.

Corbett, Steve, and Brian Fikkert. *When Helping Hurts: How to Alleviate Poverty without Hurting the Poor ... and Yourself.* Moody, 2012.

Dark, David. "Can I Get a Witness? The Righteously, Radically Campbellite Core of Nashville." Southern Foodways Alliance, January 11, 2017. https://www.southernfoodways.org/can-i-get-a-witness-the-righteously-radically-campbellite-core-of-nashville/.

Derrida, Jacques. *Given Time: I. Counterfeit Money.* Translated by Peggy Kamuf. Reprint edition. Chicago: University of Chicago Press, 1994.

Fins, Deborah. "Death Row U.S.A." NAACP Legal Defense and Educational Fund, Inc., Spring 2021. https://deathpenaltyinfo.org/death-row/overview/death-row-usa.

Flood, Derek. *Disarming Scripture: Cherry-Picking Liberals, Violence-Loving Conservatives, and Why We All Need to Learn to Read the Bible like Jesus Did.* San Francisco: Metanoia Books, 2014.

Floyd, Shawn. "Aquinas and the Obligations of Mercy." *The Journal of Religious Ethics* 37, no. 3 (2009): 449–71.

Folmer, Kaitlyn, Natasha Singh, and Suzan Clarke. "Amish School Shooter's Widow, Marie Monville, Speaks Out."

ABC News, September 30, 2013. https://abcnews.go.com/US/amish-school-shooters-widow-marie-monville-remembers-tragedy/story?id=20417790.

Foxe, John. *Foxe's Book of Martyrs*, 1563. https://www.ccel.org/f/foxe/martyrs/home.html.

Gandhi, M. K. *Non-Violent Resistance (Satyagraha)*. First ed. New York: Schocken Books, 1961.

"Global Estimates of Modern Slavery: Forced Labour and Forced Marriage." Report. Geneva: International Labour Organization (ILO), Walk Free, and International Organization for Migration (IOM), September 12, 2022. http://www.ilo.org/global/topics/forced-labour/publications/WCMS_854733/lang--en/index.htm.

"Global Prison Trends 2021." Penal Reform International and the Thailand Institute of Justice, May 2021. https://www.prisonstudies.org/sites/default/files/resources/downloads/world_prison_population_list_13th_edition.pdf.

Harnack, Adolf von. *The Mission and Expansion of Christianity in the First Three Centuries, Volume 1*. Translated by James Moffatt. London: Williams and Norgate; New York: G.P. Putnam's Sons, 1908. http://archive.org/details/TheMissionAndExpansionOfChristianityV1.

Hugo, Victor. *Les Misérables*. Translated by Norman MacAfee, Charles E Wilbour, and Lee Fahnestock. New York: New American Library, 1987. https://archive.org/stream/in.ernet.dli.2015.43835/2015.43835.Les-Miserables_djvu.txt.

"Joint Declaration on the Doctrine of Justification by the Lutheran World Federation and the Catholic Church." The Lutheran World Federation, 1999.

https://www.lutheranworld.org/sites/default/files/Joint%20Declaration%20on%20the%20Doctrine%20of%20Justification.pdf.

Kashtan, Miki. "Deserving, Gifting, and Needs." *Canadian Woman Studies* 34, no. 1–2 (June 17, 2020). https://cws.journals.yorku.ca/index.php/cws/article/view/37802.

Kasper, Walter. *Mercy: The Essence of the Gospel and the Key to Christian Life*. Translated by William Madges. New York: Paulist Press, 2014.

Keller, Timothy. *Ministries of Mercy: Learning to Care Like Jesus*. Society for Promoting Christian Knowledge, 2017.

Kierkegaard, Soren. *Works of Love*. Translated by David F. Swenson and Lillian Marvin Swenson. Princeton, NJ: Princeton University Press, 1949. http://archive.org/details/in.ernet.dli.2015.187384.

Kimmerer, Robin Wall. "The Serviceberry: An Economy of Abundance." *Emergence Magazine*, December 10, 2020. https://emergencemagazine.org/essay/the-serviceberry/.

LeBaron, Genevieve, Neil Howard, Cameron Thibos, and Penelope Kyritsis. "Confronting Root Causes: Forced Labour in Global Supply Chains." openDemocracy and the Sheffield Political Economy Research Institute, 2018. https://www.opendemocracy.net/en/beyond-trafficking-and-slavery/confronting-root-causes/.

Lederach, John Paul. *The Journey toward Reconciliation*. Scottdale, PA: Herald Press, 1999. http://archive.org/details/journeytowardrec0000lede.

Löhe, Wilhelm. "On Mercy. Volume 1." Mercy Booklet Series. The Lutheran Church - Missouri Synod, 1860. https://reporter.lcms.org/2018/mercy-essays-feature-lutheran-theologians-from-reformation-to-today/.

Luther, Martin. "Ordinance of a Common Chest." Mercy Booklet Series. The Lutheran Church, Missouri Synod, 1523. https://reporter.lcms.org/2018/mercy-essays-feature-lutheran-theologians-from-reformation-to-today/.

Marshall, Christopher D. *Beyond Retribution: A New Testament Vision for Justice, Crime, and Punishment.* Studies in Peace and Scripture. Grand Rapids, Michigan: W.B. Eerdmans, 2001.

———. *The Little Book of Biblical Justice: A Fresh Approach to the Bible's Teachings on Justice.* Little Books of Justice & Peacebuilding. Intercourse, PA: Good Books, 2005.

Mathias, Anita. *The Story of Dirk Willems: The Man Who Died to Save His Enemy,* 2019.

Moloney, Daniel P. "The Mirror of Justice: Anselm's Solution to (His Own) Paradoxes of Justice and Mercy." *Saint Anselm Journal* 13, no. 1 (Fall 2017).

———. "What Mercy Is." *First Things* March (2015). https://www.firstthings.com/article/2015/03/what-mercy-is.

Murata, Sachiko. *The Tao of Islam: A Sourcebook on Gender Relationships in Islamic Thought.* Albany: State University of New York Press, 1992.

Murphy, Jeffrie G., and Jean Hampton. *Forgiveness and Mercy.* Cambridge, UK: Cambridge University Press, 1988.

Nassal, Joseph. *Premeditated Mercy: A Spirituality of Reconciliation.* Leavenworth, KS: Forest of Peace Pub, 2000.

Nolan, Albert. *Jesus Today: A Spirituality of Radical Freedom.* Maryknoll, NY: Orbis Books, 2006.

Nussbaum, Martha C. "Equity and Mercy." *Philosophy and Public Affairs* 22, no. 2 (1993): 83–125.

———. "Pity and Mercy: Nietzsche's Stoicism." In *Nietzsche, Genealogy, Morality: Essays on Nietzsche's On the*

Genealogy of Morals, 139–64. University of California Press, 1994.

Omar, Abdul Mannan. *Dictionary of the Holy Quran: Arabic - English*, 2003. http://archive.org/details/dictionary-2018.

Plantinga, Cornelius. *Not the Way It's Supposed to Be: A Breviary of Sin*. Wm. B. Eerdmans Publishing, 1996.

Pless, John T. "Answering the Why Question: Martin Luther on Human Suffering and God's Mercy." Mercy Booklet Series. The Lutheran Church, Missouri Synod, 2019. https://reporter.lcms.org/2018/mercy-essays-feature-lutheran-theologians-from-reformation-to-today/.

Pope Francis. "Misericordiae Vultus - Bull of Indiction of the Extraordinary Jubilee of Mercy," April 11, 2015. https://www.vatican.va/content/francesco/en/apost_letters/documents/papa-francesco_bolla_20150411_misericordiae-vultus.pdf.

———. *The Name of God Is Mercy*. Edited by Andrea Tornielli. Translated by Oonagh Stransky, 2017.

Pope John Paul II. "Dives in Misericordia," 1980. http://www.vatican.va/content/john-paul-ii/en/encyclicals/documents/hf_jp-ii_enc_30111980_dives-in-misericordia.pdf.

Preus III, Jacob A. O. "The Vocation of Every Christian: Life in Christ as a Holy Calling." Mercy Booklet Series. The Lutheran Church - Missouri Synod, 2019. https://reporter.lcms.org/2018/mercy-essays-feature-lutheran-theologians-from-reformation-to-today/.

Preus, Robert D. "Clergy Mental Health and the Doctrine of Justification." Mercy Booklet Series. The Lutheran Church - Missouri Synod, 1984. https://reporter.lcms.org/2018/mercy-essays-feature-lutheran-theologians-from-reformation-to-today/.

Rollins, Peter. *The Orthodox Heretic and Other Impossible Tales*. Brewster, MA: Paraclete Press, 2009.

Rosendale, George. "Aboriginal Stories and Customs: Resources for Gospel Preaching." In *Milbi Dabaar: A Resource Book for Teachers, Leaders, Pastors and Students for Use in Christian Ministry among Aborigines of Australia*, edited by David Thompson. North Cairns, Qld.: Wontulp-Bi-Buya College, 2004.

Schmalz, Mathew N. *Mercy Matters: Opening Yourself to the Life-Changing Gift*. Huntington, IN: Our Sunday Visitor, Inc, 2016.

Scholem, Gershom. *Kabbalah*. New York: Dorset Press, 1987.

Schultz, Pamela D. *Not Monsters: Analyzing the Stories of Child Molesters*. Lanham, MD: Rowman & Littlefield, 2005.

Seneca. "Of Clemency (De Clementia)." In *L. Annaeus Seneca, Minor Dialogs Together with the Dialog "On Clemency,"* translated by Aubrey Stewart, Bohn's Classical Library Edition. London: George Bell and Sons, 1900. https://en.wikisource.org/wiki/Of_Clemency.

Stevenson, Bryan. *Just Mercy: A Story of Justice and Redemption*. Scribe Publications, 2015.

Tertullian. "Adversus Marcionem." In *The Ante-Nicene Fathers: The Writings of the Fathers down to A.D. 325*, Edited by Alexander Roberts, James Donaldson and A. Cleveland Coxe., 3:269–475. Wm B. Eerdmans, 1986.

Theodoret of Cyrus. *The Ecclesiastical History*, 455AD. https://www.documentacatholicaomnia.eu/03d/0393-0457,_Theodoretus,_Historia_Ecclesiastica,_EN.pdf.

"Thirty Nine Articles of Religion." Anglican Communion, 1571. https://www.anglicancommunion.org/media/109014/Thirty-Nine-Articles-of-Religion.pdf.

Tolkien, J. R. R. *The Letters of J.R.R. Tolkien.* Edited by Humphrey Carpenter and Christopher Tolkien. Boston: Houghton Mifflin, 1981. https://archive.org/details/lettersofjrrtolk00tolk_1.

Treece, Patricia. *A Man for Others: Maximilian Kolbe, Saint of Auschwitz, in the Words of Those Who Knew Him.* Huntington, Ind: Our Sunday Visitor Pub. Div, 1982.

Vaughan, Genevieve. *For-Giving: A Feminist Criticism of Exchange.* Plain View Press, 1997.

———. *Homo Donans: For a Maternal Economy.* Vanda ePublishing, 2016.

Vine, W. E. *An Expository Dictionary of New Testament Words.* London: Oliphants, 1975.

Wiesenthal, Simon. *The Sunflower.* Schocken, 1998.

Yoder, Perry. *Shalom: The Bible's Word for Salvation, Justice and Peace.* Spire, 1989.

Žižek, Slavoj. "Love Without Mercy." *Pli: The Warwick Journal of Philosophy* 11 (2001): 171–99.

———. *Pandemic: COVID-19 Shakes the World.* 1st edition. New York: Polity, 2020.

www.ingramcontent.com/pod-product-compliance
Lightning Source LLC
Chambersburg PA
CBHW020856020526
44107CB00076B/1839